C-4090   CAREER EXAMINATION SERIES

This is your
PASSBOOK for...

Defense Language Aptitude Battery (DLAB)

Test Preparation Study Guide
Questions & Answers

COPYRIGHT NOTICE

This book is SOLELY intended for, is sold ONLY to, and its use is RESTRICTED to individual, bona fide applicants or candidates who qualify by virtue of having seriously filed applications for appropriate license, certificate, professional and/or promotional advancement, higher school matriculation, scholarship, or other legitimate requirements of education and/or governmental authorities.

This book is NOT intended for use, class instruction, tutoring, training, duplication, copying, reprinting, excerption, or adaptation, etc., by:

1) Other publishers
2) Proprietors and/or Instructors of "Coaching" and/or Preparatory Courses
3) Personnel and/or Training Divisions of commercial, industrial, and governmental organizations
4) Schools, colleges, or universities and/or their departments and staffs, including teachers and other personnel
5) Testing Agencies or Bureaus
6) Study groups which seek by the purchase of a single volume to copy and/or duplicate and/or adapt this material for use by the group as a whole without having purchased individual volumes for each of the members of the group
7) Et al.

Such persons would be in violation of appropriate Federal and State statutes.

PROVISION OF LICENSING AGREEMENTS – Recognized educational, commercial, industrial, and governmental institutions and organizations, and others legitimately engaged in educational pursuits, including training, testing, and measurement activities, may address request for a licensing agreement to the copyright owners, who will determine whether, and under what conditions, including fees and charges, the materials in this book may be used them. In other words, a licensing facility exists for the legitimate use of the material in this book on other than an individual basis. However, it is asseverated and affirmed here that the material in this book CANNOT be used without the receipt of the express permission of such a licensing agreement from the Publishers. Inquiries re licensing should be addressed to the company, attention rights and permissions department.

All rights reserved, including the right of reproduction in whole or in part, in any form or by any means, electronic or mechanical, including photocopying, recording, or by any information storage and retrieval system, without permission in writing from the Publisher.

Copyright © 2024 by
National Learning Corporation

212 Michael Drive, Syosset, NY 11791
(516) 921-8888 • www.passbooks.com
E-mail: info@passbooks.com

PUBLISHED IN THE UNITED STATES OF AMERICA

PASSBOOK® SERIES

THE *PASSBOOK® SERIES* has been created to prepare applicants and candidates for the ultimate academic battlefield – the examination room.

At some time in our lives, each and every one of us may be required to take an examination – for validation, matriculation, admission, qualification, registration, certification, or licensure.

Based on the assumption that every applicant or candidate has met the basic formal educational standards, has taken the required number of courses, and read the necessary texts, the *PASSBOOK® SERIES* furnishes the one special preparation which may assure passing with confidence, instead of failing with insecurity. Examination questions – together with answers – are furnished as the basic vehicle for study so that the mysteries of the examination and its compounding difficulties may be eliminated or diminished by a sure method.

This book is meant to help you pass your examination provided that you qualify and are serious in your objective.

The entire field is reviewed through the huge store of content information which is succinctly presented through a provocative and challenging approach – the question-and-answer method.

A climate of success is established by furnishing the correct answers at the end of each test.

You soon learn to recognize types of questions, forms of questions, and patterns of questioning. You may even begin to anticipate expected outcomes.

You perceive that many questions are repeated or adapted so that you can gain acute insights, which may enable you to score many sure points.

You learn how to confront new questions, or types of questions, and to attack them confidently and work out the correct answers.

You note objectives and emphases, and recognize pitfalls and dangers, so that you may make positive educational adjustments.

Moreover, you are kept fully informed in relation to new concepts, methods, practices, and directions in the field.

You discover that you are actually taking the examination all the time: you are preparing for the examination by "taking" an examination, not by reading extraneous and/or supererogatory textbooks.

In short, this PASSBOOK®, used directedly, should be an important factor in helping you to pass your test.

DEFENSE LANGUAGE APTITUDE BATTERY (DLAB)

The Defense Language Aptitude Battery (DLAB) is a test used by the United States Department of Defense to test an individual's potential for learning a foreign language. It is used to determine who may pursue training as a military linguist. The test does not attempt to gauge a person's fluency in a given language, but rather to determine their ability to learn a language.

The DLAB consists of 126 multiple-choice questions, and the test is scored out of a possible 176 points. The first half of the test is audio, and the second half is written. To qualify to pursue training in a language, one needs a minimum score of 95. However, to be a linguist in the Marines or Air Force a score of 100 or better is required for all languages. The languages are broken into tiers, based on their difficulty level for a native English speaker, as determined by the Defense Language Institute.

The DLAB is typically administered to new and prospective recruits at the United States Military Entrance Processing Command sometime after the Armed Services Vocational Aptitude Battery is taken but before a final job category (frequently called NEC or MOS) is determined. An individual may usually take the DLAB if they score high enough on the ASVAB for linguist training and are interested in doing so. The DLAB is also administered to ROTC cadets while they are still attending college, as well as incoming cadets for the United States Military Academy. Military personnel interested in retraining into a linguist field typically also must pass the DLAB.

HOW TO TAKE A TEST

I. YOU MUST PASS AN EXAMINATION

A. WHAT EVERY CANDIDATE SHOULD KNOW

Examination applicants often ask us for help in preparing for the written test. What can I study in advance? What kinds of questions will be asked? How will the test be given? How will the papers be graded?

As an applicant for a civil service examination, you may be wondering about some of these things. Our purpose here is to suggest effective methods of advance study and to describe civil service examinations.

Your chances for success on this examination can be increased if you know how to prepare. Those "pre-examination jitters" can be reduced if you know what to expect. You can even experience an adventure in good citizenship if you know why civil service exams are given.

B. WHY ARE CIVIL SERVICE EXAMINATIONS GIVEN?

Civil service examinations are important to you in two ways. As a citizen, you want public jobs filled by employees who know how to do their work. As a job seeker, you want a fair chance to compete for that job on an equal footing with other candidates. The best-known means of accomplishing this two-fold goal is the competitive examination.

Exams are widely publicized throughout the nation. They may be administered for jobs in federal, state, city, municipal, town or village governments or agencies.

Any citizen may apply, with some limitations, such as the age or residence of applicants. Your experience and education may be reviewed to see whether you meet the requirements for the particular examination. When these requirements exist, they are reasonable and applied consistently to all applicants. Thus, a competitive examination may cause you some uneasiness now, but it is your privilege and safeguard.

C. HOW ARE CIVIL SERVICE EXAMS DEVELOPED?

Examinations are carefully written by trained technicians who are specialists in the field known as "psychological measurement," in consultation with recognized authorities in the field of work that the test will cover. These experts recommend the subject matter areas or skills to be tested; only those knowledges or skills important to your success on the job are included. The most reliable books and source materials available are used as references. Together, the experts and technicians judge the difficulty level of the questions.

Test technicians know how to phrase questions so that the problem is clearly stated. Their ethics do not permit "trick" or "catch" questions. Questions may have been tried out on sample groups, or subjected to statistical analysis, to determine their usefulness.

Written tests are often used in combination with performance tests, ratings of training and experience, and oral interviews. All of these measures combine to form the best-known means of finding the right person for the right job.

II. HOW TO PASS THE WRITTEN TEST

A. NATURE OF THE EXAMINATION

To prepare intelligently for civil service examinations, you should know how they differ from school examinations you have taken. In school you were assigned certain definite pages to read or subjects to cover. The examination questions were quite detailed and usually emphasized memory. Civil service exams, on the other hand, try to discover your present ability to perform the duties of a position, plus your potentiality to learn these duties. In other words, a civil service exam attempts to predict how successful you will be. Questions cover such a broad area that they cannot be as minute and detailed as school exam questions.

In the public service similar kinds of work, or positions, are grouped together in one "class." This process is known as *position-classification*. All the positions in a class are paid according to the salary range for that class. One class title covers all of these positions, and they are all tested by the same examination.

B. FOUR BASIC STEPS

1) Study the announcement

How, then, can you know what subjects to study? Our best answer is: "Learn as much as possible about the class of positions for which you've applied." The exam will test the knowledge, skills and abilities needed to do the work.

Your most valuable source of information about the position you want is the official exam announcement. This announcement lists the training and experience qualifications. Check these standards and apply only if you come reasonably close to meeting them.

The brief description of the position in the examination announcement offers some clues to the subjects which will be tested. Think about the job itself. Review the duties in your mind. Can you perform them, or are there some in which you are rusty? Fill in the blank spots in your preparation.

Many jurisdictions preview the written test in the exam announcement by including a section called "Knowledge and Abilities Required," "Scope of the Examination," or some similar heading. Here you will find out specifically what fields will be tested.

2) Review your own background

Once you learn in general what the position is all about, and what you need to know to do the work, ask yourself which subjects you already know fairly well and which need improvement. You may wonder whether to concentrate on improving your strong areas or on building some background in your fields of weakness. When the announcement has specified "some knowledge" or "considerable knowledge," or has used adjectives like "beginning principles of..." or "advanced ... methods," you can get a clue as to the number and difficulty of questions to be asked in any given field. More questions, and hence broader coverage, would be included for those subjects which are more important in the work. Now weigh your strengths and weaknesses against the job requirements and prepare accordingly.

3) Determine the level of the position

Another way to tell how intensively you should prepare is to understand the level of the job for which you are applying. Is it the entering level? In other words, is this the position in which beginners in a field of work are hired? Or is it an intermediate or advanced level? Sometimes this is indicated by such words as "Junior" or "Senior" in the class title. Other jurisdictions use Roman numerals to designate the level – Clerk I, Clerk II, for example. The word "Supervisor" sometimes appears in the title. If the level is not indicated by the title, check the description of duties. Will you be working under very close supervision, or will you have responsibility for independent decisions in this work?

4) Choose appropriate study materials

Now that you know the subjects to be examined and the relative amount of each subject to be covered, you can choose suitable study materials. For beginning level jobs, or even advanced ones, if you have a pronounced weakness in some aspect of your training, read a modern, standard textbook in that field. Be sure it is up to date and has general coverage. Such books are normally available at your library, and the librarian will be glad to help you locate one. For entry-level positions, questions of appropriate difficulty are chosen – neither highly advanced questions, nor those too simple. Such questions require careful thought but not advanced training.

If the position for which you are applying is technical or advanced, you will read more advanced, specialized material. If you are already familiar with the basic principles of your field, elementary textbooks would waste your time. Concentrate on advanced textbooks and technical periodicals. Think through the concepts and review difficult problems in your field.

These are all general sources. You can get more ideas on your own initiative, following these leads. For example, training manuals and publications of the government agency which employs workers in your field can be useful, particularly for technical and professional positions. A letter or visit to the government department involved may result in more specific study suggestions, and certainly will provide you with a more definite idea of the exact nature of the position you are seeking.

III. KINDS OF TESTS

Tests are used for purposes other than measuring knowledge and ability to perform specified duties. For some positions, it is equally important to test ability to make adjustments to new situations or to profit from training. In others, basic mental abilities not dependent on information are essential. Questions which test these things may not appear as pertinent to the duties of the position as those which test for knowledge and information. Yet they are often highly important parts of a fair examination. For very general questions, it is almost impossible to help you direct your study efforts. What we can do is to point out some of the more common of these general abilities needed in public service positions and describe some typical questions.

1) General information

Broad, general information has been found useful for predicting job success in some kinds of work. This is tested in a variety of ways, from vocabulary lists to questions about current events. Basic background in some field of work, such as sociology or economics, may be sampled in a group of questions. Often these are principles which have become familiar to most persons through exposure rather than through formal training. It is difficult to advise you how to study for these questions; being alert to the world around you is our best suggestion.

2) Verbal ability

An example of an ability needed in many positions is verbal or language ability. Verbal ability is, in brief, the ability to use and understand words. Vocabulary and grammar tests are typical measures of this ability. Reading comprehension or paragraph interpretation questions are common in many kinds of civil service tests. You are given a paragraph of written material and asked to find its central meaning.

3) Numerical ability

Number skills can be tested by the familiar arithmetic problem, by checking paired lists of numbers to see which are alike and which are different, or by interpreting charts and graphs. In the latter test, a graph may be printed in the test booklet which you are asked to use as the basis for answering questions.

4) Observation

A popular test for law-enforcement positions is the observation test. A picture is shown to you for several minutes, then taken away. Questions about the picture test your ability to observe both details and larger elements.

5) Following directions

In many positions in the public service, the employee must be able to carry out written instructions dependably and accurately. You may be given a chart with several columns, each column listing a variety of information. The questions require you to carry out directions involving the information given in the chart.

6) Skills and aptitudes

Performance tests effectively measure some manual skills and aptitudes. When the skill is one in which you are trained, such as typing or shorthand, you can practice. These tests are often very much like those given in business school or high school courses. For many of the other skills and aptitudes, however, no short-time preparation can be made. Skills and abilities natural to you or that you have developed throughout your lifetime are being tested.

Many of the general questions just described provide all the data needed to answer the questions and ask you to use your reasoning ability to find the answers. Your best preparation for these tests, as well as for tests of facts and ideas, is to be at your physical and mental best. You, no doubt, have your own methods of getting into an exam-taking mood and keeping "in shape." The next section lists some ideas on this subject.

IV. KINDS OF QUESTIONS

Only rarely is the "essay" question, which you answer in narrative form, used in civil service tests. Civil service tests are usually of the short-answer type. Full instructions for answering these questions will be given to you at the examination. But in case this is your first experience with short-answer questions and separate answer sheets, here is what you need to know:

1) Multiple-choice Questions

Most popular of the short-answer questions is the "multiple choice" or "best answer" question. It can be used, for example, to test for factual knowledge, ability to solve problems or judgment in meeting situations found at work.

A multiple-choice question is normally one of three types—
- It can begin with an incomplete statement followed by several possible endings. You are to find the one ending which *best* completes the statement, although some of the others may not be entirely wrong.
- It can also be a complete statement in the form of a question which is answered by choosing one of the statements listed.

- It can be in the form of a problem – again you select the best answer.

Here is an example of a multiple-choice question with a discussion which should give you some clues as to the method for choosing the right answer:

When an employee has a complaint about his assignment, the action which will *best* help him overcome his difficulty is to
- A. discuss his difficulty with his coworkers
- B. take the problem to the head of the organization
- C. take the problem to the person who gave him the assignment
- D. say nothing to anyone about his complaint

In answering this question, you should study each of the choices to find which is best. Consider choice "A" – Certainly an employee may discuss his complaint with fellow employees, but no change or improvement can result, and the complaint remains unresolved. Choice "B" is a poor choice since the head of the organization probably does not know what assignment you have been given, and taking your problem to him is known as "going over the head" of the supervisor. The supervisor, or person who made the assignment, is the person who can clarify it or correct any injustice. Choice "C" is, therefore, correct. To say nothing, as in choice "D," is unwise. Supervisors have and interest in knowing the problems employees are facing, and the employee is seeking a solution to his problem.

2) True/False Questions

The "true/false" or "right/wrong" form of question is sometimes used. Here a complete statement is given. Your job is to decide whether the statement is right or wrong.

SAMPLE: A roaming cell-phone call to a nearby city costs less than a non-roaming call to a distant city.

This statement is wrong, or false, since roaming calls are more expensive.

This is not a complete list of all possible question forms, although most of the others are variations of these common types. You will always get complete directions for answering questions. Be sure you understand *how* to mark your answers – ask questions until you do.

V. RECORDING YOUR ANSWERS

Computer terminals are used more and more today for many different kinds of exams.

For an examination with very few applicants, you may be told to record your answers in the test booklet itself. Separate answer sheets are much more common. If this separate answer sheet is to be scored by machine – and this is often the case – it is highly important that you mark your answers correctly in order to get credit.

An electronic scoring machine is often used in civil service offices because of the speed with which papers can be scored. Machine-scored answer sheets must be marked with a pencil, which will be given to you. This pencil has a high graphite content which responds to the electronic scoring machine. As a matter of fact, stray dots may register as answers, so do not let your pencil rest on the answer sheet while you are pondering the correct answer. Also, if your pencil lead breaks or is otherwise defective, ask for another.

Since the answer sheet will be dropped in a slot in the scoring machine, be careful not to bend the corners or get the paper crumpled.

The answer sheet normally has five vertical columns of numbers, with 30 numbers to a column. These numbers correspond to the question numbers in your test booklet. After each number, going across the page are four or five pairs of dotted lines. These short dotted lines have small letters or numbers above them. The first two pairs may also have a "T" or "F" above the letters. This indicates that the first two pairs only are to be used if the questions are of the true-false type. If the questions are multiple choice, disregard the "T" and "F" and pay attention only to the small letters or numbers.

Answer your questions in the manner of the sample that follows:

32. The largest city in the United States is
    A. Washington, D.C.
    B. New York City
    C. Chicago
    D. Detroit
    E. San Francisco

1) Choose the answer you think is best. (New York City is the largest, so "B" is correct.)
2) Find the row of dotted lines numbered the same as the question you are answering. (Find row number 32)
3) Find the pair of dotted lines corresponding to the answer. (Find the pair of lines under the mark "B.")
4) Make a solid black mark between the dotted lines.

VI. BEFORE THE TEST

Common sense will help you find procedures to follow to get ready for an examination. Too many of us, however, overlook these sensible measures. Indeed, nervousness and fatigue have been found to be the most serious reasons why applicants fail to do their best on civil service tests. Here is a list of reminders:

- Begin your preparation early – Don't wait until the last minute to go scurrying around for books and materials or to find out what the position is all about.
- Prepare continuously – An hour a night for a week is better than an all-night cram session. This has been definitely established. What is more, a night a week for a month will return better dividends than crowding your study into a shorter period of time.
- Locate the place of the exam – You have been sent a notice telling you when and where to report for the examination. If the location is in a different town or otherwise unfamiliar to you, it would be well to inquire the best route and learn something about the building.
- Relax the night before the test – Allow your mind to rest. Do not study at all that night. Plan some mild recreation or diversion; then go to bed early and get a good night's sleep.
- Get up early enough to make a leisurely trip to the place for the test – This way unforeseen events, traffic snarls, unfamiliar buildings, etc. will not upset you.
- Dress comfortably – A written test is not a fashion show. You will be known by number and not by name, so wear something comfortable.

- Leave excess paraphernalia at home – Shopping bags and odd bundles will get in your way. You need bring only the items mentioned in the official notice you received; usually everything you need is provided. Do not bring reference books to the exam. They will only confuse those last minutes and be taken away from you when in the test room.
- Arrive somewhat ahead of time – If because of transportation schedules you must get there very early, bring a newspaper or magazine to take your mind off yourself while waiting.
- Locate the examination room – When you have found the proper room, you will be directed to the seat or part of the room where you will sit. Sometimes you are given a sheet of instructions to read while you are waiting. Do not fill out any forms until you are told to do so; just read them and be prepared.
- Relax and prepare to listen to the instructions
- If you have any physical problem that may keep you from doing your best, be sure to tell the test administrator. If you are sick or in poor health, you really cannot do your best on the exam. You can come back and take the test some other time.

VII. AT THE TEST

The day of the test is here and you have the test booklet in your hand. The temptation to get going is very strong. Caution! There is more to success than knowing the right answers. You must know how to identify your papers and understand variations in the type of short-answer question used in this particular examination. Follow these suggestions for maximum results from your efforts:

1) Cooperate with the monitor

The test administrator has a duty to create a situation in which you can be as much at ease as possible. He will give instructions, tell you when to begin, check to see that you are marking your answer sheet correctly, and so on. He is not there to guard you, although he will see that your competitors do not take unfair advantage. He wants to help you do your best.

2) Listen to all instructions

Don't jump the gun! Wait until you understand all directions. In most civil service tests you get more time than you need to answer the questions. So don't be in a hurry. Read each word of instructions until you clearly understand the meaning. Study the examples, listen to all announcements and follow directions. Ask questions if you do not understand what to do.

3) Identify your papers

Civil service exams are usually identified by number only. You will be assigned a number; you must not put your name on your test papers. Be sure to copy your number correctly. Since more than one exam may be given, copy your exact examination title.

4) Plan your time

Unless you are told that a test is a "speed" or "rate of work" test, speed itself is usually not important. Time enough to answer all the questions will be provided, but this does not mean that you have all day. An overall time limit has been set. Divide the total time (in minutes) by the number of questions to determine the approximate time you have for each question.

5) Do not linger over difficult questions

If you come across a difficult question, mark it with a paper clip (useful to have along) and come back to it when you have been through the booklet. One caution if you do this – be sure to skip a number on your answer sheet as well. Check often to be sure that you have not lost your place and that you are marking in the row numbered the same as the question you are answering.

6) Read the questions

Be sure you know what the question asks! Many capable people are unsuccessful because they failed to *read* the questions correctly.

7) Answer all questions

Unless you have been instructed that a penalty will be deducted for incorrect answers, it is better to guess than to omit a question.

8) Speed tests

It is often better NOT to guess on speed tests. It has been found that on timed tests people are tempted to spend the last few seconds before time is called in marking answers at random – without even reading them – in the hope of picking up a few extra points. To discourage this practice, the instructions may warn you that your score will be "corrected" for guessing. That is, a penalty will be applied. The incorrect answers will be deducted from the correct ones, or some other penalty formula will be used.

9) Review your answers

If you finish before time is called, go back to the questions you guessed or omitted to give them further thought. Review other answers if you have time.

10) Return your test materials

If you are ready to leave before others have finished or time is called, take ALL your materials to the monitor and leave quietly. Never take any test material with you. The monitor can discover whose papers are not complete, and taking a test booklet may be grounds for disqualification.

VIII. EXAMINATION TECHNIQUES

1) Read the general instructions carefully. These are usually printed on the first page of the exam booklet. As a rule, these instructions refer to the timing of the examination; the fact that you should not start work until the signal and must stop work at a signal, etc. If there are any *special* instructions, such as a choice of questions to be answered, make sure that you note this instruction carefully.

2) When you are ready to start work on the examination, that is as soon as the signal has been given, read the instructions to each question booklet, underline any key words or phrases, such as *least, best, outline, describe* and the like. In this way you will tend to answer as requested rather than discover on reviewing your paper that you *listed without describing*, that you selected the *worst* choice rather than the *best* choice, etc.

3) If the examination is of the objective or multiple-choice type – that is, each question will also give a series of possible answers: A, B, C or D, and you are called upon to select the best answer and write the letter next to that answer on your answer paper – it is advisable to start answering each question in turn. There may be anywhere from 50 to 100 such questions in the three or four hours allotted and you can see how much time would be taken if you read through all the questions before beginning to answer any. Furthermore, if you come across a question or group of questions which you know would be difficult to answer, it would undoubtedly affect your handling of all the other questions.

4) If the examination is of the essay type and contains but a few questions, it is a moot point as to whether you should read all the questions before starting to answer any one. Of course, if you are given a choice – say five out of seven and the like – then it is essential to read all the questions so you can eliminate the two that are most difficult. If, however, you are asked to answer all the questions, there may be danger in trying to answer the easiest one first because you may find that you will spend too much time on it. The best technique is to answer the first question, then proceed to the second, etc.

5) Time your answers. Before the exam begins, write down the time it started, then add the time allowed for the examination and write down the time it must be completed, then divide the time available somewhat as follows:
   - If 3-1/2 hours are allowed, that would be 210 minutes. If you have 80 objective-type questions, that would be an average of 2-1/2 minutes per question. Allow yourself no more than 2 minutes per question, or a total of 160 minutes, which will permit about 50 minutes to review.
   - If for the time allotment of 210 minutes there are 7 essay questions to answer, that would average about 30 minutes a question. Give yourself only 25 minutes per question so that you have about 35 minutes to review.

6) The most important instruction is to *read each question* and make sure you know what is wanted. The second most important instruction is to *time yourself properly* so that you answer every question. The third most important instruction is to *answer every question*. Guess if you have to but include something for each question. Remember that you will receive no credit for a blank and will probably receive some credit if you write something in answer to an essay question. If you guess a letter – say "B" for a multiple-choice question – you may have guessed right. If you leave a blank as an answer to a multiple-choice question, the examiners may respect your feelings but it will not add a point to your score. Some exams may penalize you for wrong answers, so in such cases *only*, you may not want to guess unless you have some basis for your answer.

7) Suggestions
   a. Objective-type questions
      1. Examine the question booklet for proper sequence of pages and questions
      2. Read all instructions carefully
      3. Skip any question which seems too difficult; return to it after all other questions have been answered
      4. Apportion your time properly; do not spend too much time on any single question or group of questions

5. Note and underline key words – *all, most, fewest, least, best, worst, same, opposite,* etc.
6. Pay particular attention to negatives
7. Note unusual option, e.g., unduly long, short, complex, different or similar in content to the body of the question
8. Observe the use of "hedging" words – *probably, may, most likely,* etc.
9. Make sure that your answer is put next to the same number as the question
10. Do not second-guess unless you have good reason to believe the second answer is definitely more correct
11. Cross out original answer if you decide another answer is more accurate; do not erase until you are ready to hand your paper in
12. Answer all questions; guess unless instructed otherwise
13. Leave time for review

b. Essay questions
1. Read each question carefully
2. Determine exactly what is wanted. Underline key words or phrases.
3. Decide on outline or paragraph answer
4. Include many different points and elements unless asked to develop any one or two points or elements
5. Show impartiality by giving pros and cons unless directed to select one side only
6. Make and write down any assumptions you find necessary to answer the questions
7. Watch your English, grammar, punctuation and choice of words
8. Time your answers; don't crowd material

8) Answering the essay question

Most essay questions can be answered by framing the specific response around several key words or ideas. Here are a few such key words or ideas:

M's: manpower, materials, methods, money, management
P's: purpose, program, policy, plan, procedure, practice, problems, pitfalls, personnel, public relations

a. Six basic steps in handling problems:
1. Preliminary plan and background development
2. Collect information, data and facts
3. Analyze and interpret information, data and facts
4. Analyze and develop solutions as well as make recommendations
5. Prepare report and sell recommendations
6. Install recommendations and follow up effectiveness

b. Pitfalls to avoid
1. *Taking things for granted* – A statement of the situation does not necessarily imply that each of the elements is necessarily true; for example, a complaint may be invalid and biased so that all that can be taken for granted is that a complaint has been registered

2. *Considering only one side of a situation* – Wherever possible, indicate several alternatives and then point out the reasons you selected the best one
3. *Failing to indicate follow up* – Whenever your answer indicates action on your part, make certain that you will take proper follow-up action to see how successful your recommendations, procedures or actions turn out to be
4. *Taking too long in answering any single question* – Remember to time your answers properly

IX. AFTER THE TEST

Scoring procedures differ in detail among civil service jurisdictions although the general principles are the same. Whether the papers are hand-scored or graded by machine we have described, they are nearly always graded by number. That is, the person who marks the paper knows only the number – never the name – of the applicant. Not until all the papers have been graded will they be matched with names. If other tests, such as training and experience or oral interview ratings have been given, scores will be combined. Different parts of the examination usually have different weights. For example, the written test might count 60 percent of the final grade, and a rating of training and experience 40 percent. In many jurisdictions, veterans will have a certain number of points added to their grades.

After the final grade has been determined, the names are placed in grade order and an eligible list is established. There are various methods for resolving ties between those who get the same final grade – probably the most common is to place first the name of the person whose application was received first. Job offers are made from the eligible list in the order the names appear on it. You will be notified of your grade and your rank as soon as all these computations have been made. This will be done as rapidly as possible.

People who are found to meet the requirements in the announcement are called "eligibles." Their names are put on a list of eligible candidates. An eligible's chances of getting a job depend on how high he stands on this list and how fast agencies are filling jobs from the list.

When a job is to be filled from a list of eligibles, the agency asks for the names of people on the list of eligibles for that job. When the civil service commission receives this request, it sends to the agency the names of the three people highest on this list. Or, if the job to be filled has specialized requirements, the office sends the agency the names of the top three persons who meet these requirements from the general list.

The appointing officer makes a choice from among the three people whose names were sent to him. If the selected person accepts the appointment, the names of the others are put back on the list to be considered for future openings.

That is the rule in hiring from all kinds of eligible lists, whether they are for typist, carpenter, chemist, or something else. For every vacancy, the appointing officer has his choice of any one of the top three eligibles on the list. This explains why the person whose name is on top of the list sometimes does not get an appointment when some of the persons lower on the list do. If the appointing officer chooses the second or third eligible, the No. 1 eligible does not get a job at once, but stays on the list until he is appointed or the list is terminated.

X. HOW TO PASS THE INTERVIEW TEST

The examination for which you applied requires an oral interview test. You have already taken the written test and you are now being called for the interview test – the final part of the formal examination.

You may think that it is not possible to prepare for an interview test and that there are no procedures to follow during an interview. Our purpose is to point out some things you can do in advance that will help you and some good rules to follow and pitfalls to avoid while you are being interviewed.

What is an interview supposed to test?

The written examination is designed to test the technical knowledge and competence of the candidate; the oral is designed to evaluate intangible qualities, not readily measured otherwise, and to establish a list showing the relative fitness of each candidate – as measured against his competitors – for the position sought. Scoring is not on the basis of "right" and "wrong," but on a sliding scale of values ranging from "not passable" to "outstanding." As a matter of fact, it is possible to achieve a relatively low score without a single "incorrect" answer because of evident weakness in the qualities being measured.

Occasionally, an examination may consist entirely of an oral test – either an individual or a group oral. In such cases, information is sought concerning the technical knowledges and abilities of the candidate, since there has been no written examination for this purpose. More commonly, however, an oral test is used to supplement a written examination.

Who conducts interviews?

The composition of oral boards varies among different jurisdictions. In nearly all, a representative of the personnel department serves as chairman. One of the members of the board may be a representative of the department in which the candidate would work. In some cases, "outside experts" are used, and, frequently, a businessman or some other representative of the general public is asked to serve. Labor and management or other special groups may be represented. The aim is to secure the services of experts in the appropriate field.

However the board is composed, it is a good idea (and not at all improper or unethical) to ascertain in advance of the interview who the members are and what groups they represent. When you are introduced to them, you will have some idea of their backgrounds and interests, and at least you will not stutter and stammer over their names.

What should be done before the interview?

While knowledge about the board members is useful and takes some of the surprise element out of the interview, there is other preparation which is more substantive. It *is* possible to prepare for an oral interview – in several ways:

1) Keep a copy of your application and review it carefully before the interview

This may be the only document before the oral board, and the starting point of the interview. Know what education and experience you have listed there, and the sequence and dates of all of it. Sometimes the board will ask you to review the highlights of your experience for them; you should not have to hem and haw doing it.

2) Study the class specification and the examination announcement

Usually, the oral board has one or both of these to guide them. The qualities, characteristics or knowledges required by the position sought are stated in these documents. They offer valuable clues as to the nature of the oral interview. For example, if the job involves supervisory responsibilities, the announcement will usually indicate that knowledge of modern supervisory methods and the qualifications of the candidate as a supervisor will be tested. If so, you can expect such questions, frequently in the form of a hypothetical situation which you are expected to solve. NEVER go into an oral without knowledge of the duties and responsibilities of the job you seek.

3) Think through each qualification required

Try to visualize the kind of questions you would ask if you were a board member. How well could you answer them? Try especially to appraise your own knowledge and background in each area, *measured against the job sought*, and identify any areas in which you are weak. Be critical and realistic – do not flatter yourself.

4) Do some general reading in areas in which you feel you may be weak

For example, if the job involves supervision and your past experience has NOT, some general reading in supervisory methods and practices, particularly in the field of human relations, might be useful. Do NOT study agency procedures or detailed manuals. The oral board will be testing your understanding and capacity, not your memory.

5) Get a good night's sleep and watch your general health and mental attitude

You will want a clear head at the interview. Take care of a cold or any other minor ailment, and of course, no hangovers.

What should be done on the day of the interview?

Now comes the day of the interview itself. Give yourself plenty of time to get there. Plan to arrive somewhat ahead of the scheduled time, particularly if your appointment is in the fore part of the day. If a previous candidate fails to appear, the board might be ready for you a bit early. By early afternoon an oral board is almost invariably behind schedule if there are many candidates, and you may have to wait. Take along a book or magazine to read, or your application to review, but leave any extraneous material in the waiting room when you go in for your interview. In any event, relax and compose yourself.

The matter of dress is important. The board is forming impressions about you – from your experience, your manners, your attitude, and your appearance. Give your personal appearance careful attention. Dress your best, but not your flashiest. Choose conservative, appropriate clothing, and be sure it is immaculate. This is a business interview, and your appearance should indicate that you regard it as such. Besides, being well groomed and properly dressed will help boost your confidence.

Sooner or later, someone will call your name and escort you into the interview room. *This is it.* From here on you are on your own. It is too late for any more preparation. But remember, you asked for this opportunity to prove your fitness, and you are here because your request was granted.

What happens when you go in?

The usual sequence of events will be as follows: The clerk (who is often the board stenographer) will introduce you to the chairman of the oral board, who will introduce you to the other members of the board. Acknowledge the introductions before you sit down. Do not be surprised if you find a microphone facing you or a stenotypist sitting by. Oral interviews are usually recorded in the event of an appeal or other review.

Usually the chairman of the board will open the interview by reviewing the highlights of your education and work experience from your application – primarily for the benefit of the other members of the board, as well as to get the material into the record. Do not interrupt or comment unless there is an error or significant misinterpretation; if that is the case, do not hesitate. But do not quibble about insignificant matters. Also, he will usually ask you some question about your education, experience or your present job – partly to get you to start talking and to establish the interviewing "rapport." He may start the actual questioning, or turn it over to one of the other members. Frequently, each member undertakes the questioning on a particular area, one in which he is perhaps most competent, so you can expect each member to participate in the examination. Because time is limited, you may also expect some rather abrupt switches in the direction the questioning takes, so do not be upset by it. Normally, a board member will not pursue a single line of questioning unless he discovers a particular strength or weakness.

After each member has participated, the chairman will usually ask whether any member has any further questions, then will ask you if you have anything you wish to add. Unless you are expecting this question, it may floor you. Worse, it may start you off on an extended, extemporaneous speech. The board is not usually seeking more information. The question is principally to offer you a last opportunity to present further qualifications or to indicate that you have nothing to add. So, if you feel that a significant qualification or characteristic has been overlooked, it is proper to point it out in a sentence or so. Do not compliment the board on the thoroughness of their examination – they have been sketchy, and you know it. If you wish, merely say, "No thank you, I have nothing further to add." This is a point where you can "talk yourself out" of a good impression or fail to present an important bit of information. Remember, *you close the interview yourself*.

The chairman will then say, "That is all, Mr. _____, thank you." Do not be startled; the interview is over, and quicker than you think. Thank him, gather your belongings and take your leave. Save your sigh of relief for the other side of the door.

How to put your best foot forward

Throughout this entire process, you may feel that the board individually and collectively is trying to pierce your defenses, seek out your hidden weaknesses and embarrass and confuse you. Actually, this is not true. They are obliged to make an appraisal of your qualifications for the job you are seeking, and they want to see you in your best light. Remember, they must interview all candidates and a non-cooperative candidate may become a failure in spite of their best efforts to bring out his qualifications. Here are 15 suggestions that will help you:

1) Be natural – Keep your attitude confident, not cocky

If you are not confident that you can do the job, do not expect the board to be. Do not apologize for your weaknesses, try to bring out your strong points. The board is interested in a positive, not negative, presentation. Cockiness will antagonize any board member and make him wonder if you are covering up a weakness by a false show of strength.

2) Get comfortable, but don't lounge or sprawl

Sit erectly but not stiffly. A careless posture may lead the board to conclude that you are careless in other things, or at least that you are not impressed by the importance of the occasion. Either conclusion is natural, even if incorrect. Do not fuss with your clothing, a pencil or an ashtray. Your hands may occasionally be useful to emphasize a point; do not let them become a point of distraction.

3) Do not wisecrack or make small talk

This is a serious situation, and your attitude should show that you consider it as such. Further, the time of the board is limited – they do not want to waste it, and neither should you.

4) Do not exaggerate your experience or abilities

In the first place, from information in the application or other interviews and sources, the board may know more about you than you think. Secondly, you probably will not get away with it. An experienced board is rather adept at spotting such a situation, so do not take the chance.

5) If you know a board member, do not make a point of it, yet do not hide it

Certainly you are not fooling him, and probably not the other members of the board. Do not try to take advantage of your acquaintanceship – it will probably do you little good.

6) Do not dominate the interview

Let the board do that. They will give you the clues – do not assume that you have to do all the talking. Realize that the board has a number of questions to ask you, and do not try to take up all the interview time by showing off your extensive knowledge of the answer to the first one.

7) Be attentive

You only have 20 minutes or so, and you should keep your attention at its sharpest throughout. When a member is addressing a problem or question to you, give him your undivided attention. Address your reply principally to him, but do not exclude the other board members.

8) Do not interrupt

A board member may be stating a problem for you to analyze. He will ask you a question when the time comes. Let him state the problem, and wait for the question.

9) Make sure you understand the question

Do not try to answer until you are sure what the question is. If it is not clear, restate it in your own words or ask the board member to clarify it for you. However, do not haggle about minor elements.

10) Reply promptly but not hastily

A common entry on oral board rating sheets is "candidate responded readily," or "candidate hesitated in replies." Respond as promptly and quickly as you can, but do not jump to a hasty, ill-considered answer.

11) Do not be peremptory in your answers

A brief answer is proper – but do not fire your answer back. That is a losing game from your point of view. The board member can probably ask questions much faster than you can answer them.

12) Do not try to create the answer you think the board member wants

He is interested in what kind of mind you have and how it works – not in playing games. Furthermore, he can usually spot this practice and will actually grade you down on it.

13) Do not switch sides in your reply merely to agree with a board member

Frequently, a member will take a contrary position merely to draw you out and to see if you are willing and able to defend your point of view. Do not start a debate, yet do not surrender a good position. If a position is worth taking, it is worth defending.

14) Do not be afraid to admit an error in judgment if you are shown to be wrong

The board knows that you are forced to reply without any opportunity for careful consideration. Your answer may be demonstrably wrong. If so, admit it and get on with the interview.

15) Do not dwell at length on your present job

The opening question may relate to your present assignment. Answer the question but do not go into an extended discussion. You are being examined for a *new* job, not your present one. As a matter of fact, try to phrase ALL your answers in terms of the job for which you are being examined.

Basis of Rating

Probably you will forget most of these "do's" and "don'ts" when you walk into the oral interview room. Even remembering them all will not ensure you a passing grade. Perhaps you did not have the qualifications in the first place. But remembering them will help you to put your best foot forward, without treading on the toes of the board members.

Rumor and popular opinion to the contrary notwithstanding, an oral board wants you to make the best appearance possible. They know you are under pressure – but they also want to see how you respond to it as a guide to what your reaction would be under the pressures of the job you seek. They will be influenced by the degree of poise you display, the personal traits you show and the manner in which you respond.

ABOUT THIS BOOK

This book contains tests divided into Examination Sections. Go through each test, answering every question in the margin. We have also attached a sample answer sheet at the back of the book that can be removed and used. At the end of each test look at the answer key and check your answers. On the ones you got wrong, look at the right answer choice and learn. Do not fill in the answers first. Do not memorize the questions and answers, but understand the answer and principles involved. On your test, the questions will likely be different from the samples. Questions are changed and new ones added. If you understand these past questions you should have success with any changes that arise. Tests may consist of several types of questions. We have additional books on each subject should more study be advisable or necessary for you. Finally, the more you study, the better prepared you will be. This book is intended to be the last thing you study before you walk into the examination room. Prior study of relevant texts is also recommended. NLC publishes some of these in our Fundamental Series. Knowledge and good sense are important factors in passing your exam. Good luck also helps. So now study this Passbook, absorb the material contained within and take that knowledge into the examination. Then do your best to pass that exam.

EXAMINATION SECTION

EXAMINATION SECTION
TEST 1

DIRECTIONS: This is a test of using an artificial language.

Translation: English to Artificial Language

a = ile	officer = ule	to capture = ionet
above = hisf	prisoner = rorsea	to carry = juket
after = revo	quick = nol	to crawl = soulet
and = inklon	river = sil	to cross = sandringet
at = soe	road = jise	to elude = serenget
before = slif	she = lur	to fall = osselet
border = aille	slow = esea	to have = meneset
boy = nocrag	small = woa	to hear = urilet
but = orn	smart = brea	to hide = loet
dark = nase	the = cele	to leave = rendet
from = eiseau	they = wur	to patrol = doliet
he = nur	to = sonq	to protect = wusset
I = aol	tree = filmos	to question = parlet
in = rak	under = dun	to run = swanet
is = serrisus	was = serrilus	to say = soset
large = quin	water = ose	to search = nurret
man = emmcen	when = nand	to see = oiset
me = oa	woman = lis	to seize = femtet
morning = duren	to attempt = farret	to swim = fumet
night = tenyun	to be = serriet	

Grammar

Nouns: To make nouns plural, you must use the noun suffix –en. For example: river = sil; rivers = silen.

Although you are provided with some actual nouns, you will have to form nouns from other types of words (verbs and adjectives). The noun prefix in- when added to a verb or adjective negates the action or description and transforms it into a noun. For example: to protect = wusset; protection = inwusset; quick = nol; quickness = innol.

Nouns made from verbs or adjectives use the same plural suffix, -en. For example: to question = parlet; question = inparlet; questions = inparleten.

Pronouns: To change the case of a pronoun to the possessive, you must add the possessive suffix –ey. For example: I = aol; my = aoley; he = nur; his = nurey.

Verbs: To effectively use the given verbs, you may have to modify them, depending on their usages. Formation of verbs will vary, according to their prefixes and suffixes. The tenses of the verbs are important to the meaning of the sentences in which they are used. Notice that each verb ends with the suffix –et. When using any verb suffix, you must first drop the –et, and then add the suffix.

    sandring- + past tense suffix –lus = sandringlus
      Past tense verb sandringlus = crossed
    sandring- + present-tense suffix –sus = sandringsus
      Present tense verb sandringsus = cross, crosses
    sandring- + future tense suffix –dus = sandringdus
      Future tense verb sandringdus = will cross
    sandring- + participle suffix –mus = sandringmus
      Participial form sandringmus = crossing

Adjectives: When using an adjective, you must add the suffix that has been added to the noun you are describing. For example: Adjective large = quin; Noun tree = filmos, quin filmos = large tree; with plural suffix –en added: quinen filmosen = large trees.

Adverbs: Adverbs are used to describe verbs. The adverbs used in this test will be formed by adding the suffix -ee to adjectives. For example: Adjective slow = esea; adverbial form slowly = eseaee; verb to crawl = soulet; adverbial form = eseaee. Therefore, to crawl slowly = soulet eseaee.

Forms of adverbs are independent of verb forms. For example: soul- = past tense suffix –lus = soullus; crawled = soullus. Therefore, soullus eseaee = crawled slowly.

Negatives: The negative prefix il- applies to all words. The il- prefix does not solely represent the English prefix un-, but it is a generic negative prefix. For example: verb: to cross = sandringet; to uncross = ilsandringet.

Questions 1-20.

DIRECTIONS: Verify the translations of the underlined words. Select one of the five possible responses listed below. Print the letter of the correct answer in the space at the right.

    A – #1 word is correctly translated
    B – #2 word is correctly translated
    C – #3 word is correctly translated
    D – Two or three words are correctly translated
    E – None of the words is correctly translated

1. Wur wusssus cele aille.
    1   2   3
They protected the borders.
  1   2   3

2. Cele emmcen farrlus sandringet.
        1   2   3
The man attempted crossing.
     1   2   3

3. Cele lis dumlus nolee.
      1   2   3
The women swim quick.
     1   2   3

4. Uleen parrlus aille.
    1   2   3
Officers question the man at the borders.
    1   2   3

5. Cele rorsea serrilus swanmus nolee.
              1   2   3
The prisoner is running quick.
           1   2   3

6. Cele duren serrilus nase.
       1   2   3
The mornings were dark.
      1   2   3

7. Lur serrilus dun cele filmos.
   1   2   3
She was under the tree.
   1   2   3

1.____
2.____
3.____
4.____
5.____
6.____
7.____

8. Cele <u>emmcen</u> inklon <u>lis</u> <u>rendlus</u> soe tenyun.
       1   2   3
   The <u>woman</u> and <u>man</u> <u>left</u> at night.
        1   2   3

8._____

9. Cele <u>sil</u> <u>serrilus</u> <u>nol</u>.
        1   2   3
   The <u>river</u> <u>ran</u> <u>quickly</u>.
        1   2   3

9._____

10. Cele <u>ule</u> <u>dolimus</u> cele <u>aille</u> soe tenyun.
         1   2   3
    The <u>officers</u> <u>patrolled</u> the <u>borders</u> at night.
         1   2   3

10._____

11. Cele lis <u>urillus</u> cele <u>ule</u> rak cele <u>nase</u>.
            1   2   3
    The woman <u>heard</u> the <u>officers</u> in the <u>darkness</u>.
              1   2   3

11._____

12. <u>Nurey</u> <u>inparlet</u> <u>serengmus</u> oa.
      1   2   4
    The <u>question</u> <u>eluded</u> me.
         1   2

12._____

13. Cele <u>nocrag</u> <u>swanlus</u> <u>revo</u> cele lis.
         1   2   3
    The <u>boy</u> <u>ran</u> <u>after</u> the woman.
         1   2   3

13._____

14. Cele <u>nocragen</u> <u>lolus</u> rak cele <u>filmos</u>.
         1   2   3
    The <u>boy</u> <u>hides</u> in the <u>tree</u>.
         1   2   3

14._____

15. Cele <u>nocrag</u> <u>swanlus</u> eiseau cele <u>uleen</u>.
         1   2   3
    The <u>boys</u> <u>were running</u> from the <u>officers</u>.
         1   2   3

15._____

16. Cele <u>lis</u> <u>serrisus</u> <u>woa</u>.
         1   2   3
    The <u>woman</u> <u>was</u> <u>large</u>.
         1   2   3

16._____

17. Cele <u>ule</u> <u>rendsus</u> rak cele <u>duren</u>.
         1   2   3
    The <u>officers</u> <u>left</u> in the <u>night</u>.
         1   2   3

17._____

18. Cele ule parldus cele nocrag rak cele duren.
             1   2   3
    The officer questions the boy during the morning.
                     1   2   3

    18._____

19. Cele lis renddus nand tenyun osselsus.
           1   2   3
    The woman will leave when night falls.
                  1   3   3

    19._____

20. Cele uleen ionlus cele lisen.
          1   2   3
    The officer captured the woman.
          1   2   3

    20._____

Questions 21-30.

DIRECTIONS: Correctly translate the underlined words to English.

21. Lur juklus lurey boy.
    A. He carried his boy.   B. She carries his boy.
    C. She carried her boy   D. He carries his boy.
    E. He carries her boy.

    21._____

22. The rorsea serrisus smart and nol.
    A. The prisoner is smart and quick.
    B. The officer was smart and quick.
    C. The prisoner was smart and quick.
    D. The officer is smart and quick.
    E. The prisoner is smart and quickly.

    22._____

23. The emmcen rendlus the jise.
    A. The woman left the road.   B. The man leaves the river.
    C. The woman leaves the road.   D. The man left the road.
    E. The man is leaving the river.

    23._____

24. The woman farrlus sandringet the aille.
    A. The woman attempts crossing the border.
    B. The woman attempted to cross the border.
    C. The woman is crossing the river.
    D. The woman will attempt to cross the river.
    E. The woman will attempt to cross the border.

    24._____

25. Aol swanlus eiseau the officer.
    A. She ran to the officer.   B. She ran from the officer.
    C. I will run from the officer. D. I ran to the officer.
    E. I ran from the officer.

    25.-_____

26. A quin indoliet nurrsus the border.   26._____
    A. A small patrol searched the border.
    B. A large officer patrols the border.
    C. A large patroller is searching the border.
    D. A large patrol searches the border.
    E. A small patrol patrols the border.

27. Nur serrisus a nocrag.   27._____
    A. She is a girl.   B. She was a girl.
    C. His was a boy.   D. He was a boy.
    E. He is a boy.

28. The ule juklus the lis.   28._____
    A. The officer carried the woman.   B. The officer carries the women.
    C. The officers carry the women.   D. The officers carried the women.
    E. The officers carry the woman.

29. The rorsea farrlus serenget the officer.   29._____
    A. The prisoner attempts eluding the officer.
    B. The man attempts to elude the officer.
    C. The prisoner attempted to elude the officer.
    D. The prisoners attempted to elude the officer.
    E. The prisoners attempt eluding the officer.

30. The quinen uleen fentlus the boy.   30.-___
    A. The large officer seized the boy.
    B. The large officers seized the boy.
    C. The small officer seizes the boy.
    D. The small officers seize the boy.
    E. The large officer will seize the boy.

Questions 31-40.

DIRECTIONS: Select the correct translation for the underlined words.

The officers searched the border in their attempt to capture. The man and woman
    1   2   3
attempted to elude the officers. After the river, they hid under a large tree. In the morning, man
    4   5   6   7   8
and woman were captured and questioned.
              9   10

31. #1 would be translated: 31._____
    A. ule nurrlus   B. uleen nurrlus   C. uleen nurrsus
    D. ule nurrsus   E. uleen nurret

32. #2 would be translated:
    A. rak wur farret
    B. rak wurey farret
    C. soe wurey infarret
    D. soe wur farrsus
    E. rak wurey infarret

33. #3 would be translated:
    A. ionet rorseaen
    B. sonq ionsus rorseaen
    C. sonq ionet rorsea
    D. ionet rorsea
    E. ionsus rorseaen

34. #4 would be translated:
    A. A, farrlus sonq serengsus
    B. farrsus serenget
    C. farrsus sonq serenget
    D. farrlus serenget
    E. farrlus sonq serenget

35. #5 would be translated:
    A. Revo sandringet
    B. Revo sandringmus
    C. Nand sandringmus
    D. Revo sandringlus
    E. Nand sandringlus

36. #6 would be translated:
    A. wurey lolus
    B. wur losus
    C. wur lolus
    D. wurey lomus
    E. wur loet

37. #7 would be translated:
    A. quinen filmosen
    B. woa filmos
    C. quin filmosen
    D. woaen filmosen
    E. quin filmos

38. #8 would be translated:
    A. Rak cele duren
    B. Soe durenen
    C. Rak cele durenen
    D. Soe cele duret
    E. Rak cele duret

39. #9 would be translated:
    A. serrilus iondus
    B. serrilus ionlus
    C. serrilusen ionlus
    D. serrilusen ionlusen
    E. serrilus ionsus

40. #10 would be translated:
    A. parlmus
    B. parldus
    C. parlsus
    D. parllus
    E. parllusen

Questions 41-50.

DIRECTIONS: Select the correct usage of the underlined words.

41. Cele lisen <u>sandringet</u> <u>nol</u>. (Verb-Adverb) (The women crossed quickly.)
    A. sandringmus nolee
    B. sandringdus nol
    C. sandringlus nolee
    D. sandringlus nol
    E. sandringus nol

42. Cele nocrag farrlus cele <u>sandringet</u>. (Noun) (The boy attempted the crossing.)
    A. sandringet
    B. insandringlus
    C. sandringmus
    D. insandringet
    E. insandringmus

43. Cele ule <u>nol ionet</u> cele emmcenen. (Adverb-Verb) (The officer quickly captured the men.)
    A. nolee ionlus
    B. nol ionlus
    C. nolee inionmus
    D. nol ionmus
    E. nolee iniondus

44. Nur <u>juket</u> cele woa nocrag. (Verb) (He carried the small boy.)
    A. injukmus
    B. juklusen
    C. jukdusen
    D. juklus
    E. injuksus

45. Cele <u>nurret</u> <u>serriet</u> esea. (Singular Noun-Verb) (The search was slow.)
    A. nurrlus serrilus
    B. innurret serrilus
    C. innurrlus serrilus
    D. innurrmus serrimus
    E. nurrlus inserrimus

46. Cele uleen <u>ionet</u> cele rorseaen nand wur <u>sandringet</u>. (Verb-Verb) (The officers will capture the prisoners when they cross.)
    A. ionsus sandringdus
    B. iondus sandringmus
    C. ionlus sandringsus
    D. iondus sandringdus
    E. iondus sandringsus

47. Cele <u>filmos</u> serrisus <u>quin</u>. (Plural Nound-Adjective) (The trees are large.)
    A. filmos quinen
    B. filmosen quin
    C. filmosen quinen
    D. filmosee quin
    E. filmosee quinee

48. Cele <u>esea</u> <u>sil</u> sandringsus cele aille. (Adjective-Singular Noun) (The slow river crosses the border.)
    A. eseaen silen
    B. esea silen
    C. eseaee silee
    D. esea sil
    E. eseaee silen

49. Cele quin <u>doliet</u> <u>nurret</u> cele sil. (Singular Noun-Verb) (The large patrol searches the river.)
    A. indoliet nurrsus
    B. indolisus nurrsus
    C. indoliet innurrmus
    D. dolisus nurrsus
    E. dolimus nurrmus

50. Cele lis serrilus <u>nol</u> inklon <u>quin</u>. (Adj.-Adj.) (The woman was quick and large.)   50. ____
    A. nolen quinen
    B. nolen quin
    C. nol quin
    D. quinen nolen
    E. nolee quinee

KEY (CORRECT ANSWERS)

1.	A	11.	A	21.	C	31.	B	41.	C
2.	D	12.	B	22.	A	32.	E	42.	E
3.	E	13.	D	23.	D	33.	A	43.	A
4.	A	14.	C	24.	B	34.	D	44.	D
5.	B	15.	C	25.	E	35.	B	45.	B
6.	C	16.	A	26.	D	36.	C	46.	E
7.	D	17.	E	27.	E	37.	E	47.	C
8.	C	18.	B	28.	A	38.	A	48.	D
9.	A	19.	D	29.	C	39.	C	49.	A
10.	E	20.	B	30.	B	40.	D	50.	C

TEST 2

DIRECTIONS: This is a test of using an artificial language.

Translation: English to Artificial Language

a (or an) = ile
above = hisf
after = revo
and = inklon
at = soe
before = slif
border = aille
boy = nocrag
but = orn
dark = nase
from = eiseau
he = nur
I = aol
in = rak
is = serrisus
large = quin
man = emmcen
morning = duren
night = tenyun
officer = ule

prisoner = rorsea
quick = nol
river = sil
road = jise
she = lur
slow = esea
small = woa
smart = brea
the = cele
they = wur
to = sonq
tree = filmos
under = dun
was = serrilus
water = ose
when = nand
woman = lis
to attempt = farret
to be = serriet
to capture = ionet

to carry = juket
to crawl = soulet
to cross = sandringet
to elude = serenget
to fall = osselet
to have = meneset
to hear = urilet
to hide = loet
to leave = rendet
to patrol = doliet
to protect = wusset
to question = parlet
to run = swanet
to say = soset
to search = nurret
to see = oiset
to seize = femtet
to swim = fumet

Grammar

Nouns: To make nouns plural, you must use the noun suffix –*lins*. For example: road = jise; roads = jiselins.

Although you are provided with some actual nouns, you will have to form nouns from other types of words (verbs and adjectives). The noun prefix *al-* when added to a verb or adjective negates the action or description and transforms it into a noun. For example: to protect = wusset; protection = alwusset; quick = nol; quickness = alnol.

Nouns made from verbs or adjectives use the same plural suffix, *-lins*. For example: to question = parlet; question = alparlet; questions = alparletlins.

Pronouns: To change the case of a pronoun to the possessive, you must add the possessive suffix –*i*. For example: I = aol; my = aoli; she = lur; hers = luri.

Verbs: To effectively use the given verbs, you may have to modify them, depending on their usages. Formation of verbs will vary, according to their prefixes and suffixes. The tenses of the verbs are important to the meaning of the sentences in which they are used. Notice that each verb ends with the suffix –*et*. When using any verb suffix, you must first drop the –*et*, and then add the suffix.

ren- + past tense suffix –gon = rengon
   Past tense verb rengon = left
ren- + present-tense suffix –tin = rentin
   Present tense verb rentin = leave, leaves
ren-- + future tense suffix –nel = rennel
   Future tense verb rennel = will leave
ren- + participle suffix –ry = renry
   Participial form renry = leaving

Adjectives: When using an adjective, you must add the suffix that has been added to the noun you are describing. For example: Adjective large = quin; Noun tree = filmos, quin filmos = large tree; with plural suffix –*lins* added: quinlins filmoslins = large trees.

Adverbs: Adverbs are used to describe verbs. The adverbs used in this test will be formed by adding the suffix -*dis* to adjectives. Adjective slow= esea;adverbial form slowly = eseadis; verb to crawl = soulet + adverbial form eseadis. Therefore, to crawl slowly = soulet eseadis.

Forms of adverbs are independent of verb forms. For example: soul- = past tense suffix –*gon* = soulgon; crawled = soulgon. Therefore, soulgon eseaee = crawled slowly.

3 (#2)

Questions 1-20.

DIRECTIONS: Verify the translations of the underlined words. Select one of the five possible responses listed below. Print the letter of the correct answer in the space at the right.

    A - #1 word is correctly translated
    B – #2 word is correctly translated
    C – #3 word is correctly translated
    D – Two or three words are correctly translated
    E – None of the words is correctly translated

1. Cele <u>ule</u> <u>pargon</u> cele <u>rorsea</u> rak cele duren.
     1   2   3
The <u>officer</u> <u>will question</u> the <u>prisoner</u> in the morning.
     1   2   3

1.____

2. Cele ule <u>serrinel</u> <u>albrea</u>, orn cele <u>rorseas</u> serengtin nur.
           1   2   3
The officer <u>was</u> <u>smart</u>, but the <u>prisoners</u> eluded him.
            1 2   3

2.____

3. Aoli <u>urilry</u> cele <u>nocraglins</u> <u>sandringry</u> rak cele tenyun.
      1   2   3
I <u>heard</u> the <u>men</u> <u>crossing</u> in the night.
  1   2   3

3.____

4. Revo cele <u>alnurretlins</u>, cele <u>rorsea</u> <u>serrigon</u> jukgon.
        1   2   3
After the <u>seizures</u>, the <u>prisoners</u> <u>will be</u> captured.
      1   2   3

4.____

5. <u>Nuri</u> <u>alnol</u> <u>juktin</u> sonq cele aille.
   1   2   3
<u>His</u> <u>quickness</u> <u>carried</u> him to the border.
 1   2   3

5.____

6. Cele <u>emmcens</u> <u>serriet</u> <u>iongon</u> rak cele jise.
      1   2   3
The <u>men</u> <u>were</u> <u>captured</u> in the road.
   1   2   3

6.____

7. Nand ulelins <u>nurrgon</u> cele <u>nocrags</u>, <u>wuri</u> farrgon swanet.
          1   2   3
When officers <u>questioned</u> the <u>boys</u>, <u>they</u> attempted to run.
          1   2   3

7.____

4 (#2)

8. Slif cele duren, cele <u>ulelins</u> <u>nurrnel</u> cle <u>rorsealins</u>.
                         1   2   3
    Before the morning, the <u>officer</u> <u>will search</u> the <u>prisoner</u>.
                             1   2   3

8.____

9. Cele <u>emmcen</u> <u>menesgon</u> ile <u>alosselet</u> dun cele filmos.
           1   2   3
    The <u>man</u> <u>had</u> a <u>fall</u> under the tree.
           1   2   3

9.____

10. Cele <u>lislins</u> <u>jukgon</u> <u>wuri</u> nocraglins sonq cele aille.
            1   2   3
    The <u>women</u> <u>carry</u> <u>the</u> boys to the border.
             1   2   3

10.____

11. Cele <u>jiselins</u> <u>serrinel</u> nase <u>rak</u> tenyun.
            1   2   3
    The <u>roads</u> <u>are</u> dark <u>at</u> night.
          1   2   3

11.____

12. Revo <u>lur</u> <u>nocrags</u> serrigon pargon, cele lis <u>swangon</u>.
         1   2   3
    After <u>her</u> <u>boys</u> are questioned, the woman <u>will run</u>.
          1   2   3

12.____

13. Nur <u>menestin</u> <u>nuri</u> <u>doliet</u> rak cele duren.
          1   2   3
    He <u>had</u> <u>his</u> <u>patrol</u> in the morning.
       1   2   3

13.____

14. <u>Nand</u> wuri serritin iongon, <u>wuri</u> farrgon ile <u>alsandringet</u>.
     1   2   3
    <u>Before</u> they were captured, <u>they</u> were attempting a <u>crossing</u>.
      1   2   3

14.____

15. Cele lislins <u>dun</u> cele sil sosgon <u>wuri</u> <u>oisgon</u> cele nocraglins.
                  1   2   3

15.____

16. Ile <u>alnurret</u> <u>serritin</u> soe tenyun.
       1   2   3
    The <u>search</u> <u>will be attempted</u> at night.
        1   2   3

16.____

17. Rak cele <u>duren</u> aol <u>iongon</u> cele emmcen <u>eiseau</u> cele sil.
             1   2   3
    After the <u>patrol</u>, I <u>questioned</u> the men <u>under</u> the tree.
               1   2   3

17.____

18. <u>Revo</u> aol oisgon cele <u>emmcenlins</u>, aol <u>rengon</u>.   18._____
     1   2   3
<u>After</u> I question the <u>men</u>, I <u>will leave</u>.
  1   2   3

19. Cele <u>nocrag</u> <u>serrigon</u> <u>iongon</u> hisf cele sil.   19._____
         1   2   3
The <u>boy</u> <u>was</u> <u>captured</u> above the river.
     1   2   3

20. Nand <u>alnase</u> <u>osseltin</u>, cele ulelins <u>dolinel</u>.   20._____
         1   2   3
When <u>darkness</u> <u>fell</u>, the officers <u>patrolled</u>.
        1   2   3

Questions 21-30.

DIRECTIONS: Correctly translate the underlined words to English.

21. The <u>sil</u> <u>swantin</u> next to the <u>jise</u>.   21._____
    A. The <u>water</u> <u>is</u> next to the <u>roads</u>.
    B. The <u>men</u> <u>hid</u> next to the <u>river</u>.
    C. The <u>river</u> <u>runs</u> next to the <u>road</u>.
    D. The <u>officer</u> <u>will patrol</u> next to the <u>river</u>.
    E. The <u>river</u> <u>ran</u> next to the <u>roads</u>.

22. The <u>ulelins</u> <u>serrigon</u> the <u>aille</u> this morning.   22._____
    A. The <u>officers</u> <u>patrolled</u> the <u>border</u> this morning.
    B. The <u>man</u> <u>patrolled</u> the <u>road</u> this morning.
    C. The <u>officers</u> <u>are patrolling</u> the <u>borders</u> this morning.
    D. The <u>officer</u> <u>will patrol</u> the <u>border</u> this morning.
    E. The <u>officers</u> <u>questioned</u> the <u>prisoner</u> this morning.

23. <u>Aol</u> <u>pargon</u> the <u>lislins</u> who came to town today.   23._____
    A. <u>I will question</u> the <u>woman</u> who came to town today.
    B. <u>He seized</u> the <u>boys</u> who came to town today.
    C. <u>I have questioned</u> the <u>men</u> who came to town today.
    D. <u>I questioned</u> the <u>women</u> who came to town today.
    E. <u>He hid</u> the <u>boy</u> who came to town today.

24. <u>Revo</u> the <u>rorsealins</u> <u>rengon</u>, we discussed the situation.   24._____
    A. <u>When</u> the <u>prisoner</u> left, we discussed the situation.
    B. <u>After</u> the <u>prisoner</u> <u>ran</u>, we discussed the situation.
    C. <u>After</u> the <u>prisoners left</u>, we discussed the situation.
    D. <u>When</u> the <u>officers</u> <u>fell</u>, we discussed the situation.
    E. <u>Before</u> the <u>officers</u> <u>saw</u>, we discussed the situation.

25. The nocraglins soulgon dun the fence.   25.____
    A. The boy was captured at the fence.
    B. The boys crawled under the fence.
    C. The man crawls under the fence.
    D. The boy crawled over the fence.
    E. The boys were carried under the fence.

26. It is difficult wusset the aille soe tenyun.   26.____
    A. It is difficult to protect the road before morning.
    B. It is difficult to patrol the border after dark.
    C. It is difficult protecting the border before night.
    D. It is difficult to patrol the borders in the morning.
    E. It is difficult to protect the border at night.

27. The quinlins emmcenlins jukgon the children through the field.   27.____
    A. The large men carried the children through the field.
    B. The large man will carry the children through the field.
    C. The quick men carry the children through the field.
    D. The men quietly ran the children through the field.
    E. The smart man saw the children through the field.

28. We believe they farrnel an escape nand the officers rentin.   28.____
    A. We believe they attempted an escape after the officers left.
    B. We believe they will attempt an escape when the officers leave.
    C. We believe they attempt an escape whenever the officers leave.
    D. We believe they will attempt an escape before the officers leave.
    E. We believe they attempted an escape when the officers left.

29. The rorsealins serenggon the officers rak cele alnase.   29.____
    A. The prisoner questioned the officers at the border.
    B. The prisoners eluded the officers in the darkness.
    C. The prisoners will elude the officers in the morning.
    D. The prisoners eluded the officers under the tree.
    E. The prisoner eluded the officers in the darkness.

30. The lislins swangon song cele ose.   30.____
    A. The woman runs to the water.
    B. The officers searched at the river.
    C. The women will run to the river.
    D. The women ran to the water.
    E. The officers will patrol in the morning.

Questions 31-40.

DIRECTIONS: Select the correct translation for the underlined words.

On a <u>dark night</u>, the officers <u>patrolled the border</u> near the river that ran behind the town.
           1   2
Suddenly, an officer saw a <u>large man</u> and two <u>small boys</u> <u>attempting to cross the river</u>. The
                                                  3   4   5
officers took up positions on <u>the road above</u> them, but one of the boys <u>saw the officers</u> and
                                         6   7
began <u>to swim quickly</u> in another direction. The man and one boy were to swim quickly and
            8
the other boy was later <u>captured</u> after he was discovered <u>hiding under a tree</u>.
                                        9   10

31. #1 would be translated:
    A. naselins tenyunlins   B. alnase tenyunlins
    C. duren tenyun   D. nase tenyun
    E. nasedis tenyunlins

31.____

32. #2 would be translated:
    A. dolietlins ile aille   B. doligon cele aille
    C. dolinel cele aille   D. doliet cele aille
    E. doligon ile aille

32.____

33. #3 would be translated:
    A. alquin emmcen   B. quinlins emmcenlins
    C. alquin lislins   D. quin emmcen
    E. quin lis

33.____

34. #4 would be translated:
    A. alwoa nocraglins   B. woa nocrags
    C. brea nocrags   D. woalins nocraglins
    E. woa nograg

34.____

35. #5 would be translated:
    A. farry sandringet cele sil   B. farrnel sandringet cele jise
    C. farry sandringtin cele sil   D. farret sandringy cele sillins
    E. alfarret sandringet cele sil

35.____

36. #6 would be translated:
    A. jise hisf wur   B. ile jiselins hisflins
    C. cele jise hisf   D. alcele jise hisf
    E. cele jiselins hisf

36.____

37. #7 would be translated:
    A. oisgon celes ules   B. oiset cele ulelins
    C. aloiset ile ules   D. oistin cele ulelins
    E. oisgon cele ulelins

37.____

38. #8 would be translated:
    A. dumtin noldis
    B. dumet noldis
    C. dumry nol
    D. dumtin alnol
    E. dumet nol

39. #9 would be translated:
    A. ionet inklon parlet
    B. ionnel ile parnel
    C. iongon inklon pargon
    D. ionet inklon pargon
    E. iontin inklon partin

40. #10 would be translated:
    A. lorgon dun ile filmos
    B. lorgon dun cele filmoslins
    C. lory dun ile filmos
    D. lortin alhisf ile filmos
    E. lory dun cele filmos

Questions 41-50.

DIRECTIONS: Select the correct usage of the underlined words.

41. Aol nurret cele rorsealins soe tenyun. (Verb)
    A. nurry
    B. nurdis
    C. nurnel
    D. alnurlins
    E. alnurret

42. Wur farrgon ile doliet soe tenyun. (Noun)
    A. aldoligon
    B. dolietlins
    C. aldoliry
    D. aldoliet
    E. aldolietlins

43. Cele sil swantin esea. (Adverb)
    A. esealet
    B. eseadis
    C. alesea
    D. esealins
    E. aleseadis

44. Cele femtet farret rak cele alnase. (Noun-Verb)
    A. femtetlins alfarry
    B. alfemtetlins alfarret
    C. femgon alfarret
    D. alfemry farrnel
    E. alfemtet farrgon

45. Aol oistin ile lis swanet eiseau cele ule. (Verb)
    A. swanry
    B. swannel
    C. alswanet
    D. swanetlins
    E. alswantinlins

46. Lur serriet woa orn brea. (Verb)
    A. serrilins
    B. alserriet
    C. serritin
    D. serriry
    E. alserrigon

47. Nur menegon brea parlet. (Adjective-Noun)
    A. brealins alparletlins
    B. albrealins parletlins
    C. brealins parletlins
    D. albrea parletlins
    E. brea parletlins

9 (#2)

48. Cele nocrag <u>dumet nol</u> rak cele ose. (Verb-Adverb)   48.____
    A. dumry alnol   B. dumetlins nol
    C. dumgon noldis   D. dumet noldis
    E. aldumry noldis

49. Cele ulelins serrigon <u>esea</u> <u>sandringet</u> cele jise. (Adverb-Participle)   49.____
    A. alesea sandringet   B. eseadis sandry
    C. alesea sandringon   D. eseadis sandringry
    E. eseadis sandrinnel

50. Cele emmcenlins menestin <u>nol</u>. (Noun)   50.____
    A. nollins   B. noldis   C. alnol
    D. alnollins   E. alnoldis

KEY (CORRECT ANSWERS)

1.	D	11.	A	21.	C	31.	D	41.	C
2.	E	12.	E	22.	A	32.	B	42.	D
3.	C	13.	B	23.	D	33.	D	43.	B
4.	A	14.	C	24.	C	34.	D	44.	E
5.	D	15.	C	25.	B	35.	A	45.	A
6.	C	16.	B	26.	E	36.	C	46.	C
7.	A	17.	E	27.	A	37.	E	47.	A
8.	B	18.	D	28.	B	38.	B	48.	C
9.	D	19.	D	29.	B	39.	C	49.	D
10.	A	20.	A	30.	D	40.	C	50.	C

TEST 3

DIRECTIONS: This is a test of using an artificial language.

<u>Translation</u>: English to Artificial Language

a = ile
after = revo
alien = freyn
and = inklon
at = soe
before = slif
border = aille
boy = nocrag
but = orn
by = ota
car = milse
dark = nase
family = kwode
from = eiseau
girl = sonek
he = nur
her = lur
I = aol
illegal = lumin
in = rak
is = serrisus
large = quin
loud = sronge
man = emmcen
me = oa

morning = duren
narrow = sice
not = loted
officer = ule
plan = aloe
prisoner = rorsea
quick = nol
quiet = efern
river = sil
road = jise
she = lur
slow = esea
small = woa
smart = brea
some = isy
the = cele
they = wur
to = sonq
tree = filmos
under = dun
until = yermen
was = serrilus
water = ose
when = nand
wide = dostil

woman = lis
to admit = pladeve
to be = serrive
to capture = ionve
to carry = jukve
to climb = sosve
to cross = sandringve
to cry = slerve
to drive = ishtve
to have = menesve
to hear = urilve
to hide = loive
to hope = wessve
to patrol = dolive
to plan = ginseve
to protect = wussve
to question = parlve
to run = swanve
to search = nurrve
to see = oisve
to swim = dumve
to try = oiseve
to wait = glengave
to want = soleve

<u>Grammar</u>

Nouns: To make nouns plural, you must use the noun suffix –*der*. For example: river = sil; rivers = silder.

Although you are provided with some actual nouns, you will have to form nouns from other types of words (verbs and adjectives). The noun prefix *es-*, when added to a verb or adjective negates the action or description and transforms it into a noun. For example: to patrol = dolive; protection = esdolive; quick = nol; quickness = esnol.

Nouns made from verbs or adjectives use the same plural suffix, -*der*. For example: to question = parlve; question = esparlve; questions = esparlveder.

Pronouns: To change the case of a pronoun to the possessive, you must add the possessive suffix –*yu*. For example: I = aol; my = aolyu; he = nur; his = nuryu.

Verbs: To effectively use the given verbs, you may have to modify them, depending on their usages. Formation of verbs will vary, according to their prefixes and suffixes. The tenses of the verbs are important to the meaning of the sentences in which they are used. Notice that each verb ends with the suffix –*ve*. When using any verb suffix, you must first drop the –*ve*, and then add the suffix.

    sandring- + past tense suffix –*pau* = sandringpau
      Past tense verb sandringpau = crossed
    sandring- + present-tense suffix –*sau* = sandringsau
      Present tense verb sandringsau = cross, crosses
    sandring- + future tense suffix –*dau* = sandringdau
      Future tense verb sandringdau = will cross
    sandring- + participle suffix –*mai* = sandringmau
      Participial form sandringmau = crossing

Adjectives: When using an adjective, you must add the suffix that has been added to the noun you are describing. For example: Adjective large = quin; Noun tree = filmos, quin filmos = large tree; with plural suffix –*der* added: quinder filmosder = large trees.

Adverbs: Adverbs are used to describe verbs. The adverbs used in this test will be formed by adding the suffix -*wa* to adjectives. For example: Adjective slow = esea; adverbial form slowly = eseawa; verb to run = swanve; adverbial form = eseawa. Therefore, to run slowly = swanve eseawa.

Forms of adverbs are independent of verb forms. For example: swan- = past tense suffix –*pau* = swanpau; ran = swanpau. Therefore, swanpau eseawa = ran slowly.

Negatives: The negative prefix *po*- applies to all words. The *po*- prefix does not solely represent the English prefix *un*-, but it is a generic negative prefix. For example: verb: to cross = sandringve; to uncross = posandringve.

3 (#3)

Questions 1-20.

DIRECTIONS: Verify the translations of the underlined words. Select one of the five possible responses listed below. Print the letter of the correct answer in the space at the right.

A - #1 word is correctly translated
B – #2 word is correctly translated
C – #3 word is correctly translated
D – Two or three words are correctly translated
E – None of the words is correctly translated

1. Cele aille serrisau dostil. 1.____
          1   2   3
   The border is wide.
       1   2 3

2. Cele emmcen ishtpau eseawa. 2.____
         1   2   3
   The men drive slow.
       1   2   3

3. Cele lis pladepau sandringmau luminwa. 3.____
             1   2   3
   The woman admits crossing illegal.
             1   2   3

4. Cele esdolive glengapau ionve cele luminder freynder. 4.____
           1   2   3
   The patrol waits to capture the illegal alien.
        1   2   3

5. Cele quin emmcen loipau dun cele filmos. 5.____
         1   2   3
   The small men hid under the tree.
       1   2   3

6. Cele rorsea serripau efem. 6.____
         1   2   3
   The prisoners are loud.
         1   2 3

7. Cele kwode nurrpau rak cele nase. 7.____
        1   2   3
   The family searches in the morning.
        1   2   3

4 (#3)

8. Lur swanpau song cele jise.
      1   2   3
    She runs by the roads.
        1   2   3

8._____

9. Cele esdolive parlpau cele emmcen.
          1   2   3
    The patrol questioned the man.
         1   2   3

9._____

10. Cele uleder dolipau cele aille.
        1   2   3
    The officer patrolled the borders.
       1   2   3

10._____

11. Cele lis wesspau sandringve.
       1   2   3
    The women hope to cross.
        1   2   3

11._____

12. Lur jukpau luryu nocrag.
      1   2   3
    She carries her boy.
      1   2   3

12._____

13. Cele sil serrisau sice.
      1   2   3
    A river is wide.
    1   2   3

13._____

14. Dun parlmau, lur pladepau sandringmau cele aille luminwa.
         1   2   3
    Under questions, she admits to cross the border illegally.
            1   2   3

14._____

15. Cele nocrag glengapau rak cele milse.
                 1   2   3
    The boy waited at the cars.
         1   2   3

15._____

16. Lur serripau loted ionpau.
      1   2   3
    She was not captured.
        1   2   3

16._____

17. Cele kwode menespau swanve.
       1   2   3
    The families have to run.
       1   2   3

17._____

18. Cele <u>ose</u> <u>serripau</u> <u>sronge</u>.   18._____
           1   2   3
    The <u>river</u> <u>was</u> <u>quiet</u>.
          1   2   3

19. Cele <u>emmcender</u> swanpau <u>eiseau</u> cele <u>uleder</u>.   19._____
              1   2   3
    The <u>man</u> ran <u>to</u> the <u>officer</u>.
          1   2   3

20. <u>Wur</u> <u>nurrpau</u> cele <u>efern</u> sil.   20._____
        1   2   3
    <u>They</u> <u>search</u> the <u>wide</u> river.
         1   2   3

Questions 21-30.

DIRECTIONS: Correctly translate the underlined words to English.

21. <u>Isy</u> <u>rorseader</u> <u>serripau</u> not illegal.   21._____
    A. <u>The prisoner</u> <u>was</u> not illegal.
    B. <u>Her prionsers</u> <u>were</u> not illegal.
    C. <u>Some prisoners</u> <u>were</u> not illegal.
    D. <u>His prisoner</u> <u>was</u> not illegal.
    E. <u>Their prisoners</u> <u>were</u> not illegal.

22. The <u>sonek</u> <u>slerpau</u> <u>srongewa</u>.   22._____
    A. The <u>boy</u> <u>cries</u> <u>loudly</u>.
    B. The <u>boy</u> <u>cried</u> <u>quietly</u>.
    C. The <u>girl</u> <u>cries</u> <u>loud</u>.
    D. The <u>girl</u> <u>cried</u> <u>quietly</u>.
    E. The <u>girl</u> <u>cried</u> <u>loudly</u>.

23. The <u>sonek</u> <u>oisepau</u> <u>dummau</u>.   23._____
    A. The <u>girl</u> <u>tries</u> <u>swimming</u>.
    B. The <u>girl</u> <u>tried</u> <u>swimming</u>.
    C. The <u>boy</u> <u>tried</u> <u>to swim</u>.
    D. The <u>girl</u> <u>tried</u> <u>to swim</u>.
    E. The <u>boy</u> <u>tries</u> <u>swimming</u>.

24. She <u>glengapau</u> <u>rak</u> cele <u>nase</u>.   24._____
    A. She <u>waited</u> <u>in</u> the <u>dark</u>.
    B. She <u>is waiting</u> <u>in</u> the <u>dark</u>.
    C. She <u>waited</u> <u>in</u> the <u>water</u>.
    D. She <u>will wait</u> <u>in</u> the <u>water</u>.
    E. She <u>waited</u> <u>at</u> the <u>tree</u>.

25. The <u>nocrag</u> <u>inklon</u> <u>sonek</u> stood by the water.   25._____
    A. The <u>boys</u> <u>and</u> <u>girls</u> stood by the water.
    B. The <u>girls</u> <u>and</u> <u>boys</u> stood by the water.
    C. The <u>boy</u> <u>and</u> <u>girl</u> stood by the water.
    D. The <u>girl</u> <u>and</u> <u>boy</u> stood by the water.
    E. The <u>illegal</u> <u>boys</u> stood by the water.

26. The ule ishpau wuryu to the border.
    A. The officers drive him to the border.
    B. The officers will drive him to the border.
    C. The men drove her to the border.
    D. The officer drove them to the border.
    E. The men are driving her to the border.

26.____

27. Wur urilpau cele car.
    A. They heard the car.
    B. She hears a car.
    C. He heard a car.
    D. They hear the car.
    E. He heard his car.

27.____

28. The rorsea ginsepau glengave by the tree.
    A. The prisoners planned and waited by the tree.
    B. The prisoner wanted to wait by the tree.
    C. The officers planned to wait by the tree.
    D. The officer wanted to wait by the tree.
    E. The prisoner planned to wait by the tree.

28.____

29. The sonek swanpau nolwa.
    A. The girls run quickly.
    B. The boy ran quick.
    C. The boy runs quick.
    D. The girl ran quickly.
    E. The girls ran quickly.

29.____

30. The uleder ginspau parley the woman.
    A. The officer plans to question the woman.
    B. The officers planned to question the woman.
    C. The officer planned to capture the woman.
    D. The man plans to protect the woman.
    E. The man planned to protect the woman.

30.____

Questions 31-40.

DIRECTIONS: Select the correct translation for the underlined words.

The aille esdolive saw a family, sandringmau the river. The river
      1   2   3
serripau nase inklon dostil. The uleder dumpau to the family and jukpau the boy and girl to a
    4   5   6
woa filmos. The man and the woman pladepau song sandringmau the river luminwa.
   7   8   9   10

31. #1 would be translated:
    A. border patrols
    B. border officers
    C. border patrol
    D. borders patrol
    E. border officer

31.____

32. #2 would be translated:
    A. saw
    B. see
    C. will see
    D. is seeing
    E. sees

    32.____

33. #3 would be translated:
    A. crossed
    B. will cross
    C. crosses
    D. crossing
    E. to cross

    33.____

34. #4 would be translated:
    A. is dark and wide
    B. was dark and wide
    C. is wide and dark
    D. was quick and dark
    E. was quickly dark

    34.____

35. #5 would be translated:
    A. officers swam
    B. officer swam
    C. officers swimming
    D. man swam
    E. men swimming

    35.____

36. #6 would be translated:
    A. carry
    B. carrying
    C. will carry
    D. to carry
    E. carried

    36.____

37. #7 would be translated:
    A. large tree
    B. large trees
    C. small tree
    D. small car
    E. small cars

    37.____

38. #8 would be translated:
    A. admit
    B. admitting
    C. hid
    D. admitted
    E. hiding

    38.____

39. #9 would be translated:
    A. to cross
    B. to crossing
    C. crossing
    D. planning to cross
    E. planning

    39.____

40. #10 would be translated:
    A. hopefully
    B. hopeful
    C. quickly
    D. illegally
    E. illegal

    40.____

Questions 41-50.

DIRECTIONS: Select the correct usage of the underlined words.

41. Wur <u>swanve</u> sonq cele jise. (Verb) (They ran to the road.)
    A. swanmau
    B. swanveder
    C. swanvewa
    D. esswanve
    E. swanpau

    41.))))

42. Cele kwode <u>sandringve</u> lumen. (Verb-Adverb) (The family crossed illegally.) 42.____
    A. sandringmau luminj
    B. sandringpau luminwa
    C. sandringve luminwa
    D. sandringpau lumin
    E. essandringve luminwa

43. Cele <u>ginseve serrive</u> sandringve soe cele aille. (Singular Noun-Verb) (The plan was to cross at the border.) 43.____
    A. ginseve serripau
    B. esginseve esserrive
    C. ginseve esserrive
    D. esginseve serripau
    E. esginseve serrimau

44. Cele <u>quin emmcen</u> slerpau. (Adjective-Singular Noun) (The large man cried.) 44.____
    A. quinder emmcender
    B. esquinder emmcender
    C. quin emmcen
    D. quinder esemmcen
    E. quin emmcender

45. Cele <u>demmcen</u> serripau <u>brea</u> inklon <u>nol</u>. (Singular Noun – Adjective-Adjective) (The man was smart and quick.) 45.____
    A. emmcen brea nol
    B. emmcender breader nolder
    C. emmcender brea nol
    D. lis brea nolder
    E. lisen breader nolder

46. He <u>milse</u> ishtpau <u>esea</u> sonq cele aille. (Singular Noun-Adverb) (A car drove slowly to the border.) 46.____
    A. milse esea
    B. milseder eseader
    C. milsewa eseawa
    D. milse eseawa
    E. milsewa esea

47. Cele <u>duren serrive</u> naseder orn efernder. (Plural Noun-Verb) (The mornings were dark but quiet.) 47.____
    A. duren serripau
    B. esdurender esserive
    C. durender serrimau
    D. duren serripauder
    E. durender serripau

48. Cele <u>sandringve serrive</u> luminwa. (Singular Noun-Verb) (The crossing was illegal.) 48.____
    A. essandringpau serripau
    B. essandringveder serriveder
    C. essandringve serripau
    D. sandringve serripau
    E. sandringmau serrimau

49. Lur <u>soleve glengave</u>. (Verb-Verb) (She wanted to wait.) 49.____
    A. soleve glengapau
    B. solepau glengave
    C. essoleve essglengave
    D. essoleve glengapau
    E. solemau glengamau

50. Lur solepau <u>oiseve</u> inklon <u>dumve</u>. (Verb-Verb) (She wanted to try and swim.)
    A. oiseve dumve
    B. oisepau dumve
    C. oiseve dumpau
    D. oisemau dumpau
    E. oisemau dummau

KEY (CORRECT ANSWERS)

1. D	11. C	21. C	31. C	41. E
2. E	12. D	22. E	32. A	42. B
3. B	13. B	23. B	33. D	43. D
4. A	14. E	24. A	34. B	44. C
5. C	15. A	25. C	35. A	45. A
6. E	16. D	26. D	36. E	46. D
7. A	17. C	27. A	37. C	47. E
8. E	18. B	28. E	38. D	48. C
9. D	19. E	29. D	39. B	49. B
10. B	20. A	30. B	40. D	50. A

EXAMINATION SECTION
COMMENTARY

This section illustrates the different types of questions in a written test of general aptitude and competency. These questions are similar to actual questions in difficulty, content, and form. Competitors should carefully study every question so that they are prepared for questions of the same type in the examination. Some difficult questions are included in this section and competitors should not be discouraged if they miss some of them. No applicant is expected to answer all questions correctly on the written test.

The written test consists of several sections which measure the abilities that are considered essential in carrying out the duties of the positions filled through this examination.

QUESTIONS AND ANSWERS
EXPLANATION OF ANSWERS

DIRECTIONS: Each question or incorrect answer is followed by several suggested answers or completions. Select the one that BEST answers the question or completes the statement.

Question-type 1

Many jobs require the ability to analyze, understand, and interpret written material of varying levels of complexity and to retain the content for at least a limited period of time. Question-type 1 is primarily designed to test these comprehension and retention abilities. The following questions, therefore, require competitors to understand a given paragraph and to select an answer based on their comprehension of the conceptual content of the paragraph. The right answer is either
(1) a repetition, formulated in different terminology, of the main concept or concepts found in the paragraph, or
(2) a conclusion whose inherence in the content of the paragraph is such that it is equivalent to a restatement

1. Through advertising, manufacturers exercise a high degree of control over consumers' desires. However, the manufacturer assumes enormous risks in attempting to predict what consumers will want and in producing goods in quantity and distributing them in advance of final selection by the consumers.
   The paragraph best supports the statement that manufacturers
   A. can eliminate the risk of overproduction by advertising
   B. completely control buyers' needs and desires
   C. must depend upon the final consumers for the success of their undertakings
   D. distribute goods directly to the consumers
   E. can predict with great accuracy the success of any product they put on the market

The conclusion derived by the correct alternative, C, is inherent in the content of the paragraph; although it acknowledges that advertising plays an important role in determining consumers' desires, it affirms that final selection rests with the consumers and that manufacturers therefore take *enormous* risks in attempting to predict final selection. Alternative B contradicts the opening sentence of the paragraph which refers only to a "high degree of control." Alternatives A and E likewise affirm the opposite of what the paragraph postulates, i.e., that the manufacturer's predictions entail enormous risks. Alternative D is almost irrelevant to the paragraph since distribution techniques have not been considered.

2. The function of business is to increase the wealth of the country and the value and happiness of life. It does this by supplying the material needs of men and women. When the nation's business is successfully carried on, it renders public service of the highest value.

The paragraph best supports the statement that

A. all businesses which render public service are successful
B. human happiness is enhanced only by the increase of material wants
C. the value of life is increased only by the increase of wealth
D. the material needs of men and women are supplied by well-conducted business
E. business is the only field of activity which increases happiness

The correct alternative, D, restates the main idea in the original paragraph that business increases the value and happiness of life by supplying the material needs of men and women. Alternative A derives its conclusion incorrectly, i.e., the proposition that all successful businesses render public service, cannot be logically reversed to "all businesses which render public service are successful." Alternatives B and C assume an equation between happiness and wealth which is not supported by the content of the paragraph. Alternative E like wise equates happiness with business endeavors or their products, which the content of the paragraph does not warrant.

3. Honest people in one nation find it difficult to understand the viewpoints of honest people in another. Foreign ministries and their ministers exist for the purpose of explaining the viewpoints of one nation in terms under-stood by the ministries of another. Some of their most important work lies in this direction.

The paragraph best supports the statement that

A. people of different nations may not consider matters in the same light
B. it is unusual for many people to share similar ideas
C. suspicion prevents understanding be-tween nations
D. the chief work of foreign ministries is to guide relations between nations united by a common cause
E. the people of one nation must sympathize with the viewpoints of the people of other nations

The conclusion derived by the correct alternative, A, is inherent in the content of the paragraph; if honest people in one nation find it diffcult to understand the viewpoints of honest people in another, it is because they often see matters in different lights. Alternatives B, C and D find little or no support in the paragraph: B is concerned with "many people" whereas the paragraph refers to people of different nations; C *assumes* that nations are suspicious of each other and that suspicion prevents understanding; D contradicts the main idea expressed by the paragraph since foreign ministries should work towards mutual understanding between nations having discrepant viewpoints whether or not they have a common cause. Alternative E sets forth an ethical command which to an extent stems from the content of the paragraph but which is not completely warranted by it as is the conclusion of alternative A.

4. Education should not stop when the individual has been prepared to make a livelihood and to live in modern society. Living would be mere existence were there no appreciation and enjoyment of the riches of art, literature and science.

The paragraph best supports the statement that true education

A. is focused on the routine problems of life
B. prepares one for a full enjoyment of life
C. deals chiefly with art, literature and science

D. is not possible for one who does not enjoy scientific literature
E. disregards practical ends

The correct alternative, B, restates the main idea presented in the paragraph that living is mere existence for those individuals who lack the enjoyment of art, literature and science. Alternative A directly contradicts this main idea, and alternatives C and E also contradict the paragraph which acknowledges that education should prepare the individual to make a livelihood although it shouldn't stop there. Alternative D goes beyond the paragraph in that it affirms that each individual *must* enjoy scientific literature whereas the original statement simply suggests that life in general would be limited if the riches of science, art and literature were not available for appreciation and enjoyment.

Question-type II
Many jobs require the use of clear and succinct verbal and written expression. Basic vocabulary limitations impede the precise correspondence of words and concepts and thus hinder effective language communication. Accordingly, the following questions present a key word and five suggested answers. The competitor's task is to find the suggested answer that is closest in meaning to the key word. The wrong alternatives may have a more or less valid connection with the key word. In some cases, therefore, the right choice differs from a wrong choice only in the degree to which its meaning comes close to that of the key word.

1. *Subsume* means most nearly
   A. understate
   B. absorb
   C. include
   D. belong
   E. cover

To *subsume* means to include within a larger class or order (alternative C). Alternative A is unrelated in meaning. Alternatives D and E are somewhat related since an element included in a group or class can be said to belong to it and to be covered by it. To a degree, likewise, it may be said that an element included in a group or class is absorbed (alternative B) by the group or class, although strictly speaking, a subsumed element partially preserves its individual identity whereas an absorbed element does not.

2. *Notorious* means most nearly
   A. condemned
   B. unpleasant
   C. vexatious
   D. pretentious
   E. well-known

Notorious means being or constituting something commonly known. Thus alternative E is almost synonymous in meaning. Alternatives B, C and D are unrelated in meaning, since a notorious individual may or may not be unpleasant, vexatious or pretentious. Alternative A hinges on a secondary nuance of the word notorious: being widely and unfavorably known. However, being unfavorably well-known does not necessarily imply being condemned.

3. *Novices* means most nearly
   A. volunteers
   B. experts
   C. trainers
   D. beginners
   E. amateurs

Novice designates one who has no training or experience in a specific field or activity and is hence a beginner (alternative D). An expert (alternative B) is therefore the exact opposite. A trainer (alternative C) may or may not be an expert but must certainly have a certain amount of knowledge. Volunteers (alternative A) are in most cases not novices since they usually volunteer for something they are knowledgeable in. An amateur (alternative E) is one who engages in a particular pursuit, study or science as a pastime rather than as a profession. Thus an amateur may be a novice in the initial stages of formal training, but more often than not will be an expert who has acquired expertise in a particular field through the consistent pursuit of a pastime or pleasure.

4. To *succumb* means most nearly
   A. to aid
   B. to oppose
   C. to yield
   D. to check
   E. to be discouraged

To *succumb* is to cease to resist or contend before a superior or overpowering force or desire, hence to yield (alternative C). Alternative B expresses the stage prior to succumbing. Alternative A is not related except perhaps accidentally—an individual who succumbs may involuntarily serve the purpose of the overpowering force. Alternative D is unrelated in meaning, and alternative E is related only vaguely in the sense that the succumbing party may be susceptible to discouragement.

Question-type III
The ability to discover the underlying relations or analogies existing among specific data is important in many jobs where solving problems involves the formation and testing of hypotheses. The questions in this section test this ability. Each question consists of a series of letters arranged in a definite pattern. The competitor must discover what the pattern is and decide which alternative gives the next letter in the series.

1. b c d b c e b c f b c g

   A) b B) c C) h D) i E) e

The answer is A. The sequence maintains two letters (b c) in the same order while the third letter is in consecutive alphabetical order (d e f g). The pattern b c g has been completed and the next letter should begin the pattern b c h.

2. b c c c d e e e f g g g h i i

   A) g B) h C) i D) j E) f

The answer is C. The pattern consists of letters written in alphabetical order with every second letter repeated three times. Since the last letter in the sequence, the i, is only repeated twice, it should be repeated a third time.

3. b n c d n e f g n h i j k

   A) n B) l C) m D) i E) j

The answer is A. The sequence consists of a fixed letter (n) placed after consecutive letter periods. These periods acquire an additional letter each time and begin with the letter which alphabetically follows the last letter in the preceding period, i.e., *bn cdn efgn hijk*. The letter n must therefore be placed after the last period.

4. b c d b e f g e h i j h k l m

   A) k B) h C) l D) n E) o

The answer is A. The series is an alphabetical progression of four-letter sequences where each fourth letter repeats the first letter of each sequence: *bcdb efge hijh klmk*.

Question-type IV
As in the previous section the questions in this section measure the ability to discover the underlying relations or analogies existing among specific data. Each question consists of two sets of symbols where a common characteristic exists among the symbols in each set and where an analogy is maintained between the two sets of symbols. The competitor must discover which alternative gives the symbol that simultaneously preserves the characteristic common to the symbols in the second set and the analogy with the symbols in the first set.

1.

The answer is C. An analogy is established here between a circle and a square. Therefore a circle split into two halves is the same as a square split into two halves.

2.

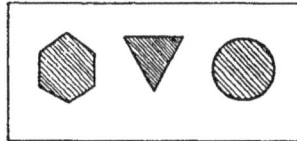 ?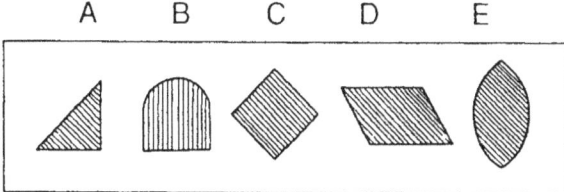

The answer is B. In this case the form of the symbols is irrelevant. The critical feature is found in the lines included within the symbols. The lines in the first three symbols are all slanted lines. The lines in the second two symbols are all vertical lines. Of the five alternatives, symbol B is the only one with vertical lines.

3.

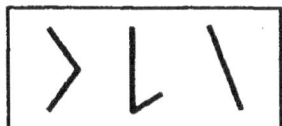  ?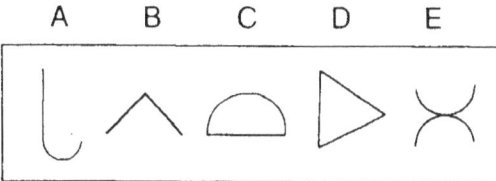

The answer is E. The symbols in the first box are made up of straight lines. The symbols in the second box are made up of curved lines. The symbol in alternative E is the only one that preserves the pattern.

4.

 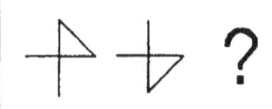 ?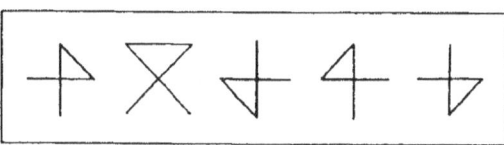

The answer is O. The first three symbols are identical except for their orientation the orientation of the second symbol is a 90 rotation of the first symbol. Likewise the third symbol is a 90° rotation of the second symbol. The symbols in the second box follow the same 90 rotation pattern. Alternative O is the only one that preserves the pattern.

Question-type V
The development of plans, systems and procedures is an essential function of many jobs. This function entails the ability to analyze given facts and discover their implications, as well as the ability to reason from general principles to the implications of these principles in specific situations. Question-type V tests these analytical abilities. Accordingly, each of the following questions consists of a statement which is to be accepted as true and should not be questioned for the purpose of this test. Following the statement are five alternatives. The correct alternative MUST derive from the information given in the original statement without drawing on additional information. By contrast, the four incorrect alternatives rest, to varying degrees, on the admission of new information.

1. No substantial alterations in the age structure took place between 2000-10 and life expectancy remained the same. A slight drop, nonetheless (from 38 to 37 percent), is noted in the proportion of the population 20 years of age and younger.
   Therefore, between 2000-10
   A. the proportion of the productive-age population increased
   B. there was a slight decrease in fertility rates
   C. there was a decrease in emigration
   D. there was a slight increase in infant mortality

E. production remained substantially the same

The correct alternative, A, follows from the data that there was a slight drop in the proportion of the population under 20 years of age and that life expectancy remained the same. Alternatives B and D are possible explanations of the slight decrease in the proportion of the younger population but do not derive from the original statement and would require additional evidence. Alternative C would likewise require additional information and would seem to apply more as a partial and possible explanation of a decrease in the productive-age population. Alternative E in no way derives from the given data since many factors affect production besides the age structure of the population.

2. A robot can take a walk in order to mail a letter; it can play chess, build other machines and generally exhibit rule-governed behavior. A robot can kill a person but, unlike a person, it cannot be ashamed. It can be annoying but not annoyed. It can *perhaps* exhibit behavior *as if* it were ashamed or annoyed.
   A. Robots are capable of thought.
   B. Robots can do things that people do but cannot be what people are.
   C. Robots and people are outwardly the same.
   D. Robots can make conscious decisions but have no moral consciousness.
   E. Robots never exhibit their inner thoughts and realities.

The correct alternative, B, derives its conclusion from the joint consideration of the actions enumerated in the original statement as actions that a robot can perform—mailing a letter, playing chess, killing a person—and the conscious states that are enumerated as impossible in a robot, i.e., being ashamed or annoyed. Furthermore, the last sentence in the original statement contrasts outward behaviors with the actual conscious states they represent. Alternative A rests on the assumption that thought can be equated with exhibited behavior and not with inner consciousness. Alternative C assumes not only that all exhibited behavior is the same but that the outward *appearance* of a robot and a person is the same. Alternative D correctly derives a section of its conclusion—the lack of moral consciousness—from the stated fact that a robot cannot be ashamed, but assumes that a robot can kill a person after making a *conscious* decision, which contradicts the original statement. Alternative E likewise affirms, in contradiction of the original statement, that robots have inner consciousness.

3. The Thirty Years' War, 1618 to 1648, established the principle of religious toleration among the German states, but it also reduced the German population by at least one-third, and much of the cultivated land became wilderness.
   Therefore, the Thirty Years' War
   A. altered the geographical boundaries of the German states
   B. was generally beneficial to the German states
   C. was fought on German soil
   D. established a large number of religions within the German states
   E. caused the German population to become widely scattered

The correct alternative, C, derives its conclusion from the given facts that the German population was reduced by one-third and much of the cultivated land became wilderness. Alternative A, on the other hand, assumes the establishment of new borders from the extraneous information that borders are usually changed by wars. Alternative B derives its conclusion from the assumption that religious tolerance creates a surrounding influence beneficial to all aspects of national life. Alternative D assumes an equation between religious tolerance and religious pluralism, and alternative E likewise assumes an equation between the reduction of the population and the scattering of the population.

4. Though easy to learn, backgammon is a surprisingly subtle and complex game to play very well. It is a game that calls for mastery of the laws of probability and the

ability to weigh and undertake frequent shifts in strategy.

Therefore, a necessary quality for playing backgammon very well is

A. the ability to deceive the opponent
B. a willingness to take calculated risks
C. a high degree of manual dexterity
D. the ability to make quick decisions
E. a mastery of advanced mathematics

The correct alternative, B, derives its conclusion from the given fact that the game is based on decisions of probability. Thus the player must take calculated risks. The four incorrect alternatives, on the other hand, rest on assumptions that, to varying degrees, go beyond the original statement. Alternative E, for example, assumes that a mastery of the laws of probability entails a more generic mastery of advanced mathematics. Alternative D assumes that frequent shifts in strategy cannot be carried out slowly.

Question-type VI
Many jobs require the ability to understand and utilize information presented in chart or table form. The following questions require competitors to deduce the missing values in a table of figures from the information in the rest of the table.

TABLE 1: GENERAL REVENUE OF STATE AND LOCAL GOVERNMENTS-STATES:
2000 Hypothetical data

STATE	Total amount (mil.do.)	REVENUE PER CAPITA [1] (dollars)						REVENUE (dollars) PER $1,000 OF PERSONAL INCOME IN CALENDAR YEAR 1999				
			From Federal Government	From own sources;					From Federal Government	From own sources		
				Taxes			Charges and miscellaneos					Charges and miscellaneous
		Total		All taxes	Property tax	Other		Total		Total	Taxes	
Ala 1,722		I	131	258	39	219	110	190	50	140	98	42
Alaska......1,259	4,168	358	417	102	315	3,393		1,001	86	915	II	815
Ariz 1,172	662	121	426	166	260	115		206	38	168	132	36
Ark 871	453	115	252	65	187	86		176	45	131	98	33
Calif 17,028	853	164	559	262	297	130		204	39	165	134	31
Colo 1,474	666	III	419	179	240	123		194	36	158	122	36
Conn 1,970	649	85	484	238	246	80		144	19	125	107	18
Del 379	692	88	450	84	366	154		172	22	150	112	38
D.C. IV	953	359	517	169	348	77		192	72	120	104	16
Fla 3,576	528	69	347	118	229	112		160	21	139	105	34

[1]Based on resident population

1. What is the value of I?
   A. 800
   B. 600
   C. 499
   D. 757
   E. None of these, or cannot be calculated from data provided

The answer is C. The figure represents the total Revenue per Capita which is obtained by adding the three major columns therein: Charges and miscellaneous, All taxes and Federal Government: 110 + 258 + 131 = 499. Alternative D represents an erroneous double addition of the Property tax and Other subcolumns, the amounts corresponding to which were already included in the All taxes column. Alternatives A and B are irrelevant values.

2. What is the value of II?
   A. 392
   B. 828
   C. 100
   D. 1814
   E. None of these, or cannot be calculated from data provided

The answer is C. It is obtained by subtracting Charges and miscellaneous from the Total Revenue from own sources: 915 - 815 = 100. Alternatives A, B and D are irrelevant values.

3. What is the value of III?
   A. 124
   B. 141
   C. 176
   D. 203
   E. None of these, or cannot be calculated from data provided

The answer is A. It is obtained by adding the two major columns for which values are given in the Revenue per Capita subdivision, All taxes and Charges and miscellaneous, and subtracting the result from the total Revenue per Capita: 419 + 123 = 542; 666 - 542 = 124. Alternatives B, C and D are irrelevant values.

4. What is the value of IV?
   A. 725
   B. 687
   C. 710
   D. 1144
   E. None of these, or cannot be calculated from data provided

The answer is E. The Total General Revenue cannot be calculated, since the total population figure is missing. This figure should be multiplied by the Per Capita Income to obtain the Total Revenue. Alternative D erroneously adds the totals for Revenue per Capita and Revenue per $1,000 of Personal Income: 192 + 953 = 1145. Alternatives A, B and C are irrelevant values.

Question-type VII
Many jobs require employees to perform or check arithmetic operations involving fractions, percentages, etc. and to solve quantitative problems of varying complexity, where the approach to be utilized is not specified. The questions in this section test these abilities. Although the arithmetical processes involved are simple, the figuring should of course be done with care.

1. 113 17/52 - 33 5/13 =
   A. 79 49/52
   B. 80 3/52
   C. 80 12/52
   D. 80 49/52
   E. None of these

The answer is A. First of all fractions are reduced to a common denominator. Additionally, since the fraction being subtracted is larger than the one it is to be subtracted from, a unit must be taken from the whole number, 113, reducing it ito 112. The borrowed unit is converted into fraction form and added to 17/52, i.e., 52/52 + 17/52 = 69/52. The subtraction is then carried out: 112 69/52 - 33 20/52 = 79 49/52.

2. $\dfrac{16 \times 17}{(57+79)4} =$
   A. .50
   B. .72
   C. 1.9
   D. 8.0
   E. None of these

The answer is A. The numbers in parentheses are added, 57 + 79 = 136 and 136 is then broken into 17 x 2 x 4. Common factors are eliminated:

$$\dfrac{16 \times 17}{(57+79)4} = \dfrac{16 \times 17}{(136)4} = \dfrac{16 \times 17}{(17 \times 2 \times 4)4} =$$

$$\dfrac{16 \times 17}{17 \times 2 \times 4 \times 4} = \dfrac{1}{2} = .50$$

3. 221 1/19 x 10 11/35 =
   A. 80.3
   B. 2510.0
   C. 2510.1
   D. 2280
   E. None of these

The answer is D. Whole numbers are reduced to fractions:

$\dfrac{4200}{19} \times \dfrac{361}{35}$. Fractions are broken into their component factors and common factors are eliminated: $\dfrac{7 \times 6 \times 100}{19} \times \dfrac{19 \times 19}{7 \times 5} =$

$\dfrac{7 \times 6 \times 5 \times 20 \times 19 \times 19}{19 \times 7 \times 5} =$

$6 \times 20 \times 19 = 2280$.

4. $\dfrac{(418 + 56 - 8)313}{77 + (50 + 9)7 - 24} =$
   A. -12378
   B. 310
   C. 313
   D. 1246.649
   E. None of these

The answer is C.

$\dfrac{(466)(313)}{77 + (59)7 - 24} = \dfrac{(466)(313)}{77 + 413 - 24} =$

$\dfrac{(466)(313)}{490 - 24} = \dfrac{(466)(313)}{466}$

Common factors are eliminated and the result is 313.

5. An office supply store buys 100 reams of special quality paper for $400. If 1 ream = 500 sheets of paper, how much must the store receive per 100 sheets to obtain a 20% gain on its cost?
   A. 83¢
   B. 85¢
   C. 96¢
   D. 98¢
   E. None of these

The answer is C. Since 1 ream = 500 sheets, 100 reams = 50000 sheets. To discover the cost of 100 sheets we set up a proportion:

$\dfrac{50000}{100} = \dfrac{400}{X}$; $50000X = 40000$; $X = \dfrac{40000}{50000} =$ 0.80. The cost of 100 sheets is 80¢. To discover the amount that the store must receive per 100 sheets to obtain a 20% gain on the 80¢ cost, we find what 20% of 80¢ is and add the result: $80 + (0.20)(80) = 80 + 16 = 96¢$.

6. A vase is packed in a carton with a 10" diameter and is surrounded by packing 2" thick at the mouth. If the diameter of the base is 1/2 the diameter of the mouth, what is the diameter of the base?
   A. 3"
   B. 4"
   C. 6"
   D. 8"
   E. None of these

The answer is A. Since the vase is surrounded by packing 2" thick at the mouth and the diameter of the carton is 10", we subtract: $10 - (2 + 2) = 10 - 4 = 6$" which is the diameter of the mouth. Since the diameter of the base is 1/2 the diameter of the mouth: $1/2(6)=3$".

7. Seventy 58" x 34" desks must be stored in a warehouse. If as many desks as possible are stored on the floor of a 15' x 25' room, how many desks will still require storage?
   A. 46
   B. 25
   C. 45
   D. 43
   E. None of these

The answer is C. First of all, the feet are reduced to inches: $15 \times 12 = 180$ and $25 \times 12 = 300$. Next we determine how many times the length of a desk fits into the length of the room and how many times the width of a desk fits into the width of the room:

$\dfrac{180}{34} = 5\dfrac{10}{34}$ and $\dfrac{300}{58} = 5\dfrac{10}{58}$ We then multiply the whole numbers, which means multiplying the number of desks per row by the number of rows: $5 \times 5 = 25$. Since 25 desks fit in the room, 45 desks will still require storage (70 - 25 = 45).

Alternative D is obtained by multiplying the width and length of the room and the width and length of a desk and dividing the total storage area by the total area of a desk: $180 \times 300 = 54000$ and $58 \times 34 = 1972$; $54000 \div 1972 = 27\dfrac{189}{493}$.

Since 70 - 27 = 43, more desks would fit in the same area. However, this solution is incorrect because it does not take into account that the storage space cannot be filled *completely* with desks. The shape of the desks is not adjustable to the shape of the room and there would always be unfilled spaces. Alternative A is obtained by determining how many times the width of a desk fits into the length of the room and the length of a desk fits into the width of the room:

$$\frac{300}{34} = 8\frac{14}{17} \text{ and } \frac{180}{58} = 3\frac{3}{29}.$$

The multiplication of the whole numbers yields 24, and 70 - 24 = 46. One more desk actually fits into the storage area if we follow the process used to obtain the correct answer, alternative C.

8. A mechanic repairs 16 cars per 8-hour day. Another mechanic in the same shop repairs 1 1/2 times this number in 3/4 the time. Theoretically, how long will it take to repair 16 cars in the shop?
   A. 2 2/3 hours
   B. 2 9/10 hours
   C. 3 hours
   D. 2 1/2 hours
   E. None of these

The answer is A. For the second mechanic we obtain 1 1/2 of 16 cars: 3/2 x 16 = 24 and 3/4 of 8 hours: 3/4 x 8 = 6 hours. The second mechanic therefore repairs 24 cars per 6-hour day. Secondly we determine how many cars each mechanic repairs per hour-the first mechanic: 2 cars/hr. and the second mechanic 4 cars/hr. Therefore 6 cars are repaired every hour if both outputs are added. Lastly we determine how many hours are required to repair 16 cars: we divide the 16 cars by the 6 cars/hr. which yields 2 2/3 hrs.

Question-type VIII
Many jobs require the ability to solve a presented problem when all the necessary facts to solve the problem are not given. Solution to the problem involves making some reasonable assumptions or anticipating what the most likely of several possible occurrences might be. This ability becomes especially important when decisions must be reached based on incomplete evidence. Accordingly, the questions in this section require competitors to select the best or most reasonable answer from five alternatives. In order to do so, competitors are required to use general knowledge not included in the original statement. Since the correct alternative consists of the best or most reasonable answer, it is essential to keep in mind that some alternatives may be plausible, although not as plausible as the correct alternative.

1. The development of a country's water power is advocated as a means of conserving natural resources CHIEFLY because such a hydroelectric policy would tend to
   A. stimulate the growth of industries in hitherto isolated regions
   B. encourage the substitution of machinery for hand labor
   C. provide a larger market for coal
   D. make cheap electricity available in rural areas
   E. lessen the use of irreplaceable fuel materials

Of the five alternatives, the correct alternative, E, derives from the fundamental or most essential reason for the endorsement of a hydroelectric policy, i.e., water is not a depletable energy resource. Alternatives A and D are plausible but are not as determinative as E. Alternative C is easily discarded since coal would have a larger market in the absence of hydroelectric power. Alternative B is also easily discarded since hydroelectric energy would increase the availability of both the fuel and/or electricity needed to run machinery.

2. Complaints by the owners of large cars that they cannot see an already-parked small car in a parking lot until they have begun to pull into a space, are BEST justified if
   A. there are few empty parking spaces in the lot
   B. the small car has been parked for a long time
   C. the owners of large cars have poor vision
   D. there is a designated parking area for small cars
   E. there are few other small cars in the lot

The correct alternative, D, hinges on the fact that strict *justification* for a complaint is more firmly rooted in legality than in individual situations or attitudes. Thus, for example, the owner of a large car who happens to find few empty parking spaces in a lot (alternative A), or who knows or assumes that a small car has been parked in a certain space for a long time (alternative B), can justify his or her annoyance only on the subjective level. On the other hand if a small car is parked in a space designated for large cars, the individual's annoyance and complaint acquire objective and formal justification.

3. A country that is newly settled usually produces very little art, music or literature. The MOST REASONABLE explanation of this fact is that
    A. its people have had few experiences to draw on
    B. there is little use for such work
    C. suitable materials for such work must be imported
    D. the physical development of the country absorbs most of the interest and energy of the people
    E. there is as yet no governmental encouragement of the arts

The correct alternative, D, presents the most basic explanation for the lack of artistic production in a newly-settled country. The development of a newly-settled country necessitates the undivided attention of its people, and manpower is thus basically unavailable for the production of art, music or literature. Alternative A is implausible since newly-settled people have many experiences which are eventually represented in the art, music and literature of later generations. Alternatives B, C and E make assumptions about conditions necessary for the production of art, music and literature which are only partially valid. Alternative B incorrectly assumes that art is always produced for utilitarian purposes. Alternative C partially applies to art and music but not at all to literature. Alternative E is only partially plausible. The government of a newly-settled country is likely to encourage the production of goods rather than the production of art, music or literature.

However, artistic production can occur without governmental encouragement.

4. The CHIEF reason why every society has certain words and concepts that are never precisely translated into the language of another society is that
    A. the art of good translation is as yet not sufficiently developed
    B. there is too great a disparity between the intellectual levels attained by different societies
    C. every society possesses cultural elements which are unique to itself
    D. words and concepts never express the true nature of a society
    E. every society has some ideas which it does not wish to share with other societies

The correct alternative, C, is the most basic reason why certain concepts are never precisely translated. Languages express the sociopolitical contexts in which they are spoken and are bound to have expressions that are unique to these contexts. Alternative A fails to distinguish between the qualitative and the quantitative. Whereas the art of good translation appears to be as yet not sufficiently widespread, it is indeed available. Furthermore its total unavailability would still constitute a secondary explanation, over and against alternative C, for the impossibility of the precise translation of certain words. Alternative B rests on the assumption that *all* existing societies are substantially disparate in their level of development, which is known not to be the case. Alternative D assumes the truth of the postulate expounded by some philosophical theories that words and concepts have no referential value. Alternative E presents a farfetched ethical judgment whose plausibility rests on the assumption that social groups are secretive and that the function of language is to exclude communication beyond the social group.

Question-type IX

As in the previous section the questions in this section measure the ability to solve a problem when all the facts relevant to its solution are not given. More specifically, many jobs require the employee to discover connections between events sometimes apparently unrelated. In order to do this the employee will find it necessary to correctly infer that unspecified events have probably occurred or are likely to occur. This ability becomes especially important when action must be taken on incomplete information. Accordingly, these questions require competitors to choose among five suggested alternatives, each of which presents a different sequential arrangement of five events. Competitors must choose the MOST logical of the five suggested sequences. In order to do so, they MAY be required to draw on general knowledge to infer missing concepts or events that are essential to sequencing the five given events. Competitors should be careful to infer only what is essential to the sequence. The plausibility of the wrong alternatives will always require the inclusion of unlikely events or of additional chains of events which are NOT essential to sequencing the five given events.

1.
    1. a body was found in the woods
    2. a man proclaimed innocence
    3. the owner of a gun was located
    4. a gun was traced
    5. the owner of a gun was questioned

    A. 4-3-5-2-1   D. 1-3-5-2-4
    B. 2-1-4-3-5   E. 1-2-4-3-5
    C. 1-4-3-5-2

The correct alternative, C, interrelates the events in the simplest and most logical sequence: if a body is found (1), it is probable that a weapon will be found and traced (4), that its owner will then be located (3) and questioned (5) and that he will proclaim his innocence (2). The plausibility of alternatives A and B rests on a more involved and less logical sequence because it requires the inclusion of an additional chain of events in order to make the discovery of a body (1) follow from a proclamation of innocence (2). The plausibility of alternative D likewise requires the inclusion of an additional chain of events to explain why a man would be located and questioned before the gun was traced. Sequence E rests on the assumption that the owner of the gun and the man proclaiming innocence are two persons. In this case the man proclaiming innocence loses his relation to the other events and becomes superfluous unless additional events are included.

2.
    1. a man was in a hunting accident
    2. a man fell down a flight of steps
    3. a man lost his vision in one eye
    4. a man broke his leg
    5. a man had to walk with a cane

    A. 2-4-5-1-3   D. 1-3-5-2-4
    B. 4-5-1-3-2   E. 1-3-2-4-5
    C. 3-1-4-5-2

The correct alternative, E, provides the most likely causal relationship for the five events. Accidents with weapons such as those used when hunting (1) can result in a loss of vision (3). One-eyed vision impedes depth perception and could result in a fall down a flight of steps (2) causing a broken leg (4) and necessitating the use of a cane (5). Alternatives A and B are less plausible because they establish a causal relationship between walking with a cane and having the type of hunting accident that results in loss of vision. In addition, it is less likely that a man with a broken leg would go hunting than that a man with impaired vision would have to go up or down steps. Alternative D is less plausible than E because a broken leg rather than impaired vision is likely to necessitate the use of a cane. Alternative C is less plausible than E because it is likely that a loss of vision will follow rather than precede a hunting accident. Also, a broken leg is more likely to result from a fall than from a hunting accident.

3.
    1. a man is offered a new job
    2. a woman is offered a new job
    3. a man works as a waiter
    4. a woman works as a waitress
    5. a woman gives notice

    A. 4-2-5-3-1   D. 3-1-4-2-5
    B. 4-2-5-1-3   E. 4-3-2-5-1
    C. 2-4-5-3-1

The correct alternative, B, provides the best temporal sequence for the five events by establishing a causal relationship where the three events concerning the woman trigger the two events concerning the man. A woman works as a waitress (4); she is offered a new job (2); gives notice to her employer (5); who offers her job to a man (1); who begins work as a waiter (3) when the woman leaves. The other four alternatives describe plausible situations but do not establish a causal relationship between the two sets of events. Thus if the new job that is offered to the man is not the one vacated by the woman, there is no way to determine whether a woman works as a waitress (4) before a man works as a waiter (3) or vice versa unless additional events are included.

4.
1. a train left the station late
2. a man was late for work
3. a man lost his job
4. many people complained because the train was late
5. there was a traffic jam

A. 5-2-1-4-3 D. 1-5-4-2-3
B. 5-1-4-2-3 E. 2-1-4-5-3
C. 5-1-2-4-3

The correct alternative, A, follows from the inference that the man who is late for work is essential to the departure of the train. This is the only assumption that leads to a logical and interrelated sequence for the five events. The other four alternatives do not really interrelate the events and become plausible only if numerous assumptions are made. In addition, the four alternatives sever the connection between the numerous complaints (4) and the lost job (3). Without this connection event 4 becomes superfluous.

EXAMINATION SECTION
TEST 1

DIRECTIONS: Each question or incomplete statement is followed by several suggested answers or completions. Select the one that BEST answers the question or completes the statement. *PRINT THE CORRECT ANSWER IN THE SPACE AT THE RIGHT.*

1. To learn a foreign LANGGWAYJ is tedious work. 1.____
   The word in capitals is misspelled. Write it correctly at the right.

2. The APRENTIS learns a trade. 2.____
   The word in capitals is misspelled. Write it correctly at the right.

3. The SOHRS of the stream is high in the hills. 3.____
   The word in capitals is misspelled. Write it correctly at the right.

4. Animals often show great INTELIJENS. 4.____
   The word in capitals is misspelled. Write it correctly at the right.

5. Our hotels AKOMODAYT many people. 5.____
   The word in capitals is misspelled. Write it correctly at the right.

6. Who determines whether a Congressman who is considered undesirable shall be seated? 6.____

   A. Congress
   B. Supreme Court
   C. President
   D. Cabinet
   E. The people

7. *Aviation in the United States is accomplishing much. The total number of miles flown annually now amounts to move than the total for any other country in the world and is about equal to the combined mileage of Germany and France.* 7.____
   According to the above paragraph, which one of the following statements is TRUE?

   A. The total number of miles flown annually in the United States is less than that of any other country.
   B. Germany leads in the number of miles flown annually.
   C. The United States surpasses every country in the world in the number of miles flown annually.
   D. Both Germany and France have greater air mileage than the United States.
   E. Because of the bigger size of the United States, our planes must fly farther than the planes in the rest of the countries combined.

8. DIG is to TRENCH as BUILD is to 8.____

   A. excavator
   B. wall
   C. mine
   D. construct
   E. replace

9. TIGER is to CAT as WOLF is to 9.____

   A. snarl B. dog C. fur D. wild E. hunted

10. GENEROUS is to MISERLY as FRIENDLY is to

    A. surly   B. kind   C. stingy   D. weak   E. clever

11. EAST is to WEST as DOWN is to

    A. earth   B. up   C. out   D. sky   E. rise

12. CLOTHES are to FABRIC as HOUSE is to

    A. lot
    D. residence
    B. shelter
    E. large
    C. wood

13. BOSTON is to SEASHORE as PITTSBURGH is to

    A. capitol
    D. city
    B. inland
    E. agriculture
    C. smaller

14. I wish to build a tank 5 feet long and 4 feet high that will hold 300 gallons. What will the width of the tank be if $7\frac{1}{2}$ gallons equal 1 cubic foot?

15. By what number is 3/4 of the product of 12 x 5 multiplied to give 405?

16. *Specimen signatures of consignee and consignor are sent on Form 6006.* What one word in the above sentence indicates the receiver?

17. CAUCASIAN is to WHITE MAN as MONGOLIAN is to

    A. Black
    D. Chinese
    B. Indian
    E. mountaineers
    C. Moor

18. *There is many a slip between the cup and the lip.*
    The above quotation means MOST NEARLY

    A. in life, as in wine, drink not to the dregs
    B. forget past troubles
    C. don't be too sure of the future
    D. a full cup spells prosperity
    E. a steady hand in all things is a necessity

19. *A new invention restores colors which were lost to some talking motion pictures when the sound track was introduced along the edge of the photographic film. By this new development, a producer may 'turn on the moonlight' for love scenes or use all the tints from blue to red in the gamut of human emotions.*
    Judging from the above paragraph, which one of the following statements is TRUE?

    A. Colors cannot be used with the talkies.
    B. Only red or blue can be used in motion pictures.
    C. A producer can now use all colors in talking films.
    D. Human emotions can be shown only with moonlight pictures.

20. LAUGHTER is to REJOICING as WEEPING is to

    A. punishment
    D. disappointment
    B. parting
    E. disillusionment
    C. sorrow

21. IRON is to HEAVY as FEATHERS are to   21.____

    A. goose   B. gray   C. light   D. grown   E. metal

22. AGREE is the opposite of   22.____

    A. quarrel   B. deny   C. warn
    D. dislike   E. unpleasant

23. ABUNDANT is the opposite of   23.____

    A. plenty   B. bouncing   C. scarce
    D. low   E. rare

24. He played the part of the VILIN.   24.____
    The word in capitals is misspelled. Write it correctly at the right.

25. These parts are INTURCHAYNJUBUL.   25.____
    The word in capitals is misspelled. Write it correctly at the right.

KEY (CORRECT ANSWERS)

1. language   11. B
2. apprentice   12. C
3. source   13. B
4. intelligence   14. 2 ft.
5. accommodate   15. 9

6. A   16. consignee
7. C   17. D
8. B   18. C
9. B   19. C
10. A   20. C

21. C
22. A
23. C
24. villain
25. interchangeable

TEST 2

DIRECTIONS: Each question or incomplete statement is followed by several suggested answers or completions. Select the one that BEST answers the question or completes the statement. *PRINT THE CORRECT ANSWER IN THE SPACE AT THE RIGHT.*

1. Extreme heat will LIKWIFY.
   The word in capitals is misspelled. Write it correctly at the right.
   1.____

2. It was his birthday ANIVURSAREE.
   The word in capitals is misspelled. Write it correctly at the right.
   2.____

3. The kittens were FROLIKING in the grass.
   The word in capitals is misspelled. Write it correctly at the right.
   3.____

4. C is to CC as AB is to
   4.____
   A. ABC B. AA C. BB D. AABB E. AAB

5. RIVER is to AMAZON as LAKE is to
   5.____
   A. deep B. Ohio C. Superior
   D. island E. Mississippi

6. Which one of the following answers may be applied to LAKE MICHIGAN but not to LAKE ERIE and LAKE ONTARIO?
   6.____
   A. Fresh water B. Inland
   C. Navigable D. St. Lawrence waterway
   E. Not adjacent to Canada

7. A tank can be filled through an intake pipe in 6 hours and emptied through an outlet pipe in 10 hours.
   If the tank is empty and both intake and outlet pipes are opened, how long will it take the tank to fill?
   7.____

8. A boy paid 36¢ for marbles. He lost three and then sold 1/3 of the remainder at cost for 90¢.
   How many marbles did he buy originally?
   8.____

9. Whenever there are urgent reasons for filling a vacancy *in any position in the competitive division and the director is unable to certify to the appointing officer, upon requisition by the latter, a list of persons eligible for appointment after a competitive examination, the appointing officer may nominate a person to the director for noncompetitive examination, and if such nominee is certified by the said director as qualified after such noncompetitive examination, he may be appointed provisionally to fill the vacancy only until a selection and appointment can be made after competitive examination, but no such appointment shall be continued for more than thirty days and successive appointments shall not be made.*
   The above paragraph states that
   9.____

   A. when no eligible register exists, appointments may be made to permanent positions by noncompetitive examinations of applicants

B. appointment is made only of the person nominated by the appointing officer
C. if an appointment continues for more than thirty days, it becomes permanent
D. permanent appointment can be made only after successful competitive examination
E. when an urgent need for filling a vacancy exists, it may be filled permanently without holding an examination

10. PHASES means

   A. varying aspects
   B. sentences
   C. frightening
   D. bluffing
   E. receptacle for flowers

11. AUGMENT means MOST NEARLY

   A. forecast
   B. increase
   C. drill
   D. hollow out
   E. sell

12. CYNICAL means MOST NEARLY

   A. cone shaped
   B. faithless
   C. morose
   D. sneering
   E. cutting

13. ALLEGES means MOST NEARLY

   A. suspects
   B. studies
   C. claims
   D. fears
   E. denies

14. ACCOSTED means MOST NEARLY

   A. reviled
   B. hated
   C. liked
   D. addressed
   E. deceived

15. ABSOLVED means MOST NEARLY

   A. acquitted
   B. responsible
   C. anointed
   D. discovered
   E. vain

16. ABANDON means MOST NEARLY

   A. enthusiasm
   B. skill
   C. loss
   D. unrestraint
   E. listlessness

17. APPREHENSIVE means MOST NEARLY

   A. angry
   B. guilty
   C. anxious
   D. generous
   E. arrested

18. Two-thirds of a hay crop was sold. One-half of the remainder was used for fodder and 60 bales still remained unused.
    How many bales were there in the entire crop?

19. A clerk threw off 1/3 of the mail sacks at A and 1/5 of the remainder at B. He then had 48 bags left.
    How many were on the train when he started?

20. A man's salary was increased by 25%. He was then earning $175 a month.
    What did he earn before the increase?

21. Street car tracks run PAIRULEL.
    The word in capitals is misspelled. Write it correctly at the right.
    21._____

22. They went KANOOING on the river.
    The word in capitals is misspelled. Write it correctly at the right.
    22._____

23. It is unwise to keep a VISHUS dog.
    The word in capitals is misspelled. Write it correctly at the right.
    23._____

24. *That which comes through hard work is most appreciated.*
    The above quotation means MOST NEARLY
    24._____

    A. easy riches lose their value
    B. easy come, easy go
    C. we appreciate that most which is hard to get
    D. hard work brings success

25. ALERTNESS is to SUCCESS as PROCRASTINATION is to
    25._____

    A. idleness   B. failure   C. postponement
    D. leisure   E. uselessness

KEY (CORRECT ANSWERS)

1. liquefy
2. anniversary
3. frolicking
4. D
5. C
6. E
7. 15
8. 12
9. D
10. A

11. B
12. D
13. C
14. D
15. A
16. D
17. C
18. 360
19. 90
20. $140

21. parallel
22. canoeing
23. vicious
24. C
25. B

TEST 3

DIRECTIONS: Each question or incomplete statement is followed by several suggested answers or completions. Select the one that BEST answers the question or completes the statement. *PRINT THE CORRECT ANSWER IN THE SPACE AT THE RIGHT.*

1. A raise in pay allowed for this month and including the previous month is called

    A. delayed
    B. postponed
    C. revertible
    D. retroactive
    E. past due

    1.____

2. Which one of the following applies to LOCK and MAILBOX but not to STAMP?

    A. Canceled
    B. Soiled
    C. Government property
    D. Metal
    E. Gummed

    2.____

3. INTEREST ON LOANS is to TIME as PARCEL POST RATES are to

    A. notes
    B. weight
    C. amount
    D. yearly
    E. distance

    3.____

4. To ATTEST is to

    A. heed
    B. bear witness
    C. make an oath
    D. try
    E. question

    4.____

5. F.O.B. is to FREIGHT SHIPMENT as C.O.D. is to

    A. charge account
    B. store sales
    C. customers
    D. package delivery
    E. purchases

    5.____

6. *Blessed is he who has found his work.*
   The above quotation means MOST NEARLY

    A. despatch is the soul of business
    B. thrice happy they who have an occupation
    C. drive your business, let not it drive you
    D. business neglected is business lost
    E. unoccupied is unprofitable

    6.____

7. *The empty vessel makes the greatest sound.*
   The above quotation means MOST NEARLY

    A. the dog that means to bite doesn't bark
    B. a boaster and a liar are cousins
    C. a deep stream flows silently
    D. aim above the mark to hit the mark
    E. the failure tells everyone how to run his business

    7.____

8. *Hitch your wagon to a star.*
   The above quotation means MOST NEARLY

   A. a bird in the hand is worth two in the bush
   B. aim high and you will hit high
   C. as good do nothing as to no purpose
   D. your ability should determine your aim
   E. let nothing stop you

9. *Little things are great to little men.*
   The above quotation means MOST NEARLY

   A. the elephant does not feel the flea bite
   B. little leaks sink great ships
   C. small minds are won by trifles
   D. drop by drop the tank is drained
   E. big oaks from little acorns grow

10. *A pound of pluck is worth a ton of luck.*
    The above quotation means MOST NEARLY

    A. lucky men are as rare as white crows
    B. good luck is often bad luck
    C. diligence is the mother of good luck
    D. luck may carry a man across the brook if he will but leap
    E. courage overcomes more than luck

11. To DISTRIBUTE is to

    A. agitate   B. collect   C. dispense
    D. derange   E. disintegrate

12. A REMARKABLE occurrence is

    A. commonplace   B. extraordinary   C. needful
    D. uneventful   E. portentous

13. WHALE is to LARGE as THUNDER is to

    A. lightning   B. injure   C. rain
    D. loud   E. distant

14. *If you are shipping canned goods from Wisconsin to San Francisco, the goods can be put down in the San Francisco market cheaper if they are hauled east by train and then carried all the way around the coast by water. For the interstate commerce commission has so built its rate structure that it is cheaper for the Wisconsin farmer to go 4,000 miles out of his way than use the direct rail route west.*
    According to the above paragraph, which one of the following statements is TRUE?

    A. The Wisconsin farmer must go 4,000 miles out of his way to ship goods to the west coast.
    B. To ship the goods by water will save time.
    C. He can save money by shipping by the direct rail route west.
    D. In sending goods to the west coast, it is cheaper for him to send them 6,000 miles by water and rail than 2,000 miles by rail only

15. The Atlantic Ocean is noted for the Gulf Stream which passes northward from the Gulf of Mexico, but which preserves its warmth until it reaches the British Isles. This is one of the reasons why England enjoys a warmer climate than Labrador, though both are in about the same latitude. The countries of southern Europe gain much of their warmth from the winds that blow across the Mediterranean Sea from the Sahara Desert.
According to the above paragraph, which one of the following statements is TRUE?
England is warmer than Labrador because

15.____

  A. the warm winds from the Sahara Desert reach England
  B. England is farther south than Labrador
  C. the Gulf Stream becomes cold before it reaches Labrador
  D. the Gulf Stream stays warm until it reaches England
  E. the Gulf of Mexico is directly across the ocean from England

16. On the west coast, a campaign for a safe and sane Fourth of July was started, resulting in laws that forbade the sale of fireworks in that section. The Fourth there is one of the quietest days of the year, the people expressing their patriotism in less harmful, though equally enjoyable, ways. In the east, where tradition is strong, there is no such law; but a tradition that brings in its wake the many tragedies that fireworks do is more honored in the breach than in the observance.
According to the above paragraph, which one of the following statements is TRUE?
The use of fireworks on the Fourth of July

16.____

  A. has been forbidden in all eastern states
  B. is traditional and so should not be prohibited
  C. is the only enjoyable way in which patriotism can be expressed
  D. is forbidden in certain western states
  E. causes very few accidents

17. A man was 69 years old on October 20th, 1992. Through 1992, in how many presidential elections could he have voted?

17.____

18. Two mechanics were repairing a motor, and one of the men, without knowing it, rubbed a smudge of grease on his face. When the job was completed, they looked at each other and the man with the clean face washed his face while the one with the dirty face did not. Which one of the following statements will explain this action?

18.____

  A. The man with the clean face wanted to impress his employer.
  B. They always washed their faces after completing a job.
  C. The man with the clean face thought his own face might be dirty.
  D. The man with the dirty face did not care about his appearance.
  E. The man with the dirty face was about to start another job.

19. In withdrawing stamps, postal cards, stamped envelopes, and newspaper wrappers from the reserve stock, postmaster should select the oldest on hand for sale to the public, provided they are in perfect condition. This will lessen the chances for stock to become shopworn and damaged, and tend to keep it fresh. Damaged or soiled stamped paper or stamps should never be offered for sale to the public.
According to the above paragraph, which one of the following statements is TRUE?

19.____

A. Postmasters should offer for sale only new, fresh stocks of stamps.
B. All old stock, regardless of condition, should be quickly sold.
C. Oldest stock, in perfect condition, should be sold first.
D. All old stock of stamps should be withdrawn and not offered for sale.
E. Imperfect stamps should be sold quickly before they become old.

20. At the time of his Gettysburg Address, Lincoln himself had no knowledge of what the final result of the Civil War was to be. He knew that the great principles for which he had stood were the principles on which the war was being fought. He knew that his own firm resolution and deep patriotism had sent thousands to their deaths and that many thousands more might die. With his mind burdened with unthinkable responsibilities, he took his place on the still scarred battlefield and spoke not only to soldiers, but to the fathers and mothers of boys who might that very day be meeting death in distant battlefields. Judging entirely from the above quotation, which one of the following statements is TRUE? 20.____

    A. The Battle of Gettysburg was in progress when Lincoln made this Address.
    B. Lincoln's patriotic principles were the underlying cause of the war.
    C. Lincoln was in sympathy with the principles on which the war was being fought.
    D. The Civil War had come to a close when Lincoln made his Gettysburg Address.
    E. The fathers and mothers of the soldiers were present at the Battle of Gettysburg.

KEY (CORRECT ANSWERS)

1.	D	11.	C
2.	D	12.	B
3.	E	13.	D
4.	B	14.	D
5.	D	15.	D
6.	B	16.	D
7.	E	17.	13
8.	B	18.	C
9.	C	19.	C
10.	E	20.	C

EXAMINATION SECTION
TEST 1

DIRECTIONS: Each question or incomplete statement is followed by several suggested answers or completions. Select the one that BEST answers the question or completes the statement. *PRINT THE LETTER OF THE CORRECT ANSWER IN THE SPACE AT THE RIGHT.*

1. An employee who is not sure how to do a job that the supervisor has just assigned should

    A. ask another employee how to do the job
    B. ask the supervisor how to do the job
    C. do some other work until the supervisor gives further instructions
    D. do the best he can

    1.____

2. An employee who is asked by the supervisor to work one hour overtime cannot stay because of previous arrangements made with the family. The employee should

    A. ask another employee who does not have a family to take over
    B. explain the situation to the supervisor and ask to be excused
    C. go home, but leave a note for the supervisor explaining the reason for not being able to stay
    D. refuse, giving the excuse that time-and-a-half is not being paid for overtime

    2.____

3. A department's MAIN purpose in setting up employee rules and regulations is to

    A. explain the department's work to the public
    B. give an official history of the department
    C. help in the efficient running of the department
    D. limit the number of employees who break the rules

    3.____

4. The MAIN reason an employee should be polite is that

    A. he may get into trouble if he is not polite
    B. he never knows when he may be talking to an official
    C. politeness is a duty which any employee owes the public
    D. politeness will make him appear to be alert and efficient

    4.____

5. Public employees would *most probably* be expected by their supervisor to do

    A. a fair day's work according to their ability
    B. more work than the employees of other supervisors
    C. more work than the supervisor really knows they can do
    D. the same amount of work that a little better than average employee can do

    5.____

6. Your supervisor gives you a special job to do without saying when it must be finished and then leaves for another job location. A little before quitting time you realize that you will not be able to finish the job that day. You should

    A. ask a few of the other employees to help you finish the job
    B. go home at quitting time and finish the job the next day
    C. stay on the job till you get in touch with your supervisor by phone and get further instructions
    D. work overtime till you finish the job

    6.____

7. "While on duty an employee is not permitted to smoke in public." Of the following, the *most likely* reason for such a rule is that

   A. government employees must be willing to surrender some of their personal liberties
   B. lighted cigarettes create a fire hazard
   C. nicotine in tobacco will lessen a city employee's ability to perform assigned duties properly
   D. smoking on duty may make an unfavorable impression on the public

8. While you are on duty someone asks you how to get somewhere. Supposing that you know how to get there, you should

   A. give him the necessary directions
   B. make believe you did not hear him
   C. tell him it is not your duty to give information
   D. tell him you are too busy to give the information

9. The BEST way to make sure that a piece of important mail will be received is to send it by

   A. first class mail
   B. fourth class mail
   C. registered mail
   D. special delivery

10. Letters, if they don't weigh more than an ounce, need a

    A. 37¢ stamp
    B. 38¢ stamp
    C. 39¢ stamp
    D. 40¢ stamp

QUESTIONS 11-15.

Answer questions 11 to 15 ONLY on the basis of the information given in the following paragraph.

If an employee thinks he can save money, time, or material for the city or has an idea about how to do something better than it is being done, he should not keep it to himself. He should send his ideas to the Employee's Suggestion Program, using the special form which is kept on hand in all departments. An employee may send in as many ideas as he wishes. To make sure that each idea is judged fairly, the name of the suggestor is not made known until an award is made. The awards are certificates of merit or cash prizes ranging from $10 to $500.

11. According to the above paragraph, an employee who knows how to do a job in a better way should

    A. be sure it saves enough time to be worthwhile
    B. get paid the money he saves for the city
    C. keep it to himself to avoid being accused of causing a speed-up
    D. send his ideas to the Employee's Suggestion Program

12. In order to send his idea to the Employee's Suggestion Program, an employee should

    A. ask the Department of Personnel for a special form
    B. get the special form in his own department

C. mail the idea, using Special Delivery
D. send it on plain, white, letter-sized paper

13. An employee may send to the Employee's Suggestion Program   13._____

    A. as many ideas as he can think of
    B. no more than one idea each week
    C. no more than ten ideas in a month
    D. only one idea on each part of the job

14. The reason the name of an employee who makes a suggestion is not made known at   14._____
    first is to

    A. give the employee a larger award
    B. help the judges give more awards
    C. insure fairness in judging
    D. make sure no employee gets two awards

15. An employee whose suggestion receives an award may be given a   15._____

    A. bonus once a year
    B. cash price of up to $500
    C. certificate for $10
    D. salary increase of $500

QUESTIONS 16-18.

Answer questions 16 to 18 ONLY on the basis of the information given in the following paragraph.

According to the rules of the Department of Personnel, the work of every permanent City employee is reviewed and rated by his supervisor at least once a year. The civil service rating system gives the employee and his supervisor a chance to talk about the progress made during the past year as well as about those parts of the job in which the employee needs to do better. In order to receive a pay increase each year, the employee must have a satisfactory service rating. Service ratings also count toward an employee's final mark on a promotion examination.

16. According to the above paragraph, a permanent City employee is rated *at least* once   16._____

    A. before his work is reviewed
    B. every six months
    C. yearly by his supervisor
    D. yearly by the Department of Personnel

17. According to the above paragraph, under the rating system the supervisor and the   17._____
    employee can discuss how

    A. much more work needs to be done next year
    B. the employee did his work last year
    C. the work can be made easier next year
    D. the work of the Department can be increased

18. According to the above paragraph, a permanent City employee will NOT receive a yearly pay increase

    A. if he received a pay increase for the year before
    B. if he used his service rating for his mark on a promotion examination
    C. if his service rating is unsatisfactory
    D. unless he got some kind of a service rating

19. "Employees on duty represent their Department to the citizens and are expected to be neat and orderly in their dress at all times." According to this statement, neat and orderly dress of employees while on duty is important because

    A. citizens don't care about the appearance of city employees who are off duty
    B. employees who are neat and orderly in their dress make better citizens
    C. if an employee dresses neatly while at work, he will dress neatly when away from work
    D. people might judge a department by the appearance of its employees

20. "In the city there are 266 shoe factories which employ 10,000 workers while in all the other cities of the state there are 62 shoe factories which employ 27,000 workers." According to this statement, the shoe factories in the city

    A. are larger than the shoe factories in any other city in the state
    B. employ more workers than all the other shoe factories in the state
    C. make cheaper shoes than the shoe factories in other cities of the state
    D. are greater in number than the shoe factories in all the other cities of the state

21. "All mail matter up to and including eight ounces in weight which is not classified as first or second class mail is third class mail. If a package weighs more than eight ounces, it is put into the fourth class and sent as parcel-post mail." According to this statement, mail weighing eight ounces or less may be

    A. classified as parcel-post mail
    B. first, second, or third class mail
    C. second class mail but not third class
    D. third or fourth class mail

QUESTIONS 22-24.

Answer questions 22 to 24 ONLY on the basis of the information given in the following paragraph.

Keeping the City of New York operating day and night requires the services of more than 200,000 civil service workers-roughly the number of people who live in Syracuse. This huge army of specialists work at more than 2,000 different jobs. The City's civil service workers are able to do everything that needs doing to keep the City running. Their only purpose is the well-being, comfort and safety of the citizens of New York.

22. Of the following titles, the one that *most nearly* gives the meaning of the above paragraph is:

    A. "Civil Service In Syracuse"
    B. "Everyone Works"

C. "Job Variety"
D. "Serving New York City"

23. According to the above paragraph, in order to keep New York City operating 24 hours a day   23._____

    A. half of the civil service workers work days and half work nights
    B. more than 200,000 civil service workers are needed on the day shift
    C. the City needs about as many civil service workers as there are people in Syracuse
    D. the services of some people who live in Syracuse is required

24. According to the above paragraph, it is MOST reasonable to assume that in New York City's civil service   24._____

    A. a worker can do any job that needs doing
    B. each worker works at a different job
    C. some workers work at more than one job
    D. some workers work at the same jobs

QUESTIONS 25-28.

Answer questions 25 to 28 ONLY on the basis of the information given in the following paragraph.

The National and City flags are displayed daily from those public buildings which are equipped with vertical or horizontal flag staffs. Where a building has only one flag staff, only the National flag is displayed. When the National flag is to be raised at the same time as other flags, the National flag shall be raised about 6 feet in advance of the other flags; if the flags are raised separately, the National flag shall always be raised first. When more than one flag is flown on horizontal staffs, the National flag shall be flown so that it is to the extreme left as the observer faces the flag.
When more than one flag is displayed, they should all by the same size. Under no circumstances should the National flag be smaller in size than any other flag in a combination display. The standard size for flags flown from City buildings is 5' x 8'.

25. From the above paragraph, a REASONABLE conclusion about flag staffs on public buildings is that a public building   25._____

    A. might have no flag staff at all
    B. needs two flag staffs
    C. should have at least one flag staff
    D. usually has a horizontal and a vertical flag staff

26. According to the above paragraph, a public building that has only one flag staff should raise the National flag   26._____

    A. and no other flag
    B. at sunrise
    C. first and then the City flag
    D. six feet in advance of any other flag

27. According to the above paragraph, the order, from left to right, in which the National flag 27._____
    flying from one of four horizontal staffs appear to a person who is facing the flag staffs is:

    A. Flag 1, flag 2, flag 3, National flag
    B. National flag, flag 1, flag 2, flag 3
    C. Flag 1, flag 2, National flag, flag 3
    D. Flag 1, National flag, flag 2, flag 3

28. According to the above paragraph, a combination display of flags on a City building 28._____
    would *usually* have

    A. a 6' x 10' National flag
    B. all flags 5' x 8' size
    C. all other flags smaller than the National flag
    D. 5' x 8' National and City flags and smaller sized other flags

QUESTIONS 29-30.

Answer questions 29 to 30 *ONLY* on the basis of the information given in the following paragraph.

Supplies are to be ordered from the stock room once a week. The standard requisition form, Form SP 21, is to be used for ordering all supplies. The form is prepared in triplicate, one white original and two green copies. The white and one green copy are sent to the stock room, and the remaining green copy is to be kept by the orderer until the supplies are received.

29. According to the above paragraph, there is a limit on the 29._____

    A. amount of supplies that may be ordered
    B. day on which supplies may be ordered
    C. different kinds of supplies that may be ordered
    D. number of times supplies may be ordered in one year

30. According to the above paragraph, when the standard requisition form for supplies is, 30._____
    prepared

    A. a total of four requisition blanks is used
    B. a white form is the original
    C. each copy is printed in two colors
    D. one copy is kept by the stock clerk

QUESTIONS 31-55.

Each of questions 31 to 55 consists of a word in capital letters followed by four suggested meanings of the word. For each question, choose the word or phrase which means *most nearly* the SAME as the word in capital letters.

31. ABOLISH 31._____

    A. count up   B. do away with
    C. give more   D. pay double for

32. ABUSE   32.____
    A. accept   B. mistreat
    C. respect   D. touch

33. ACCURATE   33.____
    A. correct   B. lost
    C. neat   D. secret

34. ASSISTANCE   34.____
    A. attendance   B. belief
    C. help   D. reward

35. CAUTIOUS   35.____
    A. brave   B. careful
    C. greedy   D. hopeful

36. COURTEOUS   36.____
    A. better   B. easy
    C. polite   D. religious

37. CRITICIZE   37.____
    A. admit   B. blame
    C. check on   D. make dirty

38. DIFFICULT   38.____
    A. capable   B. dangerous
    C. dull   D. hard

39. ENCOURAGE   39.____
    A. aim at   B. beg for
    C. cheer on   D. free from

40. EXTENT   40.____
    A. age   B. size
    C. truth   D. wildness

41. EXTRAVAGANT   41.____
    A. empty   B. helpful
    C. over   D. wasteful

42. FALSE   42.____
    A. absent   B. colored
    C. not enough   D. wrong

43. INDICATE   43.____
    A. point out   B. show up
    C. shrink from   D. take to

44. NEGLECT

    A. disregard   B. flatten
    C. likeness   D. thoughtfulness

44._____

45. PENALIZE

    A. make   B. notice
    C. pay   D. punish

45._____

46. POSTPONED

    A. put off   B. repeated
    C. taught   D. went to

46._____

47. PUNCTUAL

    A. bursting   B. catching
    C. make a hole in   D. on time

47._____

48. RARE

    A. large   B. ride up
    C. unusual   D. young

48._____

49. RELY

    A. depend   B. do again
    C. use   D. wait for

49._____

50. REVEAL

    A. leave   B. renew
    C. soften   D. tell

50._____

51. SERIOUS

    A. important   B. order
    C. sharp   D. tight

51._____

52. TRIVIAL

    A. alive   B. empty
    C. petty   D. troublesome

52._____

53. VENTILATE

    A. air out   B. darken
    C. last   D. take a chance

53._____

54. VOLUNTARY

    A. common   B. paid
    C. sharing   D. willing

54._____

55. WHOLESOME

    A. cheap   B. healthful
    C. hot   D. together

55._____

9 (#1)

56. An employee earns $96 a day and works 5 days a week. He will earn $4,320 in _____ weeks. 56._____

   A. 5   B. 7   C. 8   D. 9

57. In a certain bureau the entire staff consists of 1 senior supervisor, 2 supervisors, 6 assistant supervisors and 54 associate workers. The percent of the staff who are NOT associate workers is *most nearly* 57._____

   A. 14   B. 21   C. 27   D. 32

58. In a certain bureau, five employees each earn $2,000 a month, another three employees each earn $2,400 a month and another two employees each earn $8,200 a month. The monthly payroll for those employees is 58._____

   A. 27,200   B. 27,600   C. 33,600   D. 36,000

59. An employee contributes 5% of his salary to the pension fund. If his salary is $2,400 a month, the amount of his contribution to the pension fund in a year is 59._____

   A. 960   B. 1,440   C. 1,920   D. 2,400

60. The amount of square feet in an area that is 50 feet long and 30 feet wide is 60._____

   A. 80   B. 150   C. 800   D. 1,500

61. An injured person who is unconscious should NOT be given a liquid to drink *mainly* because 61._____

   A. cold liquid may be harmful
   B. he may choke on it
   C. he may not like the liquid
   D. his unconsciousness may be due to too much liquid

62. The MOST important reason for putting a bandage on a cut is to 62._____

   A. help prevent germs from getting into the cut
   B. hide the ugly scar
   C. keep the blood pressure down
   D. keep the skin warm

63. In first aid for an injured person, the MAIN purpose of a tourniquet is to 63._____

   A. prevent infection
   B. restore circulation
   C. support a broken bone
   D. stop severe bleeding

64. Artificial respiration is given in first aid *mainly* to 64._____

   A. force air into the lungs
   B. force blood circulation by even pressure
   C. keep the injured person awake
   D. prevent shock by keeping the victim's body in motion

65. The aromatic spirits of ammonia in a first aid kit should be used to

    A. clean a dirty wound
    B. deaden pain
    C. revive a person who has fainted
    D. warm a person who is chilled

QUESTIONS 66-70.

Read the chart below showing the absences in Unit A for the period November 1 through November 15; then answer questions 66 to 70 according to the information given.

ABSENCE RECORD-UNIT A
November 1-15

Date:	1	2	3	4	5	6	7	8	9	10	11	12	13	14	15
Employee															
Ames	X	S	H					X			H			X	X
Bloom	X		H			X	X	S	S		H	S	S		X
Deegan	X	J	H	J	J	J	X	X			H				X
Howard	X		H					X			H			X	X
Jergens	X	M	H	M	M	M		X			H			X	X
Lange	X		H			S	X	X							X
Morton	X						X	X	V	V	H				X
O'Shea	X		H			O		X			H	X		X	X

Code for Types of Absence
X-Saturday or Sunday
H-Legal Holiday
P-Leave without pay
M-Military leave
J-Jury duty
V-Vacation
S-Sick leave
O-Other leave or absence

Note: If there is no entry against an employee's name under a date, the employee worked on that date.

66. According to the above chart, NO employee in Unit A was absent on

    A. leave without pay
    B. military leave
    C. other leave of absence
    D. vacation

67. According to the above chart, all but one of the employees in Unit A were present on the

    A. 3rd   B. 5th   C. 9th   D. 13th

11 (#1)

68. According to the above chart, the *only* employees who worked on a legal holiday when the other employees were absent are   68.____

    A. Deegan and Morton
    B. Howard and O'Shea
    C. Lange and Morton
    D. Morton and O'Shea

69. According to the above chart, the employee who was absent *only* on a day that was either a Saturday, Sunday or legal holiday was   69.____

    A. Bloom   B. Howard   C. Morton   D. O'Shea

70. The employee who had more absences than anyone else are   70.____

    A. Bloom and Deegan
    B. Bloom, Deegan, and Jergens
    C. Deegan and Jergens
    D. Deegan, Jergens, and O'Shea

KEY (CORRECT ANSWERS)

1.	B	16.	C	31.	B	46.	A	61.	B
2.	B	17.	B	32.	B	47.	D	62.	A
3.	C	18.	C	33.	A	48.	C	63.	D
4.	C	19.	D	34.	C	49.	A	64.	A
5.	A	20.	D	35.	B	50.	D	65.	C
6.	B	21.	B	36.	C	51.	A	66.	A
7.	D	22.	D	37.	B	52.	C	67.	D
8.	A	23.	C	38.	D	53.	A	68.	C
9.	C	24.	D	39.	C	54.	D	69.	B
10.	C	25.	A	40.	B	55.	B	70.	B
11.	D	26.	A	41.	D	56.	D		
12.	B	27.	B	42.	D	57.	A		
13.	A	28.	B	43.	A	58.	C		
14.	C	29.	D	44.	A	59.	B		
15.	B	30.	B	45.	D	60.	D		

TEST 2

DIRECTIONS: Each question consists of a statement. You are to indicate whether the statement is TRUE (T) or FALSE (F). *PRINT THE LETTER OF THE CORRECT ANSWER IN THE SPACE AT THE RIGHT.*

QUESTIONS 1-4.

Read the paragraph below about "shock" and then answer questions 1 to 4 according to the information given in the paragraph.

SHOCK

'While not found in all injuries, shock is present in all serious injuries caused by accidents. During shock, the normal activities of the body slow down. This partly explains why one of the signs of shock is a pale, cold skin, since insufficient blood goes to the body parts during shock.

1. If the injury caused by an accident is serious, shock is sure to be present. 1.____

2. In shock, the heart beats faster than normal. 2.____

3. The face of a person suffering from shock is usually red and flushed. 3.____

4. Not enough blood goes to different parts of the body during shock. 4.____

QUESTIONS 5-8.

Read the paragraph below about carbon monoxide gas and then answer questions 5 to 8 according to the information given in this paragraph.

CARBON MONOXIDE GAS

Carbon monoxide is a deadly gas from the effects of which no one is immune. Any person's strength will be cut down considerably by breathing this gas, even though he does not take in enough to overcome him. Wearing a handkerchief tied around the nose and mouth offers some protection against the irritating fumes of ordinary smoke, but many people have died convinced that a handkerchief will stop carbon monoxide. Any person entering a room filled with this deadly gas should wear a mask equipped with an air hose, or even better, an oxygen breathing apparatus.

5. Some people get no ill effects from carbon monoxide gas until they are overcome. 5.____

6. A person can die from breathing carbon monoxide gas. 6.____

7. A handkerchief around the mouth and nose gives some protection against the effects of ordinary smoke. 7.____

8. It is better for a person entering a room filled with carbon monixide to wear a mask equipped with an air hose than an oxygen breathing apparatus. 8.____

QUESTIONS 9-17.

Read the paragraph below about moving an office and then answer questions 9 to 17 according to the information given in the paragraph.

MOVING AN OFFICE

An office with all its equipment is sometimes moved during working hours. This is a difficult task, and must be done in an orderly manner to avoid confusion. The operation should be planned in such a way as not to interrupt the progress of work usually done in the office and to make possible the accurate placement of the furniture and records in the new location. If the office moves to a place inside the same building, the desks and files are moved with all their contents. If the movement is to another building, the contents of each desk and file are placed in boxes. Each box is marked with a letter showing the particular section in the new quarters to which it is to be moved. Also marked on each box is the number of the desk or file on which the box is to be placed. Each piece of equipment must have a numbered tag. The number of each piece of equipment is put in soft chalk on the floor in the new office to show the proper location, and several floor plans are made to show where each piece of equipment goes. When the moving is done someone is stationed at each of the several exits of the old office to see that each box or piece of equipment has its destination clearly marked on it. At the new office someone stands at each of the several entrances with a copy of the floor plan, and directs the placing of the furniture and equipment according to the floor plan. No one should interfere at this point with the arrangements shown on the plan. Improvements in arrangement can be considered and made at a later date.

9. It is a hard job to move an office from one place to another during working hours. 9.____

10. Confusion CANNOT be avoided if an office is moved during working hours. 10.____

11. The work usually done in an office must be stopped for the day when the office is moved during working hours. 11.____

12. If an office is moved from one floor to another in the same building, the contents of a desk are taken out and put into boxes for moving. 12.____

13. If boxes are used to hold material from desks when moving an office, the box is numbered the same as the desk on which it is to be put. 13.____

14. Letters are marked in soft chalk on the floor at new quarters to show where the desks should go when moved. 14.____

15. When the moving begins, a person is put at each exit of the old office to check that each box and piece of equipment has clearly marked on it where it is to go. 15.____

16. A person stationed at each entrance of the new quarters to direct the placing of the furniture and equipment has a copy of the floor plan of the new quarters. 16.____

17. If, while the furniture is being moved into the new office, a person helping at a doorway gets an idea of a better way to arrange the furniture, he should change the planned arrangement and make a record of the change. 17.____

QUESTIONS 18-25.

Read the paragraph below about polishing brass fixtures and then answer questions 18 to 25 according to the information given in this paragraph.

POLISHING BRASS FIXTURES

Uncoated brass should be polished in the usual way using brass polish. Special attention need be given only to brass fixtures coated with lacquer. The surface of these fixtures will not endure abrasive cleaners or polishes and should be cleaned regularly with mild soap and water. Lacquer seldom fails to properly protect the surface of brass for the period guaranteed by the manufacturer. But, if the attendant finds darkening or corrosion, or any other symptom of failure of the lacquer, he should notify his foreman. If the guarantee period has not expired, the foreman will have the article returned to the manufacturer. If the guarantee period is over, it is necessary to first remove the old lacquer, refinish and then relacquer the fixture at the agency's shop. It is emphasized that all brass polish contains some abrasive. For this reason, no brass polish should be used on lacquered brass.

18. All brass fixtures should be cleaned in a special way. 18.____

19. A mild brass polish is good for cleaning brass fixtures coated with clear lacquer. 19.____

20. Lacquer coating on brass fixtures usually protects the surfaces for the period of the manufacturer's guarantee. 20.____

21. If an attendant finds corrosion in any lacquered brass article, he should relacquer the article. 21.____

22. The attendant should notify his foreman of failure of lacquer on a brass fixture only if the period of guarantee has expired. 22.____

23. The brass fixtures relacquered at the agency's shops are those on which the manufacturer's guarantee has expired. 23.____

24. Before a brass fixture Is relacquered, the old lacquer should be taken off. 24.____

25. Brass polish should NOT be used on lacquered surfaces because it contains acid. 25.____

QUESTIONS 26-50.

Questions 26 to 50 relate to word meaning.

26. "The foreman had received a few requests." In this sentence, the word 'requests' means *nearly* the SAME as 'complaints.' 26.____

27. "The procedure for doing the work was modified." In this sentence, the word 'modified' means *nearly* the SAME as 'discovered.' 27.____

28. "He stressed the importance of doing the job right ." In this sentence, the word 'stressed' means *nearly* the SAME as 'discovered.' 28.____

29. "He worked with rapid movements." In this sentence, the word 'rapid' means *nearly* the SAME as 'slow.' 29.____

30. "The man resumed his work when the foreman came in." In this sentence, the word 'resumed' means *nearly* the SAME as 'stopped.' 30.____

31. "The interior door would not open." In this sentence, the word 'interior' means *nearly* the SAME as 'inside.' 31._____

32. "He extended his arm." In this sentence, the word 'extended' means *nearly* the SAME as 'stretched out.' 32._____

33. "He answered promptly." In this sentence, the word 'promptly' means *nearly* the SAME as 'quickly.' 33._____

34. "He punctured a piece of rubber." In this sentence, the word 'punctured' means *nearly* the SAME as 'bought.' 34._____

35. "A few men were assisting the attendant." In this sentence, the word 'assisting' means *nearly* the SAME as 'helping.' 35._____

36. "He opposed the idea of using a vacuum cleaner for this job." In this sentence, the word 'opposed' means *nearly* the SAME as 'suggested.' 36._____

37. "Four employees were selected." In this sentence, the word 'selected' means *nearly* the SAME as 'chosen.' 37._____

38. "This man is constantly supervised." In this sentence, the word 'constantly' means *nearly* the SAME as 'rarely.' 38._____

39. "One part of soap to two parts of water is sufficient." In this sentence, the word 'sufficient' means *nearly* the SAME as 'enough.' 39._____

40. "The fire protection system was inadequate." In this sentence, the word 'inadequate' means *nearly* the SAME as 'enough.' 40._____

41. "The nozzle of the hose was clogged." In this sentence, the word 'clogged' means *nearly* the SAME as 'brass.' 41._____

42. "He resembles the man who worked here before." In this sentence, the word 'resembles,' means *nearly* the SAME as 'replaces.' 42._____

43. "They eliminated a number of items." In this sentence, the word 'eliminated' means *nearly* the SAME as 'bought.' 43._____

44. "He is a dependable worker." In this sentence, the word 'dependable' means *nearly* the SAME as 'poor.' 44._____

45. "Some wood finishes color the wood and conceal the natural grain." In this sentence, the word 'conceal' means *nearly* the SAME as 'hide.' 45._____

46. "Paint that is chalking sometimes retains its protective value." In this sentence, the word 'retains' means *nearly* the SAME as 'keeps.' 46._____

47. "Wood and trash had accumulated." In this sentence, the word 'accumulated' means *nearly* the SAME as 'piled up.' 47._____

48. An 'inflammable' liquid is one that is easily set on fire. 48._____

49. "The amounts were then compared." In this sentence, the word 'compared' means *nearly* the SAME as 'added.' 49.____

50. "The boy had fallen into a shallow pool." In this sentence, the work 'shallow' means *nearly* the SAME as 'deep.' 50.____

KEY (CORRECT ANSWERS)

1. T	11. F	21. F	31. T	41. F
2. F	12. F	22. F	32. T	42. F
3. F	13. T	23. T	33. T	43. F
4. T	14. F	24. T	34. F	44. F
5. F	15. T	25. F	35. T	45. T
6. T	16. T	26. F	36. F	46. T
7. T	17. F	27. T	37. T	47. T
8. F	18. F	28. F	38. F	48. T
9. T	19. F	29. F	39. T	49. F
10. F	20. T	30. F	40. F	50. F

EXAMINATION SECTION
TEST 1

DIRECTIONS: Each question or incomplete statement is followed by several suggested answers or completions. Select the one that BEST answers the question or completes the statement. *PRINT THE CORRECT ANSWER IN THE SPACE AT THE RIGHT.*

1. $75 \div \frac{1}{2} =$ 1._____

2. LOCOMOTIVE is to TRACKS as AUTOMOBILE is to   2._____

   A. tires   B. gas   C. chauffeur
   D. road   E. motor

3. A VAGUE statement is   3._____

   A. clear   B. frank   C. impudent
   D. cross   E. uncertain

4. A DISCREPANCY is a(n)   4._____

   A. omission   B. order   C. disagreement
   D. misdemeanor   E. change

5. The HICKERY tree has tough wood.   5._____
   The word in capitals is misspelled. Write it correctly at the right.

6. Add: $27\frac{1}{4}$ 6._____
         143 3/8
         $7\frac{1}{2}$
         ─────

7. Multiply: 8.309   7._____
              11.01
              ─────

8. Divide: .073)̄.365   8._____

9. NIGHT is to DAY as DARK is to   9._____

   A. black   B. stars   C. cold
   D. light   E. deep

10. A SLUGGISH stream is   10._____

    A. swift   B. dirty   C. muddy
    D. slow   E. active

11. A PITCHER is   11._____

    A. something used on the table

2 (#1)

    B. a useful article
    C. a container for liquids
    D. easily broken
    E. a painting

12. 100 pounds were added to the WAYT of each load.   12.____
    The word in capitals is misspelled. Write it correctly at the right.

13. If you can travel $\frac{1}{2}$ mile in one minute, how far can you travel in $\frac{1}{2}$ minute?   13.____

14. Glass is valuable because it is   14.____
        A. breakable   B. thick
        C. transparent   D. protection against cold
        E. insoluble

15. A certain garden plot contains 27 tomato plants.   15.____
    If the length and width are doubled, how many plants will it contain?
    _____ as many.
        A. Twice   B. Three times   C. Four times

16. A LOOTENENT is an officer.   16.____
    The word in capitals is misspelled. Write it correctly at the right.

17. How many square feet in a space 60 feet long and 10 feet wide?   17.____

18. He was REKWESTED to leave.   18.____
    The word in capitals is misspelled. Write it correctly at the right.

19. Canaries are kept in homes because they are   19.____
        A. useful   B. cheap
        C. amusing   D. used for food

20. PEN is to INK as SOAP is to   20.____
        A. hands   B. clean   C. water
        D. suds   E. odor

KEY (CORRECT ANSWERS)

1. 150
2. D
3. E
4. C
5. hickory

6. 178 1/8
7. 91.48209
8. E
9. D
10. D

11. C
12. weight
13. 1/4 mile
14. C
15. C

16. lieutenant
17. 600
18. requested
19. C
20. C

TEST 2

DIRECTIONS: Each question or incomplete statement is followed by several suggested answers or completions. Select the one that BEST answers the question or completes the statement. *PRINT THE CORRECT ANSWER IN THE SPACE AT THE RIGHT.*

1. Cut a 40 foot pole into 2 pieces, one 10 feet longer than the other. What is the length of the shorter piece? (If your answers are right, the shorter piece will be ten feet shorter than the longer.)   1.____

2. VELOCITY means MOST NEARLY   2.____
   - A. wind
   - B. speed
   - C. tricycle
   - D. sort of grass seed
   - E. civic plan

3. To ADHERE means to   3.____
   - A. hear easily
   - B. advertise
   - C. label
   - D. be present
   - E. cling to

4. We traveled through three KUNTREES.   4.____
   The word in capitals is misspelled. Write it correctly at the right.

5. IDENTICAL means   5.____
   - A. to recognize
   - B. to bend
   - C. exactly alike
   - D. nearly alike
   - E. an ignoramus

6. CASUALTY means   6.____
   - A. a wreck
   - B. once in a while
   - C. death by accident
   - D. insured
   - E. slight

7. FISH are to WATER as BIRDS are to   7.____
   - A. feathers
   - B. nests
   - C. flying
   - D. trees
   - E. air
   - F. molting

8. DOZEN is to TWELVE as SCORE is to   8.____
   - A. ten
   - B. fifty
   - C. eggs
   - D. baseball
   - E. gross
   - F. twenty

9. There are 60 MINITZ in an hour.   9.____
   The word in capitals is misspelled. Write it correctly at the right.

10. To be IMPARTIAL is   10.____
    - A. to take sides
    - B. not to take sides
    - C. to be unjust
    - D. to be in politics
    - E. to give

11. We want to know the height of a certain pole. Its shadow is 20 feet long. The shadow of a yardstick is 2 feet long.
    How high is the pole?

    11.____

12. If you receive a 6% increase on your invested money, and you get $6.00 for 6 months interest, how much have you invested?

    12.____

13. Which is taller, a boy 64 inches tall or a man 5 feet 3 inches?

    13.____

14. SLOW is the opposite of

    A. gaining
    B. smooth
    C. fast
    D. difficult
    E. racing

    14.____

15. CRUDE OIL

    A. is not refined
    B. has bad odor
    C. is a varnish
    D. is a plant
    E. is heavy

    15.____

16. Sold an automobile for $125, thereby gaining 25%. Cost?

    16.____

17. CAPITOL means

    A. money
    B. punishment
    C. city
    D. government building
    E. tolling of bells

    17.____

18. If cigarettes are $1.50 a package, or 2 packages for $2.50, how many cigarettes would you get for $5.00? (20 cigarettes per package)

    18.____

19. *The recent apparently increasing popularity of foolish endurance tests, such as bicycle riding, dancing, tree and flagpole sitting, suggests that those not taking, part in them are nevertheless being forced into one of their own—that of patient endurance of them.*
    According to the above quotation, which one of the following statements is TRUE?

    A. These endurance tests prove scientific facts.
    B. These *contests* are losing popular interest.
    C. Dancing, tree and flagpole sitting contests are foolish.
    D. Those not taking part now will be forced to do so later.
    E. It is foolish to endure dancing or bicycle riding.

    19.____

20. A train leaves at 10:50 A.M. and arrives at 4:26 P.M. It makes 9 stops of 4 minutes each. If it travels 50 miles an hour when running, how many miles did it cover?

    20.____

KEY (CORRECT ANSWERS)

1. 15
2. B
3. E
4. countries
5. C
6. C
7. E
8. F
9. minutes
10. B
11. 30
12. $200
13. boy
14. C
15. A
16. $100
17. D
18. 80
19. C
20. 250

EXAMINATION SECTION
TEST 1

DIRECTIONS: Each question or incomplete statement is followed by several suggested answers or completions. Select the one that BEST answers the question or completes the statement. *PRINT THE CORRECT ANSWER IN THE SPACE AT THE RIGHT.*

1. One-half of all the mail is letters, one-third is cards, and the remainder consists of 300 papers.
   What is the TOTAL number of pieces in the mail?

   1.____

2. There are 5 dozen oranges and lemons in a basket. One-fifth of all the oranges equals the total number of lemons in the basket.
   How many lemons?

   2.____

3. DISIPLIN in the army is maintained always.
   The word in capitals is misspelled. Write it correctly at the right.

   3.____

4. We pledge ALEEJUNS to our flag.
   The word in capitals is misspelled. Write it correctly at the right.

   4.____

5. Cities pass laws to curb the smoke NYOOSANS.
   The word in capitals is misspelled. Write it correctly at the right.

   5.____

6. The policeman is PUTROHLING his beat.
   The word in capitals is misspelled. Write it correctly at the right.

   6.____

7. We are SEPURAYTING the good from the bad.
   The word in capitals is misspelled. Write it correctly at the right.

   7.____

8. Which one of the following words applies to LETTERS and MAGAZINES but not to MAIL CARRIER?

   8.____

   A. Authorized   B. Regular   C. Periodical
   D. Uniform   E. Mailed

9. *No doubt the most effective way of learning spelling is to train the eye carefully to observe the forms of the words we are reading. If this habit is formed and the habit of general reading accompanies it, it is sufficient to make a nearly perfect speller. However, the observation of the general form of a word is not the observation that teaches spelling. We must have the habit of observing every letter in every word, and this we are not likely to have unless we give special attention to acquiring it. Memory works by association. If we can work up a system which will serve the memory by way of association so that the slight effort that can be given in ordinary reading will serve to fix a word more or less fully, we can soon acquire a marvelous power in the accurate spelling of words.*

   9.____

   The above paragraph tells us that the MOST effective way of learning to spell accurately is to

   A. have good eyesight
   B. observe the general form of each word
   C. form the habit of reading
   D. observe every letter in every word
   E. memorize every word we read

75

10. Each book has 200 pages.
    In a set of books standing side by side on a shelf, how many pages are there between page 1 of Volume 1 and page 200 of Volume 2?

11. Joe can sort a bag of mail in 6 minutes. Al can sort a bag of mail in 12 minutes. How long will it take them to sort one bag of mail, working together?

12. THIS is to THAT as HERE is to

    A. where   B. when   C. what   D. there   E. how

13. X is to Z as A is to

    A. Y
    D. letter
    B. C
    E. B
    C. alphabet

14. LETTER is to WORD as WORD is to

    A. alphabet
    D. spelling
    B. book
    E. chapter
    C. sentence

15. To ISOLATE is to

    A. freeze
    C. quarantine
    E. discipline
    B. separate from others
    D. be tardy often

16. UNCOUTH means MOST NEARLY

    A. youthful
    C. boorish
    E. unhealthy
    B. to straighten out
    D. masculine

17. PERJURY means MOST NEARLY

    A. to swear out a warrant
    C. to do things unlawfully
    E. jury duty
    B. to make a false oath
    D. to commit a theft

18. Law-breakers are confined in a PENITENSHAREE.
    The word in capitals is misspelled. Write it correctly at the right.

19. Birds devour INKREDIBUL numbers of insects.
    The word in capitals is misspelled. Write it correctly at the right.

20. *The Federal Reserve System, by the pooling of resources, has provided a bulwark which is destined to prevent any public nervousness from manifesting itself in money panics. An example of its service in this respect occurred last winter. The failure of the Bank of the United States in New York City caused a run on currency. The banks turned to Federal Reserve System. Within a week or so, no less than a quarter of a billion dollars had been called for. Nobody would have heard of the incident but for its record in the publications of the Federal Reserve Bank of New York. In other days, such nervousness would have precipitated a panic of the dimensions of the ones we had in 1897 and in 1907.*
    Judging from the above paragraph, it is TRUE that

    A. exactly a quarter of a billion dollars is held in reserve by the United States
    B. the United States is deeply in debt

C. by pooling its resources the Federal Reserve System can definitely prevent money panics
D. in case of a run on currency, the Federal Reserve System would be helpless
E. public nervousness may bring on any conceivable emergency

21. *In the year of Washington's birth, another illustrious American, Benjamin Franklin, announced the forthcoming appearance of the first of a long series of POOR RICHARD'S ALMANACS. These quaint publications were famous for their homely maxims advocating industry and frugality. POOR RICHARD'S proverbs, however, preached more than pinch-penny policies. They taught wise spending as well as wise saving. They counseled that neither time, energy, nor money be spent except for that which well repays its cost in real value received. By converting thousands of readers to this homely philosophy, they had a profound and lasting effect on American social and business life.* POOR RICHARD'S proverbs had a profound effect on Americans because they

    A. were published in Washington's time
    B. stated facts in a quaint manner
    C. helped to make Benjamin Franklin famous
    D. counseled wise spending, industry, and frugality
    E. suggested pinch-penny policies

21.____

22. What is simple interest on $180 at 6% for 2 years and 10 months?

22.____

23. A painter added a pint of turpentine to every gallon of paint.
In 81 quarts of this mixture, how many gallons of paint were there?

23.____

24. A man had $3.69 in change in his pocket. This consisted of an equal number of nickels, pennies, dimes, and quarters.
How many cents worth of nickels has he?

24.____

25. *The constitution of any country, whether written or traditional, is the fundamental law of that country; that is, the highest law by which the country professes to be governed. If any law is made in violation of that fundamental law, it is of no force whatever, and is, to all intents and purposes, null and void. The history of different countries shows that legislatures have sometimes attempted to pass such laws, but they have been set aside and declared inoperative by the law-interpreting branch of the government.*
Judging entirely by the preceding paragraph, which one of the following statement is TRUE?

    A. Traditional laws are never included in a constitution.
    B. A constitution must be written to be legal.
    C. History shows that legislatures enforce laws that are in opposition to the constitution.
    D. The law-interpreting branch of the government alone has the power to make laws.
    E. Laws made in violation of the constitution are not legal.

25.____

KEY (CORRECT ANSWERS)

1. 1800
2. 10
3. discipline
4. allegiance
5. nuisance

6. patrolling
7. separating
8. E
9. D
10. none

11. D
12. D
13. B
14. C
15. B

16. C
17. B
18. penitentiary
19. incredible
20. C

21. D
22. $30.60
23. 18
24. 45¢
25. E

TEST 2

DIRECTIONS: Each question or incomplete statement is followed by several suggested answers or completions. Select the one that BEST answers the question or completes the statement. *PRINT THE CORRECT ANSWER IN THE SPACE AT THE RIGHT.*

1. If 4 printing presses running together can complete a job in 12 hours, how long will it take 6 presses running together to do the same job?   1.____

2. Which one of the following answers can be applied to both BUS and STREETCAR but not to AUTOMOBILE?   2.____

   A. Carry people
   B. Have chauffeurs
   C. Motor driven
   D. Public conveyances
   E. Rubber-tired

3. LAMP-WICK is to OIL as MOTOR is to   3.____

   A. automobile
   B. locomotive
   C. mechanic
   D. gasoline
   E. alcohol

4. LOCOMOTIVE is to SMOKESTACK as HOUSE is to   4.____

   A. living quarters
   B. brick
   C. furnace
   D. chimney
   E. window

5. *That the Indian is taking a large part in administering the affairs of his own race is disclosed in a survey showing that approximately one-third of the employees of the Indian Bureau are Indians. These appointments were not made merely because the person applying was an Indian, but because he or she was found to be the best equipped person for the job. Officials at the Indian Bureau believe that the employment of Indians tends to make them more satisfied and proves an incentive to others of their race to fill responsible positions. The Indian brings to the service an understanding of his fellow men that few white people have.*   5.____
   The above paragraph states that the Indian is now taking a large part in administering the affairs of his own race because

   A. by nature he is best fitted to do this
   B. this is an incentive to others of his race
   C. he understands his people best and should, therefore, take part in administering their affairs even if he is not so competent as a white man
   D. by training he has been equipped to hold responsible positions
   E. approximately one-third of all the Indians are now in the government service

6. The postal clerk at the stamp window sold seven 3¢ stamps to every six 2¢ stamps. Altogether he sold 533 stamps. How many 3¢ stamps did he sell?   6.____

7. Art and Dave work together for 4 minutes on an assignment of 2316 pieces of mail; then Clem joins them.   7.____
   How long will it take the three of them to finish the lot if Art can sort at the rate of 57 pieces per minute, Dave at the rate of 48 per minute, and Clem at the rate of 53 per minute?

8. 2/3 of the first number equals 1/4 of the second number. This second number would be doubled by adding 24 to it. What is the FIRST number?   8.____

9. SEED is to PLANT as EGG is to
   A. food   B. nest   C. hatched
   D. chicken   E. healthful

10. *All debts contracted, and engagements entered into, shall be as valid against the United States, under this constitution, as under the Confederacy.*
    What one word in the above sentence describes the condition which is lawfully sound and good?

11. Parcels and letters shall be examined as to their condition and then recorded.
    What one word in the above sentence has the same meaning as *inspected*?

12. Who calls an election if a vacancy exists in the representation from any state?
    A. Governor   B. President   C. Congress
    D. Supreme Court   E. People

13. A VAGRANT is a
    A. land grant   B. vegetable   C. wanderer
    D. tradition   E. moron

14. AUTOMOBILE is to GARAGE as AIRSHIP is to
    A. balloon   B. pilot   C. hangar
    D. aviator   E. commander

15. WISCONSIN is to UNITED STATES as PART is to
    A. Ohio   B. whole   C. hand
    D. British Isles   E. separation

16. *The greatest wealth is health* means MOST NEARLY
    A. he who wants health wants everything
    B. a good wife and health are a man's best wealth
    C. he who is well has half won the battle
    D. health is the best wealth
    E. people with wealth can preserve their health

17. An AUTHENTIC statement is one which is
    A. false   B. true   C. formal
    D. genuine   E. likely

18. *In many foreign countries, the first one to register a trademark is considered to be the owner. Many American manufacturers who failed to register their trademarks abroad have found themselves in hot water because foreign trademark pirates have held them up for large sums of money in exchange for the stolen trademarks. As these pirates are in a position to exclude the goods of the real manufacturer from their country, the American manufacturer who happened to be asleep has to come to some agreement with them.*
    Judging from the above paragraph, which one of the following statements is TRUE?

    A. A trademark registered in a foreign country is not protected.
    B. Foreign courts are partial to their own citizens.

C. American trademarks, when not registered in many foreign countries, may be claimed and registered there by residents as their own.
D. It is necessary for Americans to pay large sums of money to register their trademarks in foreign countries.
E. Trademarks registered in the United States are thereby protected all over the world.

19. A YIELDING body is one which

    A. resists   B. forces   C. gives
    D. is obstinate   E. crumbles

20. ESTEEM is to DESPISE as FRIENDS are to

    A. lovers   B. enemies   C. men
    D. acquaintances E. people

21. *The right of citizens of the United States to vote shall not be denied or abridged by the United States or by any state on account of race, color, or previous condition of servitude.*
    According to the above paragraph, it is TRUE that any

    A. colored person who has served as a slave may not vote
    B. person who has lived in the United States for 5 years cannot vote
    C. person who has come here from abroad can vote
    D. person who has lived in the United States for 5 years can vote
    E. citizen of the United States has the right to vote

22. The legislative part of our government is the

    A. supreme court B. president   C. cabinet
    D. congress   E. people

23. ABIDE is to STAY as DEPART is to

    A. early   B. late   C. come   D. leave   E. hasten

24. *A national-origins clause added to our immigration laws would bring a heavy diminishment of immigration from Germany, Ireland, and the Scandinavian countries; but would add greatly to the number of immigrants admitted from Britain, due to the numerical rights of the original revolutionary inhabitants of this country, most of whom were British.*
    Judging from the above paragraph, which one of the following statements is TRUE?

    A. A national-origins clause would bring a heavy increase in the number of German and Irish immigrants admitted to the U.S.
    B. More British would be admitted under this clause because so many British inhabitants of this country took part in the revolutionary war.
    C. More British immigrants would be admitted because the number of British inhabitants in this country, originally, was greatest.
    D. Many Germans, Irish, and Scandinavians would be deported from the U.S.
    E. British people would be preferred to other races.

25. Which body makes the laws governing immigration? 25.___

    A. Supreme Court   B. Congress
    C. President   D. Senate
    E. Department of Labor

KEY (CORRECT ANSWERS)

1. 8 hrs.
2. D
3. D
4. D
5. D
6. 287
7. 12
8. 9
9. D
10. Valid
11. examined
12. A
13. C
14. C
15. B
16. D
17. B
18. C
19. C
20. B
21. E
22. D
23. D
24. C
25. B

TEST 3

DIRECTIONS: Each question or incomplete statement is followed by several suggested answers or completions. Select the one that BEST answers the question or completes the statement. *PRINT THE CORRECT ANSWER IN THE SPACE AT THE RIGHT.*

1. ABUDANT is to SCARCE as CHEAP is to 1.____

    A. bargain   B. buy   C. costly
    D. disagreeable   E. value

2. A WEARY horse is one which is 2.____

    A. easily refreshed   B. jaded
    C. young   D. enthusiastic
    E. breathing heavily

3. A VIRTUOUS person is a 3.____

    A. waster   B. poor friend
    C. person with morals   D. profligate
    E. friendly person

4. *Economy is a great revenue* means MOST NEARLY 4.____

    A. ask thy purse what thou shouldst buy
    B. from saving comes having
    C. penny by penny laid up will be many
    D. he who eats and saves sets the table twice
    E. thrice lucky is he who can save

5. Who is the Speaker of the House of Representatives? 5.____

    A. Vice President
    B. Sergeant-at-arms
    C. President
    D. Representative elected for this purpose
    E. Secretary of State

6. WASHINGTON is to LINCOLN as FIRST is to 6.____

    A. last   B. president   C. sixteenth
    D. Roosevelt   E. republican

7. An UNUSUAL person is 7.____

    A. odd   B. friendly   C. common
    D. kind   E. loud

8. If the President nominates most of the government's important officials, which body confirms the appointment? 8.____

    A. Senate   B. House of Representatives
    C. Supreme Court   D. Vice President
    E. People

9. PARENT is to COMMAND as CHILD is to 9.____

    A. obey   B. will   C. women
    D. achieve   E. love

10. *Safe is the man who owes nothing* means MOST NEARLY 10.___

    A. pay your debts and go to sleep
    B. he who pays his debts grows rich
    C. words pay no debts
    D. out of debt, out of danger
    E. the man who owes nothing need not fear lawsuits

11. A UNITED army is one which is 11.___

    A. attacked   B. disrupted   C. asunder
    D. joined   E. powerful

12. EYE is to HEAD as WINDOW is to 12.___

    A. ceiling   B. key   C. room
    D. door   E. wall

13. A man increased the speed of his car by 50%. After this increase, he was going 90 miles per hour. 13.___
What was his speed before the increasethe

14. *The Texas law, putting a curb on oil production, was overwhelmingly passed by both houses of the legislature. The governor had threatened to use martial law to enforce a shutdown of oil wells if the legislators took no action.* 14.___
Judging entirely from the above paragraph, it is TRUE that

    A. martial law was used to shut down oil wells in Texas
    B. legislators refused to take action in curbing oil production
    C. the legislature passed a bill which could curb oil production
    D. the Governor threatened to use martial law in compelling the legislature to take action
    E. the legislature decided to use the militia to control oil production

15. *It is evident that the fitness of the Philippine people to maintain a popular independent government will be closely dependent upon the education of the masses. It is important that a clear understanding of the educational work in the Philippines should be reached as there is much popular misapprehension on the subject. Before the Spanish-American war, the only history ever taught was that of Spain, and that under censorship; the history of other countries was a closed volume to the Filipino. The only educational advantage attainable by the common people was that afforded by the primary schools, which was a wretchedly inadequate provision.* 15.___
Judging entirely from the above paragraph, which one of the following statements is TRUE?
The fitness of the Philippine people to maintain an independent government is dependent upon

    A. the education of the people
    B. history being censored before it is taught in the schools
    C. popular support of the government
    D. their knowledge of the world's history
    E. their freedom from Spain

16. To ABANDON is to 16.____

    A. forsake   B. cherish   C. keep
    D. recall   E. forget

17. CLOTHES are to MAN as HAIR is to 17.____

    A. coat   B. dog   C. comb   D. pretty   E. cut

18. DIAMOND is to RARE as IRON is to 18.____

    A. silver   B. ore   C. common
    D. tin   E. valuable

19. *Gilbert K. Chesterton, in the course of his weekly attacks on the foibles of the day, has been turning his attention to the familiar assertion that 'in every age people have thought their own age prosaic and only the past poetical'–in other words, that, while the glamour of antiquity adds interest and prestige to the past, the present always seems dull to its people, who take a morose pleasure in comparing it unfavorably with the 'good old times.'* 19.____
    Judging entirely by the above paragraph, which one of the following statements is TRUE?
    Mr. Chesterton attacks and denies the assertion that

    A. people think the past is poetical and interesting
    B. people think their own time is commonplace and uninteresting
    C. we compare our times favorably with *the good old times*
    D. the past holds no interest for us
    E. the glamour of age is not adding prestige to our age

20. *One of the best and most cheerful signs of American interest in matters other than the purely material is the rapid increase of commercial buildings which are artistic. That a railway company should introduce decorative and ceramic art into its power house, for example, is surprising and cannot result in any immediate cash profit. Yet that is what one company has done. Located in the heart of a dingy and deserted slum district in one of our large cities, there is a great building of the finest white stone, designed by one of the best architects in America. It is simple, neither plain nor severe, but dignified and beautiful. It is already exerting an uplifting and beneficient effect upon the neighborhood.* 20.____
    Judging entirely by the statements given above, select the ONLY one of the following statements that corresponds exactly with the paragraph.

    A. All beautiful buildings are simple in design.
    B. To beautify a power house cannot result in any immediate cash return.
    C. Americans are interested only in purely material things.
    D. Beautiful buildings are always placed in slum districts to uplift and benefit the neighborhood.
    E. There would be no dingy slum districts if Americans were interested in things not only purely material.

21. To mislead is to DESEEV. 21.____
    The word in capitals is misspelled. Write it correctly at the right.

22. A small PARTIKUL remained. 22.___
    The word in capitals is misspelled. Write it correctly at the right.

23. Mules are known to be STUBURN. 23.___
    The word in capitals is misspelled. Write it correctly at the right.

24. 152 is 19% of a number. 24.___
    What is 7% of that same number.

25. If a man paid $24 for pigeons, and 12 pigeons died, and then he sold 3/7 of the rest at 25.___
    cost for $9, how many pigeons did he buy?

KEY (CORRECT ANSWERS)

1. C
2. B
3. C
4. B
5. D

6. C
7. A
8. A
9. A
10. D

11. D
12. C
13. 60
14. C
15. A

16. A
17. B
18. C
19. B
20. B

21. deceive
22. particle
23. stubborn
24. 56
25. 96

EXAMINATION SECTION
TEST 1

DIRECTIONS: Each question or incomplete statement is followed by several suggested answers or completions. Select the one that BEST answers the question or completes the statement. *PRINT THE CORRECT ANSWER IN THE SPACE AT THE RIGHT.*

1. Add: 1 1/2
         4 3/4
         9 3/8
         3 7/8

    1.____

2. Subtract: 367 3/8
              149 7/8

    2.____

3. Divide: 15.6)2496

    3.____

4. Multiply: .0035
              .56

    4.____

5. A, B, and C together can dig a ditch in 12 days. B can dig the same ditch alone in 36 days.
   How long will it take A and C to dig the ditch?

    5.____

6. This is the AYTEENTH day of the month.
   The word in capitals is misspelled. Write it correctly at the right.

    6.____

7. Which one of the following applies to both CITY DIRECTORY and TELEPHONE DIRECTORY but not to DICTIONARY?

    A. Free distribution
    B. Gives information
    C. Alphabetic listing
    D. Gives addresses
    E. Necessary business equipment

    7.____

8. Which is the Executive branch of our government?

    A. Congress   B. Supreme Court
    C. President and Cabinet   D. President and Senate
    E. Secretary of State

    8.____

9. NINE is to BASEBALL as ELEVEN is to

    A. dice   B. polo   C. sports
    D. hockey   E. football

    9.____

10. OUNCE is to POUND as QUART is to

    A. liquids   B. bottle   C. peck
    D. measurement E. milk

    10.____

11. DISC is to SPHERE as SQUARE is to

    A. flat   B. tool   C. circle   D. cube   E. box

    11.____

87

12. PRODUCT is to TRADEMARK as COUNTRY is to   12.____

    A. map   B. governed   C. flag
    D. boundary   E. political unit

13. An invitation requires an AKNAHLEJMENT.   13.____
    The word in capitals is misspelled. Write it correctly at the right.

14. The actress wanted to KANSEL her contract.   14.____
    The word in capitals is misspelled. Write it correctly at the right.

15. *Local and long distance telephone service has been an important factor in the laying of a*   15.____
    firm foundation for the modern American commercial structure. Upon its direct and personal communication depend many millions of the human contacts which must be made every day if the nation's business is to be done. Nowhere so widely as in America has the telephone been accepted as one of the essential tools of trade. Nowhere else is business transacted more swiftly and more surely. Nowhere else have been laid more securely the cornerstones of close cooperation and mutual understanding upon which sound business must be built.
    Judging from the above paragraph, which one of the following statements is TRUE?

    A. The telephone is not nearly so widely used in America as elsewhere.
    B. Business deals could not be transacted without telephone service.
    C. The modern American commercial structure has a firmer foundation because of the telephone service.
    D. Long distance telephone service is not an important factor in conducting a business.
    E. Foreign nations do not use long distance calls for business.

16. Judging entirely from the above paragraph, it is TRUE that sound business must be built   16.____
    upon

    A. a wide use of the telephone
    B. direct and personal communication
    C. swift and sure methods of doing business
    D. making millions of human contacts
    E. mutual understanding and close cooperation

17. Manufacturers BLEND coffee.   17.____
    In the above sentence, the word BLEND means

    A. drink   B. mix   C. brand
    D. ship   E. imitate

18. He BESTOWS favors.   18.____
    In the above sentence, the word BESTOWS means

    A. receives   B. collects   C. despises
    D. confers   E. refuses

19. ARSON is   19.____

    A. theft   B. murder   C. incendiarism
    D. fraud   E. suicide

20. APATHETIC is 20.____

   A. courteous B. attentive C. distracted
   D. unresponsive E. sympathetic

21. If Jim had a savings bank in which he put 1¢ Monday, three times as much Tuesday as   21.____
    Monday, three times as much Wednesday as Tuesday, etc., until he had a total of $1.21
    in the savings bank, how many days did it take to save this amount?

22. Jack's share of an estate is $6,000, which is 1/5 more than George's share.   22.____
    What is the value of the whole estate?

23. I sold a dog for $63 at a loss of $12\frac{1}{2}$%.   23.____
    If this dog had been sold for $81 instead, what would the percent of gain have been?

24. What is 1/3 of 10 added to 1/2 of 1/3 of 10?   24.____

25. Which one of the following can be applied to AUDIENCE and SPECTATORS but not to   25.____
    ACTORS?

   A. Dramatize B. Rehearsals
   C. Paying attention D. Not taking part
   E. Attendance

KEY (CORRECT ANSWERS)

1. $19\frac{1}{2}$
2. $217\frac{1}{2}$
3. .016
4. .00196
5. 18
6. eighteenth
7. D
8. C
9. E
10. C

11. D
12. C
13. acknowledgement
14. cancel
15. C

16. E
17. B
18. D
19. C
20. D

21. E
22. $11,000
23. $12\frac{1}{2}$%
24. E
25. D

TEST 2

DIRECTIONS: Each question or incomplete statement is followed by several suggested answers or completions. Select the one that BEST answers the question or completes the statement. *PRINT THE CORRECT ANSWER IN THE SPACE AT THE RIGHT.*

1. They were well EEKWIPT for the trip. 1.____
   The word in capitals is misspelled. Write it correctly at the right.

2. There was a NOTISUBUL increase in attendance. 2.____
   The word in capitals is misspelled. Write it correctly at the right.

3. *When the government caused the great Northwest to be surveyed, it divided the land into squares, each having, as nearly as possible, six miles on a side. These divisions are called townships. A row of townships along a north and south line is called a range. The township is thus seen to be a geographical unit, while a town, which is a political unit, may include one or more townships or less than a township. The town government is almost a democracy, for all the voters may meet once a year and elect their officers and vote money for necessary things for which the state law permits public money to be used.* 3.____
   According to the above paragraph, a town

   A. must be on a range line
   B. and a township are one and the same thing
   C. should be as nearly square as possible
   D. must include one or more townships
   E. is a political rather than a geographical unit

4. According to the above paragraph, 4.____

   A. the democratic party always rules in townships
   B. people in towns meet only once each year
   C. towns have a nearly democratic form of government
   D. voters in towns may appropriate money for necessary things only by special permission of the state legislature
   E. town officers vote money only for necessary things

5. ADULT is to CHILD as GOOSE is to 5.____

   A. younger   B. poultry   C. gander
   D. feathers   E. gosling

6. EAST is to WEST as CONSERVATIVE is to 6.____

   A. legal   B. travel   C. liberal
   D. politics   E. congress

7. DEER is to WOODS as WHALE is to 7.____

   A. fish   B. mammal   C. bones   D. huge   E. ocean

8. Which one of the following applies to both POSTMASTER and POST OFFICE DEPARTMENT but not to U.S. TREASURY?   8.____

    A. Municipal
    B. Public building
    C. Authorized to issue postal money orders
    D. Depository for federal funds
    E. Appointed

9. The enemy KAPITYOOLAYTED.   9.____
The word in capitals is misspelled. Write it correctly at the right.

10. A true VALYOOAYSHUN of property is made.   10.____
The word in capitals is misspelled. Write it correctly at the right.

11. He explained the PRINSIPULS of his system.   11.____
The word in capitals is misspelled. Write it correctly at the right.

12. *In 1748, George Washington, while surveying beyond the Blue Ridge, first faced real frontier life and conditions. This was one of the many experiences which taught him the true meaning of isolation and made him an ardent advocate of good highways and adequate communication facilities.*   12.____
He saw that these facilities would form strong links in the chain of federal union. To him, in large measure, Americans of his day owed their recognition of the value f effective means of keeping the widely separated sections of the country in touch with each other. While Washington was beginning to see at first hand the need for better communication facilities, Franklin was performing, in Philadelphia, a series of electrical experiments that indirectly played an important part in meeting this need. The spark that crossed the Schuylkill foreshadowed the far-flung systems of electrical communication now serving the United States.
The above paragraph clearly states that

    A. Washington installed the first line for electrical communication between the settlements
    B. Franklin invented the telephone
    C. Franklin was the first man to use electrical communication
    D. good communication facilities between settlements would strengthen the federal union
    E. in Washington's time, electrical communication was the only means of keeping the widely separated sections of the country in touch with each other

13. Audiences hear; spectators   13.____

    A. crowd   B. surge   C. see
    D. are curious   E. run

14. A newsdealer sold 18 magazines for the cost of 24. What is his percent of profit?   14.____

15. *A handsome woman is always right.*
    The above quotation means MOST NEARLY

    A. guilt is always timid
    B. he is armed without that is innocent within
    C. a pretty woman wins the lawsuit
    D. appearances are deceiving
    E. first impressions are lasting impressions

16. A freight train left Atlanta at 8:15 A.M. traveling at the rate of 22 miles per hour. A mail train left Atlanta at 9:45 A.M., passing the freight train at 11:15 A.M. What is the speed per hour of the mail train?

17. To ACCUMULATE is to

    A. scatter   B. amass   C. dissipate
    D. exploit   E. hide

18. An AFFECTIONATE person is one who is

    A. fond   B. harsh   C. kind
    D. pleasant   E. unselfish

19. *Boldly ventured is half won.*
    The above quotation means MOST NEARLY

    A. courage should have eyes as well as ears
    B. fortune gives her hand to the bold man
    C. a bold attempt is half success
    D. be not too bold
    E. looking before leaping is saving from falling

20. To COMPENSATE is to

    A. require   B. reward   C. oblige
    D. abridge   E. understand

21. To CORROBORATE is to

    A. approve   B. confirm   C. contest
    D. refute   E. agree

22. YES is to AFFIRMATIVE as NO is to

    A. knowledge   B. reason   C. negative
    D. think   E. positive

23. A wooden box four inches high and three inches long contains seventy-two cubic inches. How many inches wide is the box?

24. A man sold his house for $8,000, thereby gaining $3,000. What percent did he gain on his investment?

25. The younger male relative of an uncle is a NEFYOO.
    The word in capitals is misspelled. Write it correctly at the right.

KEY (CORRECT ANSWERS)

1. equipped
2. noticeable
3. E
4. C
5. E

6. C
7. E
8. C
9. capitulated
10. valuation

11. principles
12. D
13. C
14. 33 1/3%
15. C

16. 44
17. B
18. A
19. C
20. B

21. B
22. C
23. 6 inches
24. 60%
25. nephew

TEST 3

DIRECTIONS: Each question or incomplete statement is followed by several suggested answers or completions. Select the one that BEST answers the question or completes the statement. *PRINT THE CORRECT ANSWER IN THE SPACE AT THE RIGHT.*

1. The army is BESEEJING the city. 1.____
   The word in capitals is misspelled. Write it correctly at the right.

2. Water AKYOOMYOOLATES in low places. 2.____
   The word in capitals is misspelled. Write it correctly at the right.

3. Moderate EKSURSYZ is healthful. 3.____
   The word in capitals is misspelled. Write it correctly at the right.

4. Eighteen percent of the mail carriers were off duty. There were 164 on duty. 4.____
   How many carriers were off duty?

5. MUSIC is to SOOTHING as NOISE is to 5.____

   A. waking   B. hearing   C. annoying
   D. toiling   E. sleeping

6. REWARD is to HERO as PUNISH is to 6.____

   A. good   B. ache   C. traitor
   D. everlasting E. wound

7. BOOK is to WRITER as STATUE is to 7.____

   A. sculptor   B. city   C. beauty
   D. picture   E. stone

8. To DECREASE is to 8.____

   A. grow   B. diminish   C. settle
   D. decline   E. go

9. A HASTY person is 9.____

   A. deliberate B. meditative C. determined
   D. hurried   E. inaccurate

10. To DILATE is to 10.____

    A. contract   B. degrade   C. expand
    D. lag   E. lose

11. *Enough is great riches.* 11.____
    The above quotation means MOST NEARLY

    A. no tent so good to live in as content
    B. make the best and leave the rest
    C. he is rich who does not want
    D. he is well paid who is well satisfied
    E. he who is bright is wealthy

12. *Good instruction is better than riches.*
    The above quotation means MOST NEARLY 12.____

    A. to keep from falling, keep climbing
    B. he who plants corn sows thistles
    C. there is no royal road to learning
    D. there is no wealth like unto knowledge
    E. he who is bright is wealthy

13. How old must a senator be? 13.____

    A. 21   B. 25   C. 30   D. 35   E. 32

14. A senator may hold his seat for 14.____

    A. limit of four terms   B. limit of six terms   C. limit of two terms
    D. no limited time   E. limit of six years

15. Who calls special sessions of Congress? 15.____

    A. The Cabinet   B. Congress
    C. Vice President   D. President
    E. Supreme Court

16. *A competitor's score on an examination may indicate that he possesses ability far superior to the demands of the position for which he has applied. Another competitor may rate below the passing mark on the same examination, and thereby appear to have inferior ability for this type of work, but even though he rates low, he may receive guidance from the civil service commission as to the positions for which he is qualified.* 16.____
    From the above paragraph, it is a known fact that all applicants

    A. rate high in the examination
    B. will receive the kind of position for which they are qualified
    C. benefit by the experience
    D. may learn their qualifications from their examination ratings
    E. rate low in the examination

17. I sold a house for $9,000 and received $1,200 as my share of the profits. My partner had invested 60% of the amount required to build the house, and I had invested 40%. 17.____
    How many dollars had I invested in the house?

18. It is FATEEGING to run fast. 18.____
    The word in capitals is misspelled. Write it correctly at the right.

19. Four ATURNEES appeared in court. 19.____
    The word in capitals is misspelled. Write it correctly at the right.

20. His illness at this time is REGRETUBUL. 20.____
    The word in capitals is misspelled. Write it correctly at the right.

KEY (CORRECT ANSWERS)

1. besieging
2. accumulates
3. exercise
4. 36
5. C

6. C
7. A
8. B
9. D
10. C

11. C
12. D
13. 30
14. D
15. D

16. D
17. $2400
18. fatiguing
19. attorneys
20. regrettable

EXAMINATION SECTION

TEST 1

DIRECTIONS: Each question or incomplete statement is followed by several suggested answers or completions. Select the one that BEST answers the question or completes the statement. *PRINT THE LETTER OF THE CORRECT ANSWER IN THE SPACE AT THE RIGHT.*

1. Add: 37.10
          .006
        300.105
         16.02
       7341.
         72.50

2. Add: 25 7/8
         31 3/4
         72 1/8
         96 1/2
         89 3/8

3. Multiply: .18902
               .018

4. Divide: .063)6048

5. To OSCILLATE means to
   A. quiver
   B. freeze
   C. swing back and forth
   D. hate
   E. rebound

6. *A New York broker who studied in Scotland during his younger years took a keen interest in the game of golf as it was played there. When he returned to the United States back in the seventies, he introduced the game over here by reproducing one of England's most famous courses.*
   According to the above paragraph, which one of the following statements is TRUE?
   A. Golf originated in the United States.
   B. The first golf course was built in England seventy years ago.
   C. Golf was introduced in the United States in the seventies.
   D. Golf was formerly played only by students.

7. CAT is to FELINE as COW is to
   A. quadruped
   B. pedigreed
   C. canine
   D. bovine
   E. equine

8. BILL is to PAPER as COIN is to 8.____
   A. money   B. heavy   C. shiny   D. metal   E. round

9. WATER is to FLUID as IRON is to 9.____
   A. metal   B. rusty   C. solid   D. rails   E. mines

10. OVER is to UNDER as TRESTLE is to 10.____
    A. tunnel   B. bridge   C. trains
    D. skeleton   E. river

11. VAGUE means MOST NEARLY 11.____
    A. style   B. definite   C. not clear
    D. silly   E. tired

12. To AGGRAVATE is to 12.____
    A. indulge   B. counsel   C. inflate
    D. help   E. make worse

13. PRECISION means MOST NEARLY 13.____
    A. cutting   B. exactness   C. risky
    D. measurement   E. training

14. A TERSE statement is 14.____
    A. long   B. condensed   C. rude
    D. wild   E. exact

15. A car will go 3/8 of a given distance in one hour. What part will it cover in 5/8 of an hour? 15.____

16. An incubator was set with 120 eggs. If 18 eggs failed to hatch, what percent hatched? 16.____

17. At $2.00 a case, what fraction of a case can be bought for 7/8 of a dollar? 17.____

18. A earns $3.50 a day. B earns ¼ more a day than A does. How many days will it take B to earn the same amount that A earns in 10 days? 18.____

19. What is the postage on a package weighing 12 lbs., if the rate is 8 cents for the first pound and 4 cents for each additional pound? 19.____

20. *Money order may be cashed without gain or profit by any post office having surplus money order funds.* What one word in the above sentence is synonymous to *excess*? 20.____

21. The jury AKWITED the prisoner. The word in capitals is misspelled. Write it correctly at the right. 21.____

22. Dogs are SUGAYSHUS animals. The word in capitals is misspelled. Write it correctly at the right. 22.____

3 (#1)

23. The parade caused a TRAFIK jam. 23._____
    The word in capitals is misspelled. Write it correctly at the right.

24. The soldiers were ready to drop with FATEEG. 24._____
    The word in capitals is misspelled. Write it correctly at the right.

25. To TOLERATE is to 25._____
    A. prohibit   B. spoil   C. endure
    D. liberate   E. rejoice

KEY (CORRECT ANSWERS)

1. 7766.731
2. 315 5/8
3. .00340236
4. 9.6
5. C

6. C
7. D
8. D
9. C
10. A

11. C
12. E
13. B
14. B
15. 15/64

16. 85%
17. 7/16
18. 8
19. 52¢
20. surplus

21. acquitted
22. sagacious
23. traffic
24. fatigue
25. C

TEST 2

DIRECTIONS: Each question or incomplete statement is followed by several suggested answers or completions. Select the one that BEST answers the question or completes the statement. *PRINT THE LETTER OF THE CORRECT ANSWER IN THE SPACE AT THE RIGHT.*

1. To CONCUR means to
   A. gather
   B. repeat
   C. assent
   D. cause
   E. put together

   1._____

2. *The world never knows its great men until it buries them* means MOST NEARLY
   A. worry kills more men than work
   B. when a thing is lost, its worth is known
   C. every shoe fits not every foot
   D. no man really lives who is buried in conceit

   2._____

3. *The Congress of the United States provided for the cooperation of the federal government with the states in the construction of rural roads all over the country and was a powerful force in the development of highways.*
   Judging from the above paragraph, which one of the following statements is TRUE?
   A. Each state builds its highways and rural post roads unaided.
   B. Congress builds all highways in the United States.
   C. The state receive federal cooperation in the building of all roads.
   D. The federal government assists in the building of post roads.

   2._____

4. LAKE is to LAND as ISLAND is to
   A. separated
   B. land
   C. lonely
   D. water
   E. large

   4._____

5. NOVELIST is to FICTION as HISTORIAN is to
   A. war
   B. fact
   C. books
   D. school
   E. primitive

   5._____

6. Four men agreed to dig a ditch in 20 days. After 10 days, only one-fourth of the ditch was completed.
   How many more men must be engaged to finish on time?

   6._____

7. *Let a man be true to his intentions and his efforts to fulfill them, and the point is gained, whether he succeed or not.*
   The above statement states that
   A. a man cannot succeed unless he makes an effort to be true to his intentions
   B. he may be satisfied with himself if he makes an effort to be true to his intentions
   C. every point is gained whether a man succeeds or fails
   D. no special effort is necessary for success
   E. a certain amount of accomplishment always attends conscientious effort

   7._____

2 (#2)

8. MASS is to the WHOLE as ATOM is to
   A. physics   B. weight   C. solids   D. part   E. theory

9. DIME is to CENT a DOLLAR is to
   A. silver   B. dime   C. nickel   D. paper   E. coin

10. WISE is to FOOLISH as KNOWLEDGE is to
    A. simple   B. ignorance   C. books
    D. learned   E. intolerance

11. REPUBLIC is to PRESIDENT as MONARCHY is to
    A. communists   B. ruler   C. constitution
    D. elections   E. emperor

12. The distance from A to C is 423 miles. Tourists left A at 7 A.M. and traveled 225 miles at 45 miles an hour, then stopped 30 minutes for lunch. The remainder of the trip was made at 36 miles an hour.
    At what time did they arrive at C?

13. The TRANSHENT population is quite large.
    The word in capitals is misspelled. Write it correctly at the right.

14. The LYOOTENANT wore a new uniform.
    The word in capitals is misspelled. Write it correctly at the right.

15. He stepped on the AKELURAYTER.
    The word in capitals is misspelled. Write it correctly at the right.

16. Paper is easily PUNGKTYOORD.
    The word in capitals is misspelled. Write it correctly at the right.

17. Even in hot weather, the water supply is ADEKWAYT.
    The word in capitals is misspelled. Write it correctly at the right.

18. PLAUSIBLE explanations are
    A. ample   B. untrue   C. courageous
    D. apparently right   E. impossible

19. Which one of the following words may be applied to OPTION but not to PURCHASE or SALE?
    A. Legal   B. Document   C. Permanent
    D. Abstract   E. Temporary   F. Concession

20. ATTENTUATE means to
    A. wire   B. flatter   C. heed
    D. lessen   E. be present   F. extend

21. GIVING is to LENDING as TAKING is to   21.____
    A. alms   B. prison   C. thieves
    D. stealing   E. kindness   F. borrowing

22. A and B together earned $180.00 on piece work. B worked only 2/3 as fast   22.____
    as A, but he worked 6 days more and received $90.00.
    How many days did A work?

23. CHEAP is to ABUNDANT as COSTLY is to   23.____
    A. plenty   B. inexpensive   C. high priced
    D. scarce   E. frugal

24. *Two-thirds of all American fires are home fires, and the preponderant cause*   24.____
    is carelessness. This source of economic waste and human suffering can be
    checked only as we exercise greater care to eliminate such fire hazards as the
    accumulation of inflammable rubbish, careless smoking habits, overheated
    stoves, etc. Remember this, that even though you have no fire loss, you share
    in the loss of every fire in the country.
    According to the above paragraph, which one of the following statements is
    TRUE?
    A. There are fewer fires in homes than in industrial plants.
    B. Fires are no loss when they are covered by insurance.
    C. This economic waste can be overcome only as we exercise greater care.
    D. Waste is the preponderant cause of home fires.
    E. Carelessness in the accumulation of rubbish causes fires.

25. If a stock of 500 rungs is divided into two parts, one of which contains 2/3 as   25.____
    many as the other, how many rugs are there in the smaller part?

KEY (CORRECT ANSWERS)

1. C
2. B
3. D
4. D
5. B

6. 8
7. E
8. D
9. B
10. B

11. E
12. 6:00 P.M
13. transient
14. lieutenant
15. accelerator

16. accumulated
17. adequate
18. D
19. E
20. D

21. F
22. 12
23. D
24. C
25. 200

TEST 3

DIRECTIONS: Each question or incomplete statement is followed by several suggested answers or completions. Select the one that BEST answers the question or completes the statement. *PRINT THE LETTER OF THE CORRECT ANSWER IN THE SPACE AT THE RIGHT.*

1. John travels a mile in 1/3 of an hour. Ben travels a mile in 3/10 of an hour. How many minutes does Ben finish before John, each traveling 12 miles?   1._____

2. KITTEN is to CAT as COLT is to   2._____
    A. young   B. pasture   C. horse
    D. donkey   E. cattle

3. WOLF is to HOWL as DOG is to   3._____
    A. bite   B. pet   C. bark
    D. pedigree   E. whine

4. DYNAMYT is used for blasting.   4._____
    The word in capitals is misspelled. Write it correctly at the right.

5. The champion's OPOHNENT won the boxing match.   5._____
    The word in capitals is misspelled. Write it correctly at the right.

6. The hungry man's appetite was APEEZD.   6._____
    The word in capitals is misspelled. Write it correctly at the right.

7. WHEN is to WHERE as TIME is to   7._____
    A. hour   B. place   C. clock   D. here   E. work

8. ATLANTIC is to OCEAN as BRAZIL is to   8._____
    A. South America   B. country   C. river
    D. large   E. small

9. REGIMENT is to ARMY as SHIP is to   9._____
    A. marines   B. wars   C. navy
    D. submarine   E. commerce

10. *Substitute or temporary clerks shall be paid at the rate of $9.76 an hour for each hour or part hour after 6:00 P.M.*   10._____
    What one word in the above quotation is synonymous to a fixed value?

11. *The United States leads the world in the amount of sugar consumed per capita, more than a hundred pounds annually for every person in the nation. The rest of the world is just as fond of sugar but not so able to buy it.*   11._____
    Judging from the above paragraph, which one of the following statements is TRUE?

A. The United States leads in sugar production.
B. Europeans pay more for sugar.
C. Each person in the United States consumes a pound of sugar each week.
D. The per capita consumption of sugar in the United States is the largest in the world.
E. Americans are not so able to buy sugar as the rest of the world.
F. More sugar is consumed in the United States than in the rest of the world.

12. HABITUAL means MOST NEARLY
    A. healthy   B. customary   C. clothing
    D. harness   E. deadly

13. A COMPETENT man is one who is
    A. capable   B. clever   C. idle
    D. ambitious   E. punctual

14. To ADHERE is to
    A. hate   B. tape   C. degrade
    D. cling to   E. listen

15. To CALCULATE is to
    A. number   B. compute   C. whitewash
    D. tell tales   E. think

16. Which one of the following terms may be applied to MOTORCYCLE and AIRPLANE but not to BICYCLE?
    A. High speed   B. Padded seats   C. Metal
    D. Rubber tires   E. Two wheels

17. *He can who believes he can.*
    The above quotation means MOST NEARLY
    A. to believe a thing impossible is the way to make it go
    B. we are able when we feel so
    C. the man who believes is the man who achieves
    D. we walk by faith, not by sight
    E. nothing is impossible to him who tries

18. *How many acquaintances, but few friends.*
    The above quotation means MOST NEARLY
    A. be courteous to all, but intimate with few
    B. a true friend is forever a friend
    C. friends in distress make trouble less
    D. the only way to have a friend is to be one
    E. make friends of all you meet

19. *A man of many trades begs his bread on Sunday.*
    The above quotation means MOST NEARLY
    A. with too many irons in the fire some will burn
    B. doing everything is doing nothing
    C. one cannot do many things profitably at the same time
    D. an intense hour will do more than two dreamy years
    E. A man without a trade will beg his bread

19.____

20. *Caution is the parent of safety.*
    The above quotation means MOST NEARLY
    A. all things belong to the prudent
    B. better a mistake avoided than two corrected
    C. look before you leap
    D. better go around than jump and fall short

20.____

KEY (CORRECT ANSWERS)

1.	24 min.	11.	D
2.	C	12.	B
3.	C	13.	A
4.	dynamite	14.	D
5.	opponent	15.	B
6.	appeased	16.	A
7.	B	17.	C
8.	B	18.	A
9.	C	19.	C
10.	rate	20.	D

GENERAL AND MENTAL ABILITY
COMMENTARY

No matter what the level of the examination tested for, be it for trainee or administrator, whether a specific substantive examination is drawn up *ad hoc* for the position announced or whether a brief, simple qualifying test is given, keen analysis of current testing practices reveals that the type of question indicative of general or mental ability or aptitude, or *intelligence*, is an inevitable component and/or element of most examinations.

In other words, the examiners assume that all candidates must possess, or show, a certain level of understanding or *good sense* in matters or situations that may be considered common or general to all. This, then, is the purpose of the general-or-mental-type question: it seems to delimn, in objective terms, the basic, clearly definable, mental or intellectual status of the examinee, no matter what his education or his training or his experience of his present position or reputation.

In some cases, and for certain whole fields of job positions, tests of general and mental ability have even supplanted the specialized subject-area or position-information examination.

Moreover, even in the latter type of examination, e.g., the specific position-type, it will be found that questions testing general qualities study the examination at point after point.

This section should be of inestimable value to the candidate as he prepares not only for the job-examination, but also for any other examination that he may take at this time or in the future.

Now the candidate should *take* the tests of general and mental ability that follow, because of this special importance. These, particularly, portray the extended and rounded examination of general and/or mental ability.

The *Tests* that follow also serve to focus the candidate's attention on the variety and types of questions to be encountered, and to familiarize him with answer-patterns-and-nuances.

GENERAL AND MENTAL ABILITY

COMMENTARY

No matter what the level of the examination tested for, be it for trainee or administrator, whether a specific substantive examination is drawn up *ad hoc* for the position announced or whether a brief, simple qualifying test is given, keen analysis of current testing practices reveals that the type of question indicative of general or mental ability or aptitude, or "intelligence," is an inevitable component and/or element of most examinations.

In other words, the examiners assume that all candidates must possess, or show, a certain level of understanding or "good sense" in matters or situations that may be considered common or general to all. This, then, is the purpose of the general-or-mental-type question: it seems to delimn, in objective terms, the basic, clearly definable, mental or intellectual status of the examinee, no matter what his education or his training or his experience or his present position or reputation.

In some cases, and for certain whole fields of job positions, tests of general and mental ability have even supplanted the specialized subject-area or position-information examination.

Moreover, even in the latter type of examination, e.g., the specific position-type, it will be found that questions testing general qualities stud the examination at point after point.

This section should be of inestimable value to the candidate as he prepares not only for the job-examination, but also for any other examination that he may take at this time or in the future.

Now the candidate should "take" the tests of general and mental ability that follow, because of this special importance. These, particularly, portray the extended and rounded examination of general and/or mental ability.

The "Tests" that follow also serve to focus the candidate's attention on the variety and types of questions to be encountered, and to familiarize him with answer-patterns-and-nuances.

EXAMINATION SECTION
TEST 1

DIRECTIONS: Each question or incomplete statement is followed by several suggested answers or completions. Select the one that *BEST* answers the question or completes the statement. *PRINT THE LETTER OF THE CORRECT ANSWER IN THE SPACE AT THE RIGHT.*

1. The *opposite* of despair is 1.____

   A. hate   B. shame   C. despondent   D. hope   E. loyal

2. The *opposite* of constant is 2.____

   A. feeble   B. fickle   C. sober   D. thorough   E. standing

3. A person *always* has 3.____

   A. teeth   B. nerves   C. money   D. children   E. house

2 (#1)

4. A mare is *always* _____ than her colt. 4.____
   A. bigger   B. faster   C. stronger   D. older   E. slower

5. A sculptor is to a statue as a writer is to a 5.____
   A. book   B. clay   C. human   D. pencil   E. library

6. If the words below are rearranged to make a good sentence, with what letter would the *last* word of the sentence *begin*? 6.____
   always   are   on   hung   walls   pictures
   A. h   B. w   C. p   D. o   E. a

7. An event which might happen is said to be _____. 7.____
   A. probably   B. possible   C. obvious   D. fixed   E. planned

8. The wind is to a sailboat as _____ is to a locomotive. 8.____
   A. water   B. steam   C. a siren   D. a sail   E. a track

9. The *opposite* of victory is 9.____
   A. prosperity   B. outcome   C. defeat   D. glory   E. chagrin

10. Gold is *more* costly than silver because it is 10.____
    A. attractive   B. scarcer   C. stylish   D. colorful   E. heavier

11. The *opposite* of rough is 11.____
    A. quiet   B. kindly   C. robust   D. docile   E. gentle

12. The idea that the earth is flat is 12.____
    A. ridiculous   B. improbable   C. deceitful   D. evil   E. unjust

13. The two words *pertinent* and *permanent* mean _____. 13.____
    A. the opposite
    B. the same
    C. *neither* the same *nor* the opposite
    D. *both* the same *and* the opposite
    E. *all* of the above or *none* of the above

14. Darkness is related to sunlight in the same way as quiet is related to 14.____
    A. dungeon   B. sound   C. din   D. clamor   E. tranquility

15. One number is *wrong* in the following series. *Which one?* 15.____
    A. 5   B. 6   C. 7   D. 9   E. 9

16. A seed is related to a plant as a(n) _____ is related to a bird. 16.____
    A. worm   B. shell   C. tree   D. root   E. egg

17. The air is to an airplane as a _____ is to an automobile. 17.____
    A. driver   B. road   C. mechanic   D. tire   E. gas station

3 (#1)

18. A boat race *always* has

    A. wind   B. swimmers   C. trophy   D. contestants   E. masts

    18.____

19. *Which one* of the five things below is *MOST* like these three: giraffe, lizard, eagle?

    A. Leg   B. Wing   C. Bird   D. Mouth   E. Tail

    19.____

20. Temperature is related to thermometer as time is related to

    A. day   B. month   C. spring   D. year   E. clock

    20.____

21. *Which one* of the five words following is *MOST* unlike the other four?

    A. Violent   B. Evil   C. Pretty   D. Good   E. Went

    21.____

22. *Which* of the following is a trait of character?

    A. Affluent   B. Famous   C. Lavish   D. Unreliable   E. Tough

    22.____

23. *Which* word means the *opposite* of pride?

    A. Happiness   B. Humility   C. Fickleness
    D. Comical   E. Loyalty

    23.____

24. *What* is related to physiology as stars is to astronomy?

    A. Veins   B. Corpuscles   C. Blood   D. Food   E. Color

    24.____

25. Write the letter that *precedes* the letter M in the alphabet.

    A. N   B. O   C. P   D. L   E. J

    25.____

KEYS (CORRECT ANSWERS)

1.	D	11.	E
2.	B	12.	B
3.	B	13.	C
4.	D	14.	D
5.	A	15.	D
6.	B	16.	E
7.	B	17.	B
8.	B	18.	D
9.	C	19.	C
10.	B	20.	E

21. E
22. D
23. B
24. C
25. D

TEST 2

DIRECTIONS: Each question or incomplete statement is followed by several suggested answers or completions. Select the one that BEST answers the question or completes the statement. PRINT THE LETTER OF THE CORRECT ANSWER IN THE SPACE AT THE RIGHT

1. Which word is spelled the *same* backwards and forward? 1.____
   A. SOON   B. POOR   C. SEWER   D. MOO   E. SEES

2. Evolution is to revolution as crawl is to 2.____
   A. floor   B. infant   C. totter   D. run   E. stand

3. A debate *always* involves 3.____
   A. people   B. a meeting place   C. a trophy
   D. a controversy E. an opinion

4. Order is to confusion as _____ is to war. 4.____
   A. bombs   B. peace   C. planes   D. army   E. generals

5. *What* is related to ordinary as few is to less? 5.____
   A. More   B. Several   C. Alone   D. Exceptional   E. Plain

6. Of the things following, four are alike in a certain way. 6.____
   Which one is NOT like these four?
   A. Milk   B. Soot   C. Snow   D. Cotton   E. Ivory

7. To insist that stones have thoughts is 7.____
   A. nonsense   B. psychological   C. evil   D. rumor   E. futile

8. Wood is to table as brick is to a(n) _____ . 8.____
   A. color   B. oven   C. seat   D. wall   E. bricklayer

9. *Which* of these grouped numbers is *equal to* 5? 9.____
   A. 11-5   B. 6-2   C. 13-8   D. 9-5   E. 13-9

10. If one finds a kind of flower that was never seen before, one has made a(n) 10.____
    A. gem   B. idea   C. fixation   D. style   E. discovery

11. A city *always* has _____. 11.____
    A. tall buildings   B. restaurants   C. motels
    D. people   E. parks

12. Find the letter which in this sentence itself appears a *second time NEAREST* the beginning. 12.____
    A. F   B. I   C. N   D. T   E. E

112

13. A person who pretends to be anything other than what he is, is said to be

    A. honest   B. insincere   C. loyal   D. sorry   E. kind

14. If an act conforms to recognized principles or standards, it is said to be

    A. impartial   B. punitive   C. lawful
    D. recognized   E. accepted

15. A general is to an army as a _____ is to a state.

    A. city   B. mayor   C. governor   D. parks   E. laws

16. *Which one* of the five words below is *MOST* unlike the other four?

    A. Agile   B. Fast   C. Speedy   D. Run   E. Alert

17. A man who acquires the property of others by deceit is called a

    A. liar   B. swindler   C. convict   D. bailiff   E. counterfeiter

18. Feathers are to a bluebird as fur is to a _____.

    A. coat   B. duck   C. leopard   D. stole   E. store

19. The *opposite* of joy is

    A. sneer   B. wishful   C. affluent   D. happy   E. sorrow

20. If the first two statements following are true, the third is _____.
    All members of this club are Progressives. John is not a Progressive. John is a member of this club.

    A. true   B. false   C. not certain
    D. not enough information given   E. indeterminable

21. If the first two statements following are true, the third is _____.
    Some of Albert's friends are Mormons. Some of Albert's friends are lawyers. Some of Albert's friends are Mormon lawyers.

    A. true   B. false   C. not certain
    D. not enough information given   E. indeterminable

22. If the first two statements following are true, the third is _____.
    It takes perfect motor coordination to become a good fighter. Peter has perfect motor coordination. Peter will become a fighter.

    A. true   B. false   C. not certain
    D. not enough information given   E. indeterminable

23. A gulf is to an ocean as a peninsula is to a _____.

    A. pond   B. pool   C. continent   D. cape   E. fortress

24. A coin or bill made by dishonest people to deceive the public and pass for real money is said to be _____.

    A. a token   B. counterfeit   C. a reproduction
    D. foreign   E. larceny

25. Today is to yesterday as modern is to 25._____

    A. the next day   B. current   C. modernistic
    D. ancient   E. today

KEYS (CORRECT ANSWERS)

1.	E	11.	D
2.	D	12.	E
3.	D	13.	B
4.	B	14.	C
5.	E	15.	C
6.	B	16.	D
7.	A	17.	B
8.	D	18.	C
9.	C	19.	E
10.	E	20.	B
21.	C		
22.	C		
23.	C		
24.	B		
25.	D		

TEST 3

DIRECTIONS: Each question or incomplete statement is followed by several suggested answers or completions. Select the one that BEST answers the question or completes the statement. PRINT THE LETTER OF THE CORRECT ANSWER IN THE SPACE AT THE RIGHT.

1. A person who is confident he can complete a task is said to be _____.   1.____
   A. courageous   B. sure   C. bright   D. successful   E. alert

2. Do what this mixed-up sentence tells you to do. total seven Write four the one and of _____.   2.____
   A. 8   B. 12   C. 11   D. 5   E. 7

3. If a child sleeping peacefully is awakened by a sudden cry, he is *likely* to be   3.____
   A. ill   B. uncomfortable   C. startled   D. hungry   E. morbid

4. A bank is to money as a _____ is to books.   4.____
   A. authors   B. building   C. library   D. librarian   E. teacher

5. The SHORTEST distance between two points is a(n)   5.____
   A. cross-section   B. straight line   C. angle
   D. drawing   E. circle

6. "No time was set for the conference." The word below that BEST describes this fact is   6.____
   A. indefinite   B. decisive   C. ignored   D. powerful   E. irrational

7. *What* is related to accident as sanitation is related to disease?   7.____
   A. Nurse   B. Hospital   C. Ambulance   D. Medication   E. Caution

8. A person who is influenced in making a decision by preconceived opinions is said to be   8.____
   A. subjective   B. obstinate   C. hateful   D. ignorant   E. objective

9. The *opposite* of extravagant is _____.   9.____
   A. affluent   B. costly   C. frugal   D. cheap   E. heavier

10. A dinner *always* involves   10.____
    A. service   B. waitress   C. cloth   D. food   E. forks

11. *Which* word is the OPPOSITE of rotund?   11.____
    A. Tremendous   B. Muscular   C. Strong   D. Skinny   E. Elongated

12. A person who works hard and strives to achieve success is said to be _____.   12.____
    A. ambitious   B. lucky   C. patient   D. clever   E. strong

13. A person who says things he knows to be wrong is said to be   13.____
    A. hateful   B. deliberate   C. kind   D. craven   E. lying

14. The *opposite* of abolish is _____.

    A. announce   B. nullify   C. continue   D. refresh   E. expunge

15. *Which one* of these five things is *most* unlike the other four?

    A. Cucumber   B. Fig   C. Rose   D. Tomato   E. Cherry

16. A home *always* has a

    A. radio   B. television   C. relationship
    D. parent   E. dining room

17. Which word makes the *truest* sentence?
    Parents are _____ wiser than their children.

    A. usually   B. rarely   C. always   D. exceedingly   E. never

18. Of the five items listed below, four are alike in a certain way. *Which one* is NOT like the other four?

    A. Misery   B. Love   C. Sorrow   D. Despondent   E. Despair

19. A grandmother is always _____ than her grandchild.

    A. good   B. generous   C. older   D. kinder   E. wiser

20. *Which one* of the five words below tells BEST what a weapon is?

    A. Knife   B. Target   C. Aim   D. Bullet   E. Gangster

21. A cat does not *always* have

    A. a tail   B. a collar   C. whiskers   D. eyes   E. paws

22. A horse *cannot*

    A. talk   B. run   C. neigh   D. kick   E. trot

23. *Which* group is NOT in sequence?

    A. abcde   B. fghij   C. kmnop   D. rstuv   E. xyzab

24. The father of *my* mother is *my*

    A. cousin   B. nephew   C. uncle   D. grandfather   E. godfather

25. One number is *wrong* in the following series. *Which one?*
    1,   3,   9,   27,   82,   243......

    A. 1   B. 3   C. 27   D. 82   E. 243

KEYS (CORRECT ANSWERS)

1.	B	11.	D
2.	B	12.	A
3.	C	13.	E
4.	C	14.	C
5.	B	15.	C
6.	A	16.	C
7.	E	17.	A
8.	A	18.	B
9.	C	19.	C
10.	D	20.	A

21.	B
22.	A
23.	C
24.	D
25.	D

EXAMINATION SECTION

TEST 1

DIRECTIONS: Each question or incomplete statement is followed by several suggested answers or completions. Select the one that BEST answers the question or completes the statement. *PRINT THE LETTER OF THE CORRECT ANSWER IN THE SPACE AT THE RIGHT.*

1. Which one of the five things below does NOT belong with the others? 1.____
   A. Horse   B. Dog   C. Camel   D. Fish   E. Bear

2. Which one of the five words below tells BEST what a sword is? 2.____
   A. Cut   B. Weapon   C. Officer   D. Tool   E. Fight

3. Which one of the five words below means the OPPOSITE of south? 3.____
   A. West   B. Arctic   C. North   D. Tropics   E. Pole

4. A banana is to the peeling and an ear of corn is to the husk as an egg is to 4.____
   A. omelet   B. shell   C. cob   D. hen   E. food

5. A person who shares what he has with his friends is said to be 5.____
   A. kind   B. generous   C. courteous
   D. meek   E. loyal

6. Which one of the five things below is the LARGEST? 6.____
   A. Knee   B. Toe   C. Leg   D. Ankle   E. Foot

7. Feathers are to a bird as fur is to a(n) 7.____
   A. coat   B. swan   C. rabbit   D. glove   E. ostrich

8. Which word means the OPPOSITE of fail? 8.____
   A. Lose   B. Rise   C. Succeed
   D. Recede   E. Give up

9. Which one of the things below is MOST like these three: carrot, bean, cabbage? 9.____
   A. Bush   B. Apple   C. Lettuce   D. Salad   E. Cherry

10. Which one of the ten numbers below is the LARGEST? 10.____
    A. 4456   B. 6968   C. 2265   D. 3061   E. 2108
    F. 5549   G. 1335   H. 7472   I. 1286   J. 6970

11. Parasol is to sunshine as umbrella is to 11.____
    A. rain   B. night   C. promenade
    D. winter   E. black

12. If the below words were rearranged to make a good sentence, with what letter would the LAST word of the sentence begin?
    usually   are   on   hung   walls   pictures

    12.____

13. At 4 cents each, how many pencils can be bought for 32 cents?

    13.____

14. Which expression tells BEST just what a floor is?
    A. Part of a house   B. An inverted wall
    C. It is made of wood   D. The lower part of a room
    E. Something to step on

    14.____

15. A knee is to a leg the same as an elbow is to a(n)
    A. arm   B. shoulder   C. bone   D. wrist   E. hand

    15.____

16. If I find a kind of plant that was never seen before, I have made a(n)
    A. invention   B. adoption   C. creation
    D. novelty   E. discovery

    16.____

17. 5 10 15 20 25 30 35 41 45 50
    One number is wrong in the above series.
    What should that number be? (Write the CORRECT number in the space at the right.)

    17.____

18. What is the MOST important reason that airplanes were invented?
    A. Trains were unsafe.
    B. Roads were crowded.
    C. There was a demand for more rapid transportation.
    D. Airplanes furnish work for mechanics.
    E. Trains were getting too crowded.

    18.____

19. Railroad tracks are to a locomotive as _____ is to an automobile.
    A. tires   B. steam   C. speed   D. road   E. gasoline

    19.____

20. Which one of the words below would come FIRST in the dictionary?
    A. Trail   B. Salt   C. Raving
    D. Quarry   E. Grave   F. Naught
    G. Padded

    20.____

21. 7 1 7 2 7 3 7 4 7 5 7 6 7 8
    One number is wrong in the above series.
    What should that number be?

    21.____

22. A bicycle is to a motorcycle as a wagon is to
    A. an engine   B. an airplane   C. a horse
    D. slower   E. an automobile

    22.____

23. A boy who often tells stories he knows are not true is said to
    A. brag   B. cheat   C. lie
    D. exaggerate   E. lie

    23.____

3 (#1)

24. Which one of the five words below means the OPPOSITE of easy? 24._____
    A. Simple   B. Slow   C. Tough
    D. Difficult   E. Baffling

25. Which one of the five things below is MOST like these three: eagle, giraffe, lizard? 25._____
    A. Wing   B. Neck   C. Sparrow
    D. Grass   E. Spots

KEY (CORRECT ANSWERS)

1.	D		11.	A
2.	B		12.	W
3.	C		13.	8
4.	B		14.	D
5.	B		15.	A
6.	C		16.	E
7.	C		17.	40
8.	C		18.	C
9.	C		19.	D
10.	H		20.	E

21. 7
22. E
23. E
24. D
25. C

TEST 2

DIRECTIONS: Each question or incomplete statement is followed by several suggested answers or completions. Select the one that BEST answers the question or completes the statement. *PRINT THE LETTER OF THE CORRECT ANSWER IN THE SPACE AT THE RIGHT.*

1. A church is to a preacher as a school is to
   - A. study
   - B. pupils
   - C. religion
   - D. a teacher
   - E. a choir

    1.____

2. Which tells BEST just what a cat is?
   - A. Something that walks quietly
   - B. It has soft fur
   - C. A thing that climbs trees
   - D. A small domestic animal
   - E. It drinks milk

    2.____

3. October   June   December   August   April
   If the above words were arranged in order, with what letter would the middle word begin?

    3.____

4. Which one of the words below would come FIRST in the dictionary?
   - A. Brass
   - B. Button
   - C. Broad
   - D. Bully
   - E. Breakable
   - F. Brush
   - G. Buckle
   - H. Bright

    4.____

5. Worse is to bad as better is to
   - A. very bad
   - B. medium
   - C. good
   - D. much better
   - E. worst

    5.____

6. Which tells BEST just what a colt is?
   - A. An animal with hoofs
   - B. An awkward little beast
   - C. An animal that runs fast
   - D. A young horse
   - E. A little animal that eats hay

    6.____

7. houses   stone   built   of   men   wood   and
   If the above words were rearranged to make a good sentence, with what letter would the third word of the sentence begin? (Make the letter like a printed capital.)

    7.____

8. There is a saying, *All's well that ends well.*
   This means:
   - A. All comes out well in the end.
   - B. The success of anything is judged by the final result.
   - C. Stick to a job until it is finished.
   - D. Don't worry how things will turn out.

    8.____

9. Bread is to man as hay is to
   - A. wheat
   - B. barn
   - C. grass
   - D. horse
   - E. flour

    9.____

10. Which tells BEST just what a guess is?
    A. A mistaken idea
    B. A statement we think is most likely correct
    C. A statement we know is correct
    D. A statement that is almost correct
    E. Something we cannot find out

11. The daughter of my mother's brother is my
    A. niece   B. aunt   C. cousin
    D. stepsister   E. granddaughter

12. If Harry is shorter than Arthur and Arthur is shorter than Tom, then Harry is _____ Tom.
    A. shorter than   B. taller than
    C. just as tall as   D. cannot say which

13. A king is to a kingdom as _____ is to a republic.
    A. a democrat   B. a monarchy   C. a president
    D. laws   E. a voter

14. 9 4 6 9 3 4 9 6 7 9 9 3 6 9 4 5 9 9 6 3 1 9 6
    9 0 4 9 3 6 2 9 1 7 6 9
    Count each 6 above that has a 9 next after it. Tell how many 6's you count.

15. An event which might happen is said to be
    A. doubtful   B. possible   C. certain
    D. probable   E. unreasonable

16. Which one of the five things below is MOST like these three: king, general, dictator?
    A. War   B. Power   C. President
    D. Order   E. Monarchy

17. Loud is to sound as bright is to
    A. noise   B. shiny   C. dull   D. quiet   E. light

18. Eleven Thirteen Nine Twelve Ten
    If the above words were arranged in order, with what letter would the middle word begin?

19. A quantity which grows larger is said to
    A. prosper   B. increase   C. fatten
    D. rise   E. burst

20. In a foreign language:
    boy = Puero
    good boy = Puero Duko
    The word that means GOOD begins with what letter?

21. A governor is to a state as a general is to
    A. a king B. war C. an army
    D. a captain E. a commander

22. 4 3 4 2 4 3 4 2 4 2
    One number is wrong in the above series.
    What should that number be?

23. If Frank is younger than George and George is just as old as James, then James is _____ Frank.
    A. younger than B. older than
    C. just as old as D. cannot say which

24. alphabet the letter Write twenty-third the of
    Do what this mixed-up sentence tells you to do.

25. Clothes are to a man as _____ are to a bird.
    A. nests B. colors C. wings
    D. trees E. feathers

KEY (CORRECT ANSWERS)

1. D   11. C
2. D   12. A
3. A   13. C
4. A   14. 4
5. C   15. B

6. D   16. C
7. H   17. E
8. B   18. E
9. D   19. B
10. B   20. D

21. C
22. 3
23. B
24. W
25. E

TEST 3

DIRECTIONS: Each question or incomplete statement is followed by several suggested answers or completions. Select the one that BEST answers the question or completes the statement. *PRINT THE LETTER OF THE CORRECT ANSWER IN THE SPACE AT THE RIGHT.*

1. If Carl is younger than Edward and Carl is older than John, then John is _____ Edward.
    A. younger than
    B. older than
    C. just as old as
    D. cannot say which

    1._____

2. What is the MOST important reason that glass is used in windows?
    A. It is cheaper than wood.
    B. It permits light to pass through the window.
    C. It keeps out the rain and snow.
    D. It does not collect dust and germs.
    E. The people inside can watch their friends go by outside.

    2._____

3. cook chocolate the a cake made layer
    If the above words were rearranged to make a good sentence, with what letter would the third word of the sentence begin? (Make the letter like a printed capital.)

    3._____

4. A person who is sure he can accomplish a task is said to be
    A. successful
    B. confident
    C. proud
    D. fearless
    E. brave

    4._____

5. Minute Month Day Second Hour Year Week
    If the above words were arranged in order, with what letter would the middle word begin?

    5._____

6. If a man has walked west from his home 8 blocks and then walked east 5 blocks, how many blocks is he from home?

    6._____

7. In a foreign language, very hot = Sano Gur, very cold = Fros Guro.
    The word that means VERY begins with what letter?

    7._____

8. Which one of the five things below is MOST like these three: skate, baseball, jump-rope?
    A. Shoe   B. Club   C. String   D. Ice   E. Scooter

    8._____

9. There is a saying: *Any port in a storm.*
    This means:
    A. Ships should not venture out to sea in storms.
    B. Stormy weather causes large waves in harbors.
    C. In emergencies any aid is acceptable.
    D. Ships usually sink in storms.

    9._____

10. sum five Write two the one and of
Do what this mixed-up sentence tells you to do.

11. An object or institution that will last only a short time is said to be
   A. temporary   B. changeable   C. unsound
   D. worthless   E. unstable

12. In a foreign language, some bread = Pani Anko, some milk = Lecha Anko, some bread and milk = Pani Oto Lecha Anko.
With what letter does the word that means AND begin?

13. Which word means the OPPOSITE of humility?
   A. Joy   B. Pride   C. Dry
   D. Funny   E. Recklessness

14. Tree Limb Twig Trunk Bud
If the above words were arranged in order, with what letter would the middle word begin?

15. There is a saying, *Birds of a feather flock together.*
This means:
   A. Birds fly in large flocks.
   B. Some birds can't fly.
   C. People associate with others like themselves.
   D. Birds in a flock have the same color.
   E. People settle inn cities to be near others.

16. Which tells BEST just what a neck is?
   A. It is something to wear a collar on.
   B. It is that which joins the head to the body.
   C. A giraffe has a long one.
   D. It is something to fasten a necklace on.
   E. It is the connecting part of the body.

17. 1 2 4 8 24 32 64
One number is wrong in the above series.
What should that number be?

18. Write the letter that precedes the letter that comes next before *O* in the alphabet.

19. State Park Nation City Yard
If the above words were arranged in order, with what letter would the middle word begin?

20. There is a saying, *Kill not the goose that lays the golden eggs.* 20.____
    This means:
    A. Geese that lay golden eggs are too touch to eat.
    B. Don't destroy the things that do you good.
    C. Don't kill birds.
    D. Not many geese can lay golden eggs.
    E. Golden eggs are valuable.

21. If I have a large box with 3 small boxes in it and 3 very small boxes in each 21.____
    small box, how many boxes are there in all?

22. If a boy can run 200 feet in 10 seconds, how many feet can he run in 1/4 of 22.____
    a second?

23. Which one of the following words would come LAST in the dictionary? 23.____
    A. Health   B. Juggle   C. Grateful
    D. Never   E. House   F. Normal
    G. Latin

24. 4 5 8 9 12 13 16 18 20 21 24.____
    One number is wrong in the above series.
    What should that number be?

25. A feeling that each of two persons has for the other is said to be 25.____
    A. friendship   B. mutual   C. incompatible
    D. contemporary   E. deference

KEY (CORRECT ANSWERS)

1.	A		11.	A
2.	B		12.	O
3.	M		13.	B
4.	B		14.	L
5.	D		15.	C
6.	3		16.	B
7.	G		17.	16
8.	E		18.	M
9.	C		19.	C
10.	8		20.	B

21. 13
22. 5
23. F
24. 17
25. B

EXAMINATION SECTION

TEST 1

DIRECTIONS: Each question or incomplete statement is followed by several suggested answers or completions. Select the one that BEST answers the question or completes the statement. *PRINT THE LETTER OF THE CORRECT ANSWER IN THE SPACE AT THE RIGHT.*

1. Which one of the five things below does NOT belong with the others?
   A. Rose
   B. Violet
   C. Pansy
   D. Grape
   E. Morning-glory

2. Which one of the five words below tells BEST what a gun is?
   A. Shoot
   B. A weapon
   C. A tool
   D. An apparatus
   E. A thing

3. Which one of the five words below means the OPPOSITE of north?
   A. East
   B. Star
   C. South
   D. Pole
   E. Equator

4. A boy is to a man and a lamb as to a sheep as a kitten is to a
   A. girl   B. cat   C. dog   D. wolf   E. son

5. A child who accidentally hurts another child should
   A. hurt himself
   B. say he didn't do it
   C. run away
   D. do nothing
   E. say *I'm sorry*

6. Which one of the five things below is the SMALLEST?
   A. ankle   B. leg   C. toe   D. knee   E. foot

7. Which one of the five thins below is MOST like these three: a chair, a bed, and a stove?
   A. Iron
   B. Steps
   C. Wood
   D. A table
   E. A floor

8. Which one of the five words below means the OPPOSITE of thin?
   A. Strong
   B. Fat
   C. Healthy
   D. Tall
   E. Large

9. An elbow is to an arm as a knee is to
   A. a leg
   B. an ankle
   C. trousers
   D. a bone
   E. a man

10. Which word means the OPPOSITE of joy?
    A. Sickness
    B. Bad
    C. Happiness
    D. Sorrow
    E. Cry

11. Which one of the nine numbers below is the SMALLEST?
    A. 5084   B. 4160   C. 3342   D. 6521   E. 2918
    F. 3296   G. 6475   H. 2657   I. 7839

12. Which word means the OPPOSITE of ugly?
    A. Witch   B. Pretty   C. Colored
    D. Deformed   E. Mean

13. If the following numbers were arranged in order, what would the middle number be?
    A. 5   B. 9   C. 1   D. 7   E. 3

14. If you are sure you are right, you have
    A. pride   B. confidence   C. doubt
    D. confusion   E. safety

15. A sculptor is to a statue as an author is to a
    A. book   B. man   C. name
    D. bookcase   E. pen

16. Which is the MOST important reason we use money?
    A. It is made of silver.
    B. It makes goods cheaper.
    C. It makes exchanging goods easier.
    D. We have used it for a long time.
    E. It is fun to jingle.

17. Which one of the five things below is MOST like these three: a saw, a hammer, and a file? A
    A. bottle   B. pen   C. screwdriver
    D. fork   E. carpenter

18. At 3 cents each, how many pencils can be bought for 27 cents?

19. If a person sleeping quietly is awakened by a sudden cry, he is likely to be
    A. sick   B. dreaming   C. startled
    D. paralyzed   E. asleep

20. A seed is to a plant as a _____ is to a bird.
    A. tree   B. egg   C. feather   D. nest   E. flying

21. 6 1 6 2 6 3 6 4 6 5 6 7
    One number is wrong in the above series.
    What should that number be?

22. Which one of the five things below is MOST like these three: a goat, a frog, and a dove?
    A. A flower   B. A nest   C. Grass
    D. A snake   E. A tree

23. usually cans made tin of are   23.____
    If the above words were rearranged to make the best sentence, with what letter would the LAST word of the sentence begin? (Make the letter like a printed capital.)

24. A man who acquires the property of others by deceit is called a   24.____
    A. traitor   B. swindler   C. burglar
    D. prisoner   E. lawyer

25. Steam is to a locomotive as _____ is to a sailboat.   25.____
    A. the ocean   B. the wind   C. a rudder
    D. a whistle   E. a mast

KEY (CORRECT ANSWERS)

1.	D		11.	H
2.	B		12.	B
3.	C		13.	A
4.	B		14.	B
5.	E		15.	A
6.	C		16.	C
7.	D		17.	C
8.	B		18.	9
9.	A		19.	C
10.	D		20.	B

21. 6
22. D
23. T
24. B
25. B

TEST 2

DIRECTIONS: Each question or incomplete statement is followed by several suggested answers or completions. Select the one that BEST answers the question or completes the statement. *PRINT THE LETTER OF THE CORRECT ANSWER IN THE SPACE AT THE RIGHT.*

1. Which tells BEST what a cup is? 1.____
   A. A small drinking vessel
   B. Something to hold coffee
   C. A thin, breakable object
   D. It is used on a table
   E. It has a hand

2. If John is older than Peter, and Peter is older than Harry, then John is _____ Harry. 2.____
   A. older than
   B. younger than
   C. just as old as
   D. cannot say which

3. 5 3 1 8 7 5 1 5 6 3 5 2 0 9 5 3 5 1 0 2 5 8 7 1 5 3 3 5 0 1 3 5 5 3 2 5 3.____
   Count each 5 above that has a 3 next after it.
   Tell how many 5's you count.

4. heavier   lead   cork   is   than 4.____
   If the words above were rearranged to make a good sentence, with what letter would the FIRST word of the sentence begin? (Make the letter like a printed capital.)

5. A lamp is to light as _____ is to a breeze. 5.____
   A. a fan
   B. bright
   C. a sailboat
   D. a window
   E. blow

6. Which one of the seven words below would come FIRST in a dictionary? 6.____
   A. Mary
   B. Obey
   C. House
   D. Porch
   E. Elephant
   F. Newly
   G. Fairy

7. The son of my father's sister is my 7.____
   A. nephew
   B. uncle
   C. cousin
   D. stepbrother
   E. grandson

8. 5 4 5 6 5 4 5 6 5 6 8.____
   One number is wrong in the above series.
   What should that number be?

9. Which one of the five things below is MOST like these three: a ship, a bicycle, and a truck? 9.____
   A. A sail
   B. A wheel
   C. A train
   D. The ocean
   E. A tire

132

10. If Henry is taller than Tom and Henry is shorter than George, then George is _____ Tom.
    A. taller than
    B. shorter than
    C. just as tall as
    D. cannot say which

    10.____

11. What is the MOST important reason that we use telephones?
    A. To call the fire department
    B. To save time in communication
    C. To chat with our neighbors
    D. To hear the bell ring
    E. They give jobs to operators

    11.____

12. A government in which there are graft and bribery is said to be
    A. anarchistic
    B. corrupt
    C. autocratic
    D. inefficient
    E. disorganized

    12.____

13. A road is to an automobile as _____ is to an airplane.
    A. flying
    B. a propeller
    C. speed
    D. the air
    E. wings

    13.____

14. letter   Print   first   year   the   the   word   of
    Do what this mixed-up sentence tells you to do.

    14.____

15. 5   10   15   20   25   31   35   40   45   50
    One number is wrong in the above series.
    What should that number be?

    15.____

16. Which word means the OPPOSITE of guilty?
    A. Tarnished
    B. Brave
    C. Unselfish
    D. Cordial
    E. Innocent

    16.____

17. Peace is to war as _____ is to confusion.
    A. explosion
    B. order
    C. armistice
    D. riot
    E. police

    17.____

18. In an artificial language, bad water = Mullo Nero, bad air = Batti Nero. The word that means *bad* begins with what letter?

    18.____

19. A man who strives and hopes to achieve success is said to be
    A. ambitious
    B. lazy
    C. contented
    D. faithful
    E. loyal

    19.____

20. Which one of the five things below is MOST like these three: towel, shirt, and handkerchief?
    A. laundry   B. store   C. bath   D. sail   E. shoe

    20.____

21. A library is to books as a _____ is to money.
    A. store
    B. school
    C. bank
    D. knowledge
    E. gold

    21.____

22. If George is taller than Frank and Frank is just as tall as James, then James is _____ George. 22.____
   A. taller than   B. shorter than
   C. just as tall as   D. cannot say which

23. Sentence   Letter   Paragraph   Word   Chapter 23.____
    If the above words were arranged in order, with what letter would the MIDDLE word begin?

24. always   father   A   younger   his   than   boy   is 24.____
    If the above words were rearranged to make a good sentence, with what letter would the SECOND word of the sentence begin? (Make the letter like a printed capital.)

25. If an act conforms to recognized principles or standards, it is said to be 25.____
    A. legislative   B. wicked   C. legitimate
    D. harmonious   E. wrong

KEY (CORRECT ANSWERS)

1.	A		11.	B
2.	A		12.	B
3.	4		13.	D
4.	L		14.	Y
5.	A		15.	360
6.	E		16.	E
7.	C		17.	B
8.	4		18.	N
9.	C		19.	A
10.	A		20.	D

21. C
22. B
23. S
24. B
25. C

TEST 3

DIRECTIONS: Each question or incomplete statement is followed by several suggested answers or completions. Select the one that BEST answers the question or completes the statement. *PRINT THE LETTER OF THE CORRECT ANSWER IN THE SPACE AT THE RIGHT.*

1. In an artificial language, rose = Raab, red rose = Raab Lupo. The word that means *red* begins with what letter? 1.____

2. If a man has walked north from his home 11 blocks and then walked south 6 blocks, how many blocks is he from home? 2.____

3. A vase is to flowers as _____ is to milk 3.____
   A. drink   B. a cow   C. white   D. a pitcher   E. cream

4. sum three Write one the five and of 4.____
   Do what this mixed-up sentence tells you to do.

5. There is a saying, *Every rose has its thorn*. 5.____
   This means:
   A. All rosebushes have thorns.   B. There is no joy without some sorrow.
   C. Some rose petals are sharp.   D. All flowers come from bushes.

6. Which tells BEST what a wheel is? 6.____
   A. Something that turns
   B. It goes around
   C. A circular rim and hub connected by spokes
   D. A round thing to put on an automobile
   E. A bicycle always has two of them

7. Brick is to a wall as _____ is to a table. 7.____
   A. a chair   B. red   C. eat
   D. wood   E. a kitchen

8. sentence the letter Write fifth this in 8.____
   Do what this mixed-up sentence tells you to do.

9. Which one of the words below would come LAST in the dictionary? 9.____
   A. Emerge   B. Eject   C. Edible
   D. Estate   E. Enter   F. Eternal
   G. Easily   H. Emulate

10. There is a saying, *People who live in glass houses should not throw stones*. 10.____
    This means:
    A. Those who have faults should not criticize others.
    B. People should not live in glass houses.
    C. The stones thrown are likely to break the glass in the houses.
    D. People who live in glass houses need all the stones they have.

11. Lunch Dress Undress Supper Breakfast
    If the above words were arranged in order, with what letter would the MIDDLE word begin?

11.____

12. In an artificial language, little dogs = Puri Kamo, little cats = Gatti Kamo, little dogs and cats = Puri Erno Gatti Kamo.
    The word that means *and* begins with what letter?

12.____

13. A coin or bill made by dishonest people to deceive the public and pass for real money is said to be
    A. a duplicate   B. counterfeit   C. an imitation
    D. stage money   E. a slug

13.____

14. There is a saying, *As you make your bed, so must you lie on it.*
    This means:
    A. You should learn to make your own bed.
    B. You must bear the consequences of your own acts.
    C. You must lie down as soon as your bed is made up.
    D. Sleep is necessary to have good health.

14.____

15. Which one of the words below would come LAST in the dictionary?
    A. Harmony   B. Graft   C. Leader
    D. Gallop   E. Lively   F. Know
    G. Habit

15.____

16. Which tells BEST what an automobile is?
    A. A horseless carriage   B. A thing with tires
    C. Something to travel in   D. A vehicle propelled by an engine
    E. An engine mounted on wheels

16.____

17. Steam is to water as water is to
    A. hot   B. ice   C. an engine
    D. a solid   E. gas

17.____

18. Which statement tells BEST just what a hallway is?
    A. A small room
    B. A place to hang your hat and coat
    C. It is long and narrow
    D. A passage giving entrance to a building
    E. Where to say goodbye

18.____

19. Which one of the five words below is MOST like these three: small, back, and hard?
    A. Thick   B. Coal   C. Very   D. Soot   E. Color

19.____

20. Write the letter that precedes the letter that comes before Q in the alphabet.

20.____

21. 1 2 4 8 16 36 64
    One number is wrong in the above series.
    What should that number be?

    21._____

22. A son is to a daughter as an uncle is to a(n)
    A. mother   B. aunt   C. relation
    D. woman   E. sister

    22._____

23. If I have a large box with 5 small boxes in it and 2 very small boxes in each of the small boxes, how many boxes are there in all?

    23._____

24. 3 4 6 7 9 10 12 14
    One number is wrong in the above series.
    What should that number be?

    24._____

25. There is a saying, *An ounce of practice is worth a pound of preaching.*
    This means:
    A. Don't preach   B. Deeds count more than words.
    C. Preaching takes practice

    25._____

KEY (CORRECT ANSWERS)

1. L
2. 5
3. D
4. 9
5. B

6. C
7. D
8. E
9. F
10. A

11. L
12. E
13. B
14. B
15. E

16. D
17. B
18. D
19. A
20. O

21. 32
22. B
23. 16
24. 13
25. B

EXAMINATION SECTION
TEST 1

DIRECTIONS: Each question or incomplete statement is followed by several suggested answers or completions. Select the one that BEST answers the question or completes the statement. *PRINT THE CORRECT ANSWER IN THE SPACE AT THE RIGHT.*

1. The OPPOSITE of hate is

   A. enemy B. fear C. love D. friend E. joy

2. If 3 pencils cost 5 cents, how many pencils can be bought for 50 cents?

3. A bird does not always have

   A. wings B. eyes C. feet D. a nest E. a bill

4. The OPPOSITE of honor is

   A. glory B. disgrace C. cowardice
   D. fear   E. defeat

5. A fox MOST resembles a

   A. wolf B. goat C. pig D. tiger E. cat

6. Quiet is related to sound in the same way that darkness is related to

   A. a cellar   B. sunlight   C. noise
   D. stillness   E. loud

7. A party consisted of a man and his wife, his two sons and their wives, and four children in each son's family.
   How many were there in the party?

8. A tree ALWAYS has

   A. leaves   B. fruit   C. buds
   D. roots   E. a shadow

9. The OPPOSITE of economical is

   A. cheap   B. stingy   C. extravagant
   D. value   E. rich

10. Silver is more costly than iron because it is

    A. heavier   B. scarcer   C. whiter
    D. harder   E. prettier

139

Questions 11–13.

DIRECTIONS: Answer Questions 11 through 13 by choosing the CORRECT proverb of the following:
- A. Don't do the impossible.
- B. Weeping is bad for the eyes.
- C. Don't worry over troubles before they come.
- D. Early birds like worms best.
- E. Prompt persons often secure advantages over tardy ones.
- F. It is foolish to fret about things we can't help.

11. Which statement above tells the meaning of the proverb: *The early bird catches the worm?* 11.___

12. Which statement above tells the meaning of the proverb: *Don't cry over spilt milk?* 12.___

13. Which statement above explains the proverb: *Don't cross a bridge till you get to it?* 13.___

14. An electric light is related to a candle as an automobile is to 14.___

    - A. a carriage
    - B. electricity
    - C. a tire
    - D. speed
    - E. glow

15. If a boy can run at the rate of 6 feet in $\frac{1}{4}$ of a second, how many feet can he run in 10 seconds? 15.___

16. A meal ALWAYS involves 16.___

    - A. a table
    - B. dishes
    - C. hunger
    - D. food
    - E. water

17. Of the five words below, four are alike in a certain way. Which is the one NOT like these four? 17.___

    - A. Bend
    - B. Shave
    - C. Chop
    - D. Whittle
    - E. Shear

18. The OPPOSITE of never is 18.___

    - A. often
    - B. sometimes
    - C. occasionally
    - D. always
    - E. frequently

19. A clock is related to time as a thermometer is to 19.___

    - A. a watch
    - B. warm
    - C. a bulb
    - D. mercury
    - E. temperature

20. Which word makes the TRUEST sentence? 20.___
    Men are _____ shorter than their wives.

    - A. always
    - B. usually
    - C. much
    - D. rarely
    - E. never

21. 1 4 2 5 3 6 4 7 5 9 6 9   21.____
     One number is wrong in the above series.
     What should that number be?

22. All members of this club are Republicans.   22.____
     Smith is not a Republican.
     Smith is a member of this club.
     If the first two statements above are true, the third is

     A. true   B. false   C. not certain

23. A contest ALWAYS has   23.____

     A. an umpire   B. opponents   C. spectators
     D. applause   E. victory

24. 6 4 5 3 7 8 0 9 5 9 8 8 6 5 4 7 3 0 8   24.____
     9 1
     Which number in the above series appears a second time NEAREST the beginning?

25. The moon is related to the earth as the earth is to   25.____

     A. Mars   B. the sun   C. clouds
     D. stars   E. the universe

KEY (CORRECT ANSWERS)

1. C   11. E
2. 30   12. F
3. D   13. C
4. B   14. A
5. A   15. 240

6. B   16. D
7. 14   17. A
8. D   18. D
9. C   19. E
10. B   20. D

21. 8
22. B
23. B
24. E
25. B

TEST 2

DIRECTIONS: Each question or incomplete statement is followed by several suggested answers or completions. Select the one that BEST answers the question or completes the statement. *PRINT THE CORRECT ANSWER IN THE SPACE AT THE RIGHT.*

1. Which word makes the TRUEST sentence?
   Fathers are _____ wiser than their sons.

   A. always   B. usually   C. much
   D. rarely   E. never

   1.___

2. The OPPOSITE of awkward is

   A. strong   B. pretty   C. short
   D. graceful   E. swift

   2.___

3. A mother is always _____ than her daughter.

   A. wiser   B. taller   C. stouter
   D. older   E. more wrinkled

   3.___

Questions 4–6.

DIRECTIONS: Answer Questions 4 through 6 by choosing the CORRECT meanings of the following proverbs:
   A. Frivolity flourishes when authority is absent.
   B. Unhappy experiences teach us to be careful.
   C. A thing must be tried before we know its value.
   D. A meal is judged by the dessert.
   E. Small animals never play in the presence of large ones.
   F. Children suffer more from heat than grown people.

4. Which statement above explains the proverb, *The burnt child dreads the fire?*   4.___

5. Which statement above explains the proverb, *When the cat is away the mice will play?*   5.___

6. Which statement above explains the proverb, *The proof of the pudding is in the eating?*   6.___

7. If the settlement of a difference is made by mutual concession, it is called a

   A. promise   B. compromise   C. injunction
   D. coercion   E. restoration

   7.___

8. _____ related to disease as carefulness is to accident?

   A. Doctor   B. Surgery   C. Medicine
   D. Hospital   E. Sanitation

   8.___

9. Of the five things below, four are alike in a certain way. Which is the one NOT like these four?

   A. Smuggle   B. Steal   C. Bribe
   D. Cheat   E. Sell

   9.___

10. If 10 boxes full of apples weigh 400 pounds, and each box when empty weighs 4 pounds, how many pounds do all the apples weigh?

10.____

11. The OPPOSITE of hope is

    A. faith   B. misery   C. sorrow   D. despair   E. hate

11.____

12. A B C D E F G H I J K L M N O P Q R S T U V W X Y Z
If all the odd–numbered letters in the above alphabet were crossed out, what would be the TENTH letter not crossed out?

12.____

13. What letter in the word *superfluous* is the same number in the word (counting from the beginning) as it is in the alphabet?

13.____

14. What people say about a person constitutes his

    A. character   B. gossip   C. reputation
    D. disposition   E. personality

14.____

15. If $2\frac{1}{2}$ yards of cloth cost 30 cents, how many cents will 10 yards cost?

15.____

16. same means big large the as
If the words above were arranged to make a good sentence, with what letter would the SECOND word of the sentence begin? (Make it like a printed capital.)

16.____

17. George is older than Frank.
James is older than George.
Frank is younger than James.
If the first two statements above are true, the third is

    A. true   B. false   C. not certain

17.____

18. Suppose the first and second letters in the word *constitutional* were interchanged, also the third and fourth letters, the fifth and sixth, etc.
Print the letter that would then be the twelfth letter counting to the right.

18.____

19. 0 1 3 6 10 15 21 28 34
One number is wrong in the above series.
What should that number be?

19.____

20. If $4\frac{1}{2}$ yards of cloth cost 90 cents, how many cents will $2\frac{1}{2}$ yards cost?

20.____

21. A man's influence in the community should depend upon his

    A. wealth   B. dignity   C. wisdom
    D. ambition   E. political power

21.____

22. _____ is related to few as ordinary is to exceptional.

    A. None   B. Some   C. Many   D. Less   E. More

22.____

23. The OPPOSITE of treacherous is 23.___

    A. friendly   B. brave   C. wise
    D. cowardly   E. loyal

24. Which one of the five words below is MOST unlike the other four? 24.___

    A. Good   B. Large   C. Red   D. Walk   E. Thick

25. Some of Brown's friends are Baptists. 25.___
    Some of Brown's friends are dentists.
    Some of Brown's friends are Baptist dentists.
    If the first two statements are TRUE, the third is

    A. true   B. false   C. not certain

KEY (CORRECT ANSWERS)

1.	B	11.	D
2.	D	12.	T
3.	D	13.	F
4.	B	14.	C
5.	A	15.	120
6.	C	16.	M
7.	B	17.	A
8.	E	18.	O
9.	E	19.	36
10.	360	20.	50

21. C
22. C
23. E
24. D
25. C

TEST 3

DIRECTIONS: Each question or incomplete statement is followed by several suggested answers or completions. Select the one that BEST answers the question or completes the statement. *PRINT THE CORRECT ANSWER IN THE SPACE AT THE RIGHT.*

1. How many of the following words can be made from the letters in the word *largest,* using any letter any number of times? great, stagger, grasses, trestle, struggle, rattle, garage, strangle   1.____

2. The statement that the moon is made of green cheese is   2.____

    A. absurd B. misleading C. improbable
    D. unfair E. wicked

3. Of the five things following, four are alike in a certain way. Which is the one NOT like these four?   3.____

    A. Tar B. Snow C. Soot D. Ebony E. Coal

4. What is related to a cube in the same way in which a circle is related to a square?   4.____

    A. Circumference B. Sphere C. Corners
    D. Solid E. Thickness

5. If the following words were seen on a wall by looking in a mirror on an opposite wall, which word would appear exactly the same as if seen directly?   5.____

    A. Ohio B. Saw C. Noon D. Motor E. Otto

6. If a strip of cloth 24 inches long will shrink to 22 inches when washed, how many inches long will a 36-inch strip be after shrinking?   6.____

7. Which of the following is a trait of character?   7.____

    A. Personality B. Esteem C. Love
    D. Generosity E. Health

8. A B C D E F G H I J K L M N O P Q R S T U V W X Y Z   8.____
Find the two letters in the word *doing* which have just as many letters between them in the word as in the above alphabet. Print the one of these letters that comes FIRST in the alphabet.

9. Revolution is related to evolution as flying is to   9.____

    A. birds B. whirling C. walking
    D. wings E. standing

10. 1 3 9 27 81 108   10.____
One number is wrong in the above series.
What should that number be?

11. If Frank can ride a bicycle 30 feet while George runs 20 feet, how many feet can Frank ride while George runs 30 feet?   11.____

12. N O N T Q M N O T M O N O O N Q M N N O Q N O T O N A M O N O M

    Count each N in this series that is followed by an O next to it if the O is not followed by a T next to it. Tell how many N's you count.

13. A man who is averse to change and progress is said to be

    A. democratic B. radical C. conservative
    D. anarchistic E. liberal

14. Print the letter which is the fourth letter to the left of the letter which is midway between 0 and S in the alphabet.

Questions 15-17.

DIRECTIONS: Questions 15 through 17 are to be answered on the basis of the following figure.

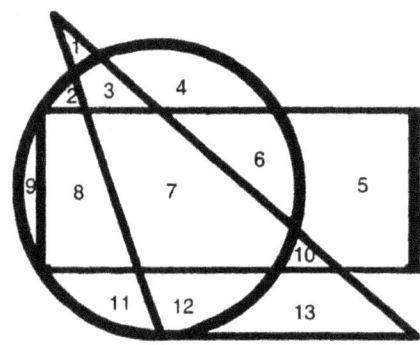

15. What number is in the space which is in the rectangle and in the triangle but not in the circle?

16. What number is in the same geometrical figure or figures as the number 8?

17. How many spaces are there that are in any two but only two geometrical figures?

18. A surface is related to a line as a line is to

    A. solid B. plane C. curve D. point E. string

19. One cannot become a good violinist without much practice. Charles practices much on the violin.
    Charles will become a good violinist.
    If the first two statements are TRUE, the third is

    A. true B. false C. not certain

20. Sincerity traits courtesy character of desirable and are
    If the words above were arranged to make the best sentence, with what letter would the LAST word of the sentence end?(Print the letter as a capital.)

21. A man who is influenced in making a decision by preconceived opinions is said to be 21.____

    A. influential B. prejudiced C. hypocritical
    D. decisive   E. impartial

22. A hotel serves a mixture of 2 parts cream and 3 parts milk. 22.____
    How many pints of cream will it take to make 15 pints of the mixture?

23. _____ is related to blood as physics is to motion. 23.____

    A. Temperature B. Veins   C. Body
    D. Physiology   E. Geography

24. A statement, the meaning of which is not definite, is said to be 24.____

    A. erroneous B. doubtful   C. ambiguous
    D. distorted E. hypothetical

25. If a wire 20 inches long is to be cut so that one piece is 2/3 as long as the other piece, 25.____
    how many inches long must the shorter piece be?

KEY (CORRECT ANSWERS)

1. 6
2. A
3. B
4. B
5. E

6. 33
7. D
8. G
9. C
10. 243

11. 45
12. D
13. C
14. M
15. 10

16. 6
17. 5
18. D
19. C
20. R

21. B
22. 6
23. D
24. C
25. 8

EXAMINATION SECTION
TEST 1

DIRECTIONS: Each question or incomplete statement is followed by several suggested answers or completions. Select the one that BEST answers the question or completes the statement. *PRINT THE CORRECT ANSWER IN THE SPACE AT THE RIGHT.*

1. The OPPOSITE of defeat is   1.____
   - A. glory
   - B. honor
   - C. victory
   - D. success
   - E. hope

2. If 3 pencils cost 10 cents, how many pencils can be bought for 50 cents?   2.____

3. A dog does NOT always have   3.____
   - A. eyes
   - B. bones
   - C. a nose
   - D. a collar
   - E. lungs

4. The OPPOSITE of strange is   4.____
   - A. peculiar
   - B. familiar
   - C. unusual
   - D. quaint
   - E. extraordinary

5. A lion MOST resembles a   5.____
   - A. dog
   - B. goat
   - C. cat
   - D. cow
   - E. horse

6. Sound is related to quiet in the same way that sunlight is to   6.____
   - A. darkness
   - B. evaporation
   - C. bright
   - D. a cellar
   - E. noise

7. A party consisted of a man and his wife, his three sons and their wives, and two children in each son's family. How many were there in the party?   7.____

8. A man ALWAYS has   8.____
   - A. children
   - B. nerves
   - C. teeth
   - D. home
   - E. wife

9. The OPPOSITE of stingy is   9.____
   - A. wealthy
   - B. extravagant
   - C. poor
   - D. economical
   - E. generous

10. Lead is cheaper than silver because it is   10.____
    - A. duller
    - B. more plentiful
    - C. softer
    - D. uglier
    - E. less useful

Questions 11-13.

DIRECTIONS: Answer Questions 11 through 13 by choosing the CORRECT proverb meaning given below.

A. Eat heartily at a good feast.
B. Only exceptional misfortunes harm all concerned.
C. Don't invite trouble by stirring it up.
D. Strong winds blow harder than weak ones.
E. Too much of anything is no better than a sufficiency.
F. Tired dogs need lots of sleep.

11. Which statement above explains the proverb, *Let sleeping dogs lie?*   11.____

12. Which statement above explains the proverb, *Enough is as good as a feast?*   12.____

13. Which statement above explains the proverb, *It's an ill wind that blows nobody good?*   13.____

14. A radio is related to a telephone as _____ is to a railroad train.   14.____

    A. a highway   B. an airplane   C. gasoline
    D. speed   E. noise

15. If a boy can run at the rate of 8 feet in 1/3 of a second, how far can he run in 10 seconds?   15.____

16. A debate ALWAYS involves   16.____

    A. an audience   B. judges   C. a prize
    D. a controversy   E. an auditorium

17. Of the five words below, four are alike in a certain way. Which one is NOT like these four?   17.____

    A. Walk   B. Run   C. Kneel   D. Skip   E. Jump

18. The OPPOSITE of frequently is   18.____

    A. seldom   B. occasionally   C. never
    D. sometimes   E. often

19. A thermometer is related to temperature as a speedometer is to   19.____

    A. fast   B. automobile   C. velocity
    D. time   E. heat

20. Which word makes the TRUEST sentence? Women are _____ shorter than their husbands.   20.____

    A. always   B. usually   C. much
    D. rarely   E. never

21. 1 6 2 7 3 8 4 9 5 10 7 11   21.____
One number is wrong in the above series.
What should that number be?

22. All children in this class are good students.   22.____
John is not a good student.
John is a member of this class.
If the first two statements are true, the third is

    A. true   B. false   C. not certain

23. A boat race ALWAYS has   23._____

    A. oars B. spectators C. victory
    D. contestants E. sails

24. 4 2 3 1 5 6 8 7 3 4 6 6 4 3 2 5 1 8 6 7 9   24._____
    Which number in this row appears a second time nearest the beginning?

25. The sun is related to the earth as the earth is to   25._____

    A. clouds B. rotation C. the universe
    D. the moon E. circumference

KEY (CORRECT ANSWERS)

1. C	11. C
2. 15	12. E
3. D	13. B
4. B	14. B
5. C	15. 240
6. A	16. D
7. 14	17. C
8. B	18. A
9. E	19. C
10. B	20. B

21. 6
22. B
23. D
24. 3
25. D

TEST 2

DIRECTIONS: Each question or incomplete statement is followed by several suggested answers or completions. Select the one that BEST answers the question or completes the statement. *PRINT THE CORRECT ANSWER IN THE SPACE AT THE RIGHT.*

1. Which word makes the TRUEST sentence?
   A youth is _____ wiser than his father.

   A. never   B. rarely   C. much
   D. usually   E. always

   1.____

2. The OPPOSITE of graceful is

   A. weak   B. ugly   C. slow
   D. awkward   E. uncanny

   2.____

3. A grandmother is always _____ than her granddaughter.

   A. smarter   B. more quiet   C. older
   D. smaller   E. slower

   3.____

Questions 4-6.

DIRECTIONS: Answer Questions 4 through 6 by choosing the CORRECT proverb meaning given below.

    A. Even the darkest situations have their bright aspects.
    B. The final result is more important than the intermediate steps.
    C. Handsome persons always do pleasing things.
    D. All comes out well in the end.
    E. Persons whose actions please us seem good-looking.
    F. Clouds shimmer as if they were made of silver.

4. Which statement above explains the proverb, *All's well that ends well?*

   4.____

5. Which statement above explains the proverb, *Every cloud has a silver lining?*

   5.____

6. Which statement above explains the proverb, *Handsome is that handsome does?*

   6.____

7. If the settlement of a difference between two parties is made by a third party, it is called a(n)

   A. compromise   B. truce   C. promise
   D. injunction   E. arbitration

   7.____

8. Oil is to toil as _____ is to hate.

   A. love   B. work   C. boil   D. ate   E. hat

   8.____

9. Of the five words below, four are alike in a certain way.
   Which one is NOT like these four?

   A. Push   B. Hold   C. Lift   D. Drag   E. Pull

   9.____

10. If 10 boxes full of apples weigh 300 pounds and each box when empty weighs 3 pounds, how many pounds do all the apples weigh?   10._____

11. The OPPOSITE of sorrow is   11._____

    A. fun   B. success   C. hope
    D. prosperity   E. joy

12. A B C D E F G H I J K L M N O P Q R S T U V W X Y Z   12._____
If all the odd-numbered letters in the alphabet were crossed out, what would be the twelfth letter NOT crossed out?

13. What letter in the word *unfortunately* is the same number in the word (counting from the beginning) as it is in the alphabet?   13._____

14. Such traits as honesty, sincerity, and loyalty constitute one's   14._____

    A. personality   B. reputation   C. wisdom
    D. character   E. success

15. If 3 1/3 yards of cloth cost 25 cents, what will 10 yards cost?   15._____

16. same means small little the as   16._____
If the above words were arranged to make a good sentence, with what letter would the second word of the sentence begin? (Make it like a printed capital.)

17. George is younger than Frank.   17._____
James is younger than George.
Frank is older than James.
If the first two statements are true, the third is

    A. true   B. false   C. not certain

18. Suppose that the first and second letters in the word *abolitionist* were interchanged, also the third and fourth letters, the fifth and sixth, etc.   18._____
Print the letter that would be the tenth letter counting to the right.

19. 0 1 3 6 10 15 21 29 36   19._____
One number is wrong in the above series.
What should that number be?

20. If 3 1/2 yards of cloth cost 70 cents, what will 4 1/2 yards cost?   20._____

21. A person who never pretends to be anything other than what he is, is said to be   21._____

    A. loyal   B. hypocritical   C. sincere
    D. meek   E. courageous

22. Which of these words is related to many as exceptional is to ordinary?   22._____

    A. None   B. Each   C. More   D. Much   E. Few

23. The OPPOSITE of cowardly is   23._____

    A. brave   B. strong   C. treacherous
    D. loyal   E. friendly

24. Which one of the five words below is MOST unlike the other four? 24._____

    A. Fast   B. Agile   C. Quick   D. Run   E. Speedy

25. Some of Brown's friends are Catholics. 25._____
Some of Brown's friends are lawyers.
Some of Brown's friends are Catholic lawyers.
If the first two statements are true, the third is

    A. true   B. false   C. not certain

KEY (CORRECT ANSWERS)

1.	B	11.	E
2.	D	12.	X
3.	C	13.	L
4.	B	14.	D
5.	A	15.	75
6.	E	16.	M
7.	E	17.	A
8.	D	18.	N
9.	B	19.	28
10.	270	20.	90

21.	C
22.	E
23.	A
24.	D
25.	C

TEST 3

DIRECTIONS: Each question or incomplete statement is followed by several suggested answers or completions. Select the one that BEST answers the question or completes the statement. *PRINT THE CORRECT ANSWER IN THE SPACE AT THE RIGHT.*

1. How many of the following words can be made from the letters in the word *strangle*, using any letter any number of times: greatest, tangle, garage, stresses, related, grease, nearest, reeling?

   1.____

2. To insist that trees can talk to one another is

   A. absurd   B. misleading   C. improbable
   D. unfair   E. wicked

   2.____

3. Of the things following, four are alike in a certain way. Which one is NOT like these four?

   A. Snow   B. Soot   C. Cotton   D. Ivory   E. Milk

   3.____

4. A square is related to a circle in the same way in which a pyramid is related to

   A. a solid   B. Egypt   C. height
   D. a cone   E. a circumference

   4.____

5. If the following words were seen on a wall by looking in a mirror on the opposite wall, which word would appear exactly the same as if seen directly?

   A. Meet   B. Rotor   C. Mama   D. Deed   E. Toot

   5.____

6. If a strip of cloth 32 inches long will shrink to 28 inches when washed, how many inches long will a 24-inch strip of the same cloth be after shrinking?

   6.____

7. Which of the following is a trait of character?

   A. Ability   B. Reputation   C. Hate
   D. Stinginess   E. Nervousness

   7.____

8. Find the two letters in the word *coming* which have just as many letters between them in the word as in the alphabet. Print the one of these letters that comes FIRST in the alphabet.

   8.____

9. Modern is to ancient as _____ is to yesterday.

   A. tomorrow   B. time   C. up-to-date
   D. history   E. today

   9.____

10. 1 2 4 8 16 32 64 96
    One number is wrong in the above series.
    What should that number be?

    10.____

11. If George can ride a bicycle 40 feet while Frank runs 30 feet, how far can George ride while Frank runs 45 feet?

    11.____

12. L U L R V E L U R E U L U U L V E L L U V L U R U L O E V L U E
    Count each L in this series that is followed by a U next to it if the U is not followed by an R next to it.
    Tell how many L's you count.

    12.___

13. A man who is in favor of marked change is said to be

    A. democratic
    B. conservative
    C. radical
    D. anarchistic
    E. republican

    13.___

14. Print the letter which is the fourth letter to the left of the letter midway between N and R in the alphabet.

    14.___

Questions 15-17.

DIRECTIONS: Questions 15 through 17 are to be answered on the basis of the following figure.

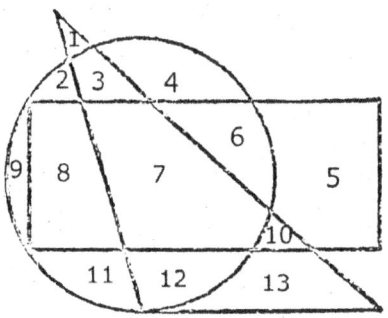

15. What number is in the space which is in the rectangle but not in the triangle or in the circle?

    15.___

16. What number is in the same geometrical figure or figures (and no other) as the number 3?

    16.___

17. How many spaces are there that are in any one but only one geometrical figure?

    17.___

18. A line is related to a surface as a point is to a

    A. circle
    B. line
    C. solid
    D. dot
    E. intersection

    18.___

19. One cannot become a good lawyer without diligent study.
    George studies law diligently.
    George will become a good lawyer.
    If the first two statements are true, the third is

    A. true
    B. false
    C. not certain

    19.___

20. honesty traits Generosity character of desirable and are
    If the above words are arranged to make the BEST sentence, with what letter will the last word of the sentence end? (Print the letter as a capital.)

    20.___

21. A man who carefully considers all available information before making a decision is said to be

    A. influential B. prejudiced C. decisive
    D. hypocritical E. impartial

22. A hotel serves a mixture of 2 parts cream and 3 parts milk. How many pints of milk will it take to make 25 pints of the mixture?

23. _____ is related to stars as physiology is to blood.

    A. Telescope B. Darkness C. Astronomy
    D. Light waves E. Chemistry

24. A statement based upon a supposition is said to be

    A. erroneous B. ambiguous C. distorted
    D. hypothetical E. doubtful

25. If a wire 40 inches long is to be cut so that one piece is 2/3 as long as the other piece, how many inches long must the shorter piece be?

KEY (CORRECT ANSWERS)

1. 6
2. A
3. B
4. D
5. E
6. 21
7. D
8. G
9. E
10. 128
11. 60
12. 4
13. C
14. L
15. 5
16. 12
17. 7
18. B
19. C
20. R
21. E
22. 15
23. C
24. D
25. 16

EXAMINATION SECTION
TEST 1

DIRECTIONS: Each question or incomplete statement is followed by several suggested answers or completions. Select the one that BEST answers the question or completes the statement. *PRINT THE CORRECT ANSWER IN THE SPACE AT THE RIGHT.*

1. The OPPOSITE of familiar is 1.____

   A. friendly   B. old   C. strange
   D. aloof   E. different

2. If 4 pencils cost 10 cents, how many pencils can be bought for 50 cents? 2.____

3. A man does not always have 3.____

   A. arteries   B. hair   C. muscle
   D. skin   E. blood

4. What letter in the word *Washington* is the same number in the word (counting from the beginning) as it is in the alphabet? 4.____

5. tests children intelligence hundreds have of taken If the above words were arranged to make the best sentence, the LAST word of the sentence would begin with what letter? (Make it like a printed capital.) 5.____

6. A word meaning the same as change is 6.____

   A. endure   B. cause   C. result
   D. alter   E. anticipate

7. Copper is cheaper than gold because it is 7.____

   A. duller   B. more plentiful   C. harder
   D. uglier   E. less useful

8. An egg is related to a bird in the same way that a _____ is related to a plant. 8.____

   A. shell   B. leaf   C. root
   D. feather   E. seed

9. If 10 boxes full of oranges weigh 600 pounds and each box when empty weighs 6 pounds, how many pounds do all the oranges weigh? 9.____

10. The OPPOSITE of skillful is 10.____

    A. lazy   B. clumsy   C. weak
    D. slow   E. novice

Questions 11-13.

DIRECTIONS: Answer Questions 11 through 13 by choosing the CORRECT proverb meaning given below.

   A. A conscientious worker needs no prodding.
   B. Geese that lay golden eggs are too tough to eat.

159

C. In dire distress, any aid is acceptable.
D. Don't destroy the things that do you good.
E. A willing horse should be whipped lightly.
F. Ships should not venture out to sea in stormy weather.

11. Which statement above explains the proverb, *Kill not the goose that lays the golden eggs?* 11.___

12. Which statement above explains the proverb, *Any port in a storm?* 12.___

13. Which statement above explains the proverb, *Don't spur a willing horse?* 13.___

14. In general, it is safer to judge a woman's character by her 14.___

    A. face   B. cooking   C. clothes
    D. deeds   E. speeches

15. An ellipse is related to a circle as a diamond is to a 15.___

    A. ring   B. square   C. rectangle
    D. oval   E. cube

16. A mare is always _____ than her colt. 16.___

    A. faster   B. sleeker   C. bigger
    D. older   E. stronger

17. The OPPOSITE of wasteful is 17.___

    A. wealthy   B. quiet   C. stingy
    D. economical   E. extravagant

18. 1 5 2 6 3 7 4 9 5 9 18.___
    One number is wrong in the above series.
    What should that number be?

19. Such things as looks, dress, likes, and dislikes indicate one's 19.___

    A. character   B. wisdom   C. personality
    D. gossip   E. reputation

20. A picnic consisted of a minister, six deacons and their wives, and three children in each of the deacons' families. How many were there at the picnic? 20.___

21. At a dinner there is ALWAYS 21.___

    A. soup   B. wine   C. food
    D. waiters   E. dishes

22. The idea that the earth is flat is 22.___

    A. absurd   B. misleading   C. improbable
    D. unfair   E. wicked

23. Which word is needed to begin the following sentence? 23.___
    _____ a geometrical figure has three straight sides, it is a triangle.

    A. Although   B. If   C. Since
    D. Now that   E. Because

24. All residents in this block are Republicans.
Smith is not a Republican.
Smith resides in this block.
If the first two statements are true, the third is

    A. true   B. false   C. not certain

24.____

25. The OPPOSITE of seldom is

    A. never   B. many   C. invariably
    D. always   E. frequently

25.____

KEY (CORRECT ANSWERS)

1. C
2. 20
3. B
4. G
5. T

6. D
7. B
8. E
9. 540
10. B

11. D
12. C
13. A
14. D
15. B

16. D
17. D
18. 8
19. C
20. 31

21. C
22. A
23. B
24. B
25. E

TEST 2

DIRECTIONS: Each question or incomplete statement is followed by several suggested answers or completions. Select the one that BEST answers the question or completes the statement. *PRINT THE CORRECT ANSWER IN THE SPACE AT THE RIGHT.*

1. Which one of these things is MOST unlike the other four? 1.____
   A. Bean   B. Cherry   C. Pea   D. Carrot   E. Beet

2. A sewing machine is related to a needle as a typewriter is to 2.____
   A. a pin   B. a cloth   C. ink
   D. a pen   E. a page

3. The two words *repentant* and *reluctant* mean 3.____
   A. the same
   B. the opposite
   C. neither same nor opposite

4. The OPPOSITE of brave is 4.____
   A. intrepid   B. weak   C. treacherous
   D. cowardly   E. fragile

5. Z F Z S E Y Z F S Y F Z F F S Y S Z F E Z F S F Z Y F Z F Y 5.____
   Count each Z in this series that is followed by an F next to it if the F is now followed by an S next to it.
   Tell how many Z's you count.

6. If a boy can run 2 feet in 1/10 of a second, how many feet can he run in 10 seconds? 6.____

Questions 7-9.

DIRECTIONS: Answer Questions 7 through 9 by choosing the CORRECT proverb meaning given below.

   A. Chickens are easier to count than eggs.
   B. People tend to associate with others like themselves.
   C. Prying into the affairs of others may bring trouble.
   D. Birds fly in large flocks.
   E. Don't rely too much on your anticipations.
   F. Cats are often too curious.

7. Which statement above explains the proverb, *Curiosity killed the cat?* 7.____

8. Which statement above explains the proverb, *Don't count your chickens before they are hatched?* 8.____

9. Which statement above explains the proverb, *Birds of a feather flock together?* 9.____

10. best hard road the work success to is 10.____
    If the above words were arranged to make a good sentence, the FOURTH word of the sentence would begin with what letter?

11. Frank is older than George.
    James is older than Frank.
    George is younger than James.
    If the first two statements are true, the third is

    A. true B. false C. not certain

12. One who says things he knows to be wrong is said to be

    A. careless B. misled C. conceited
    D. untruthful E. prejudiced

13. The OPPOSITE of create is

    A. sustain B. evolution C. transform
    D. explode E. abolish

14. If $3\frac{1}{2}$ yards of cloth cost $9, how many dollars will 7 yards cost?

15. Which of the five things following is MOST unlike the other four?

    A. Nail B. Hammer C. Screw
    D. Bolt E. Tack

16. Darkness is to sunlight as _____ is to sound.

    A. noise B. brightness C. air
    D. echo E. quiet

17. The OPPOSITE of gentle is

    A. strong B. careless C. humane
    D. thoughtless E. rough

18. Some members of this club are Baptists.
    Some members of this club are lawyers.
    Some members of this club are Baptist lawyers.
    If the first two statements above are true, the third is

    A. true B. false C. not certain

19. If $4\frac{1}{2}$ yards of cloth cost 90 cents, how many cents will $3\frac{1}{2}$ yards cost?

20. A line is to a point as a surface is to

    A. flat B. line C. solid D. square E. plane

21. The two words *precise* and *indefinite* mean

    A. the same
    B. the opposite
    C. neither same nor opposite

22. When two windows have the same shape, the dimensions of one are _____ the dimensions of the other. 22.___

    A. equal to   B. greater than
    C. less than   D. proportional to
    E. double

23. Suppose that the first and second letters of the alphabet were interchanged, also the third and fourth, the fifth and sixth, etc. 23.___
Write the letter which would then be the sixteenth letter of the series.

24. If a strip of cloth 32 inches long will shrink to 28 inches when washed, how many inches long will a 48-inch strip be after shrinking? 24.___

25. Which one of the following five words is MOST unlike the other four? 25.___

    A. Was   B. Came   C. Have   D. Stay   E. Here

KEY (CORRECT ANSWERS)

1. B	11. A
2. D	12. D
3. C	13. E
4. D	14. 18
5. 4	15. B
6. 200	16. E
7. C	17. E
8. E	18. C
9. B	19. 70
10. T	20. E

21. B
22. D
23. O
24. 42
25. E

TEST 3

DIRECTIONS: Each question or incomplete statement is followed by several suggested answers or completions. Select the one that BEST answers the question or completes the statement. *PRINT THE CORRECT ANSWER IN THE SPACE AT THE RIGHT.*

1. A city ALWAYS has   1.____

   A. street cars B. a mayor
   C. traffic officers D. residents
   E. churches

2. A word meaning the same as congratulate is   2.____

   A. felicitate B. commemorate C. reward
   D. console E. promote

3. Find the two letters in the word *canal* which have just as many letters between them in the word as in the alphabet. Write the one of these two letters that comes FIRST in the alphabet.   3.____

4. The mandates of a dictator are   4.____

   A. obsolete B. arbitrary C. omnipotent
   D. conditional E. optional

5. Which one of the five words below is MOST like these three: love, hate, joy?   5.____

   A. Memory B. Taste C. Anger
   D. Health E. Life

6. A gulf is to the ocean as a _____ is to a continent.   6.____

   A. mountain B. river C. land
   D. peninsula E. island

7. A B C D E F G H I J K L M N O P Q R S T U V W X Y Z   7.____
   If all the even-numbered letters in the alphabet were crossed out, the TWELFTH letter left not crossed out would be what letter?

8. Write the letter of the alphabet which is the third to the right of the letter which is midway between O and S.   8.____

9. A hotel serves a mixture of 2 parts cream and 3 parts milk. How many pints of milk will it take to make 15 pints of the mixture?   9.____

10. Which of the following is a trait of character?   10.____

    A. Reputation B. Wealth C. Influence
    D. Fickleness E. Strength

11. A man who spends his money lavishly for non-essentials is considered to be   11.____

    A. fortunate B. thrifty C. extravagant
    D. generous E. economical

12. 1 4 9 16 25 36 45 64   12.____
    One number is wrong in the above series.
    What should that number be?

165

13. Democracy is to monarchy as corporation is to 13.___
    A. board of directors
    B. stockholders
    C. partnership
    D. general manager
    E. individual enterprise

14. How many of the following words can be made of the letters in the word *celebrate,* using any letter twice: create, better, traceable, erect, tattle, rabble, crated, prattle, barter? 14.___

15. If George can ride a bicycle 60 feet while Frank runs 40 feet, how many feet can George ride while Frank runs 60 feet? 15.___

16. choose care man A friends should with his If the above words were arranged to make a good sentence, the FIFTH word in the sentence would begin with what letter? 16.___

17. It takes a good sense of balance to become a tight-rope walker. 17.___
    John has a good sense of balance.
    John will become a tight-rope walker.
    If the first two statements above are true, the third is

    A. true   B. false   C. not certain

18. If a wire 40 inches long is to be cut so that one piece is 2/3 as long as the other piece, how many inches must the longer piece be? 18.___

19. Find the letter which in this sentence itself appears a third time nearest the beginning. 19.___

20. Which of the following five things is MOST like these three: cotton, show, ivory? 20.___

    A. Soot   B. Milk   C. Ice   D. Ebony   E. Water

21. 1 2 4 7 11 16 22 28 21.___
    One number is wrong in the above series.
    What should that number be?

Questions 22-24.

DIRECTIONS: Questions 22 through 24 are to be answered on the basis of the following figure.

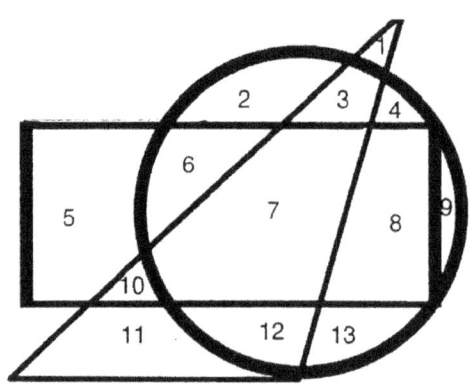

22. What number is in the space which is in the rectangle but not in the triangle or in the circle? 22.____

23. What number is in the same geometrical figure or figures (and no others) as the number 12? 23.____

24. How many spaces are there which are in any one but only one geometrical figure? 24.____

25. The OPPOSITE of *because* is 25.____
    A. but   B. since   C. hence   D. for   E. and

KEY (CORRECT ANSWERS)

1. D
2. A
3. L
4. B
5. C

6. D
7. W
8. T
9. 9
10. D

11. C
12. 49
13. E
14. 6
15. 90

16. H
17. C
18. 24
19. T
20. B

21. 29
22. 5
23. 6
24. 6
25. A

EXAMINATION SECTION
TEST 1

DIRECTIONS: Each question or incomplete statement is followed by several suggested answers or completions. Select the one that BEST answers the question or completes the statement. *PRINT THE LETTER OF THE CORRECT ANSWER IN THE SPACE AT THE RIGHT.*

Questions 1-10.

DIRECTIONS: In answering Questions 1 through 10, select the alternative that means the *same as* or the *opposite* of the word in italics.

1. *acquire*
    A. judge
    B. identify
    C. surrender
    D. educate
    E. happen

2. *begrudge*
    A. envy
    B. hate
    C. annoy
    D. obstruct
    E. punish

3. *obsolete*
    A. fatal
    B. modern
    C. distracting
    D. untouched
    E. broken

4. *inflexible*
    A. weak
    B. righteous
    C. harmless
    D. unyielding
    E. secret

5. *nominal*
    A. just
    B. slight
    C. cheerful
    D. familiar
    E. ceaseless

6. *debt*
    A. insane
    B. artificial
    C. skillful
    D. determined
    E. humble

7. *censure*
    A. focus
    B. exclude
    C. baffle
    D. portray
    E. praise

8. *nebulous*
    A. imaginary
    B. spiritual
    C. distinct
    D. starry-eyed
    E. unanswerable

9. *impart*
    A. hasten
    B. adjust
    C. gamble
    D. address
    E. communicate

10. *terminate*
    A. gain B. graduate C. harvest
    D. start E. paralyze

Questions 11-20.

DIRECTIONS: In answering Questions 11 through 20, select the word which, if inserted in the blank space, agrees MOST closely with the thought of the sentence.

11. Every good story is carefully contrived; the elements of the story are _____ to fi with one another in order to make an effect on the reader.
    A. read B. learned C. emphasized
    D. reduced E. planned

12. Their work was commemorative in character and consisted largely of _____ erected upon the occasion of victories.
    A. towers B. tombs C. monuments
    D. castles E. fortresses

13. Before criticizing the work of an artist, one needs to _____ the artist's purpose.
    A. understand B. reveal C. defend
    D. correct E. change

14. Because in the administration it hath respect not to the group but to the _____, our form of government is called a democracy.
    A. courts B. people C. majority
    D. individual E. law

15. Deductive reasoning is that form of reasoning in which the conclusion must necessarily follow if we accept the premise as true. In deduction, it is _____ for the premise to be true and the conclusion false.
    A. impossible B. inevitable C. reasonable
    D. surprising E. unlikely

16. Mathematics is the product of thought operating by means of _____ for the purpose of expressing general laws.
    A. reasoning B. symbols C. words
    D. examples E. science

17. No other man loss so much, so _____, so absolutely, as the beaten candidate for high public office.
    A. bewilderingly B. predictably C. disgracefully
    D. publicly E. cheerfully

18. Many television watchers enjoy stories which contain violence. Consequently, those television producers who are dominated by rating systems aim to _____ the popular taste.
    A. raise B. control C. gratify
    D. ignore e. lower

19. The latent period for the contractile response to direct stimulation of the muscle has quite another and shorter value, encompassing only a utilization period. Hence, it is that the term *latent period* must be _____ carefully each time that it is used.
    A. checked B. timed C. introduced
    D. defined E. selected

20. A man who cannot win honor in his own _____ will have a very small chance of winning it from posterity.
    A. right B. field C. country
    D. way E. age

Questions 21-35.

DIRECTIONS: In answering Questions 21 through 35, select the word that BEST completes the analogy.

21. Albino is to color as traitor is to
    A. patriotism B. treachery C. socialism
    D. integration E. liberalism

22. Senile is to infantile as supper is to
    A. snack B. breakfast C. dinner
    D. daytime E. evening

23. Snow shovel is to sidewalk as eraser is to
    A. writing B. pencil C. paper
    D. desk E. mistake

24. Lawyer is to court as soldier is to
    A. battle B. victory C. training
    D. rifle E. discipline

25. Faucet is to water as mosquito is to
    A. swamp B. butterfly C. cistern
    D. pond E. malaria

26. Astronomy is to geology as steeplejack is to
    A. mailman B. surgeon C. pilot
    D. miner E. skindiver

27. Chimney is to smoke as guide is to
    A. snare   B. compass   C. hunter
    D. firewood E. wild game

28. Prodigy is to ability as ocean is to
    A. water   B. waves   C. ships
    D. icebergs E. current

29. War is to devastation as microbe is to
    A. peace   B. flea   C. dog
    D. germ   E. pestilence

30. Blueberry is to pea a sky is to
    A. storm   B. world   C. star
    D. grass   E. purity

31. Pour is to spill as lie is to
    A. deception   B. misstatement   C. falsehood
    D. perjury   E. fraud

32. Disparage is to despise as praise is to
    A. dislike   B. adore   C. acclaim
    D. advocate   E. compliment

33. Wall is to mortar as nation is to
    A. family   B. people   C. patriotism
    D. geography E. boundaries

34. Servant is to butter as pain is to
    A. cramp   B. hurt   C. illness
    D. itch   E. anesthesia

35. Fan is to air as newspaper is to
    A. literature   B. reporter   C. information
    D. subscription E. reader

36. A set of papers is arranged and numbered from 1 to 49. If the paper numbered 3 is drawn first and every ninth paper thereafter, what will be the number of the last paper drawn?
    A. 45   B. 46   C. 47   D. 48   E. 49

37. Which quantity can be measured *exactly* from a tank of water by using only a 10-pint can and an 8-pint can? _____ pint(s)
    A. 1   B. 6   C. 3   D. 7   E. 5

38. If city R has more fires than city S, and city T has more fires than cities P and S combined, then the number of fires in city
    A. P must be less than in city T
    B. T must be less than in city R
    C. T must be greater than in city R
    D. R must be greater than in city P
    E. S must be greater than in city T

39. The average of three numbers is 25.
    If one of the numbers is increased by 4, the average will remain unchanged if each of the other two numbers is reduced by
    A. 1   B. 2   C. 2/3   D. 4   E. 1 1/3

40.
```
                    1
                 1     1
              1    2     1
           1    3    3     1
        1    4    6    4    1
     1    5   10    X    5    1
```
Above are the first six rows of a triangular array constructed according to a fixed law.
What number does the letter X represent?
A. 8   B. 10   C. 15   D. 20   E. 5

41. If all A are C and no C are B, it necessarily follows that
    A. all B are C   B. all B are A   C. no A are B
    D. no C are A   E. some B are A

42. What number is missing in the series 7, ____, 63, 189?
    A. 9   B. 11   C. 19   D. 21   E. 24

43. A clock that gains one minute each hour is synchronized at noon with a clock that loses two minutes an hour.
    How many minutes apart will the minute hands of the two clocks be at midnight?
    A. 0   B. 12   C. 14   D. 24   E. 30

44. The pages of a typewritten report are numbered by hand from 1 to 100.
    How many times will it be necessary to write the numeral 5?
    A. 10   B. 11   C. 12   D. 19   E. 20

45. The number 6 is called a *perfect* number because it is the sum of all its integral divisors except itself.
    Another *perfect* number is
    A. 12   B. 16   C. 24   D. 28   E. 36

KEY (CORRECT ANSWERS)

1.	C	11.	E	21.	A	31.	B	41.	C
2.	A	12.	C	22.	B	32.	B	42.	D
3.	B	13.	A	23.	C	33.	C	43.	D
4.	D	14.	D	24.	A	34.	A	44.	E
5.	B	15.	A	25.	E	35.	C	45.	D
6.	C	16.	B	26.	D	36.	D		
7.	E	17.	D	27.	C	37.	B		
8.	C	18.	C	28.	A	38.	A		
9.	E	19.	D	29.	E	39.	B		
10.	D	20.	E	30.	D	40.	B		

BASIC WORD VOCABULARY TEST (BWVT)

COMMENTARY

Verbal ability plays a central role in intellectual development and informal human communications. It forms a basic staple of practically every test of general and mental ability.

In assessing level of development in verbal ability, a vocabulary test called the Basic Word Vocabulary Test (BWVT) has been developed.

The rationale of this test is of great importance in providing a more complete assessment of the status, health, and well-being of our population.

The test was developed to provide a measurement instrument of word-knowledge acquisition with two additional properties that are not extant in any other standardized vocabulary test. These two properties are reflected in its content representation (content validity) of a carefully specified population of words and in its range of application from about the third grade level of literacy to the highest level of word-knowledge acquisition. These two properties permit assessment of a wide range of vocabulary development in terms of absolute level (as estimates of the word population) and relative standing in reference to various normative groups, i.e., age-education standing, on one continuous scale.

Thus, this test extends measurement-capability in assessing vocabulary development practically along the full range of the psychosocial aspects of functioning.

This is the only standardized test of vocabulary that provides, in a single instrument, for the evaluation of vocabulary on the elementary, high school, college, and university levels.

EXAMINATION SECTION

TEST 1

DIRECTIONS: Select the word or phrase which has the same meaning, or most nearly, the same meaning as the CAPITALIZED word. *PRINT THE LETTER OF THE CORRECT ANSWER IN THE SPACE AT THE RIGHT.*

1. A CAR is to
   A. start fires with
   B. eat on
   C. take pictures with
   D. ride in
   E. draw with

   1.____

2. The SHORE is by the
   A. sea B. train C. letter D. table E. paper

   2.____

3. INK is used to
   A. walk on
   B. write with
   C. cut with
   D. serve with
   E. stand on

   3.____

4. POOR means having very little
   A. money B. hair C. sun D. time E. snow

   4.____

5. SHOWER
   A. field B. doctor C. rain D. post E. battle

   5.____

6. EAGLE
   A. family B. cup C. lake D. coat E. bird

   6.____

7. A TRICYCLE is to
   A. hear with
   B. ride on
   C. lie on
   D. walk under
   E. see through

   7.____

8. COMBAT
   A. point B. report C. fight D. start E. admit

   8.____

9. STABLE
   A. husband
   B. window
   C. ocean
   D. building
   E. street

   9.____

10. A MISTAKE is something done
    A. first B. wrong C. next D. often E. alone

    10.____

11. VIOLET
    A. plant B. ship C. story D. home E. river

    11.____

12. A DESERT is very
    A. kind B. strong C. dry D. brave E. dark

    12.____

13. A WITNESS
    A. trains animals
    C. observes actions
    E. grows wheat
    B. bakes cakes
    D. fixes machines
    13.____

14. AMBUSH
    A. attitude   B. address   C. artist   D. attack   E. authority
    14.____

15. HOWL
    A. roar   B. design   C. propose   D. depart   E. succeed
    15.____

16. QUIT
    A. hope   B. trade   C. learn   D. take   E. stop
    16.____

17. PUSS
    A. factory   B. devil   C. exercise   D. camp   E. cat
    17.____

18. ENCYCLOPEDIA
    A. woman   B. reason   C. nation   D. food   E. book
    18.____

19. PHONY
    A. tough   B. neutral   C. vivid   D. fake   E. hasty
    19.____

20. CRISP
    A. safe and warm   B. hard and thin   C. deep and wide
    D. soft and short   E. round and heavy
    20.____

21. ADVICE
    A. record   B. visit   C. bridge   D. opinion   E. minute
    21.____

22. TOMB
    A. baby   B. market   C. grave   D. roof   E. scale
    22.____

23. CORPS
    A. angry teacher   B. tired worker   C. sick animal
    D. military unit   E. special vacation
    23.____

24. BURLAP
    A. tunnel   B. medicine   C. soil   D. engine   E. fabric
    24.____

25. DAME
    A. lady   B. voice   C. bay   D. party   E. region
    25.____

26. A SEAMSTRESS is a woman who
    A. writes   B. sews   C. sings   D. paints   E. bakes
    26.____

27. TREMENDOUS
    A. serious   B. enormous   C. religious
    D. famous   E. precious
    27.____

28. PLATEAU
    A. large post   B. big present   C. kind prince
    D. great play   E. high plain

29. A JURIST is an expert in
    A. law   B. business   C. weather   D. art   E. history

30. APPROACH means to come
    A. through   B. with   C. into   D. between   E. near

31. EVENT
    A. occasion   B. temper   C. notion
    D. monument   E. explanation

32. BRISTLE
    A. difficult problem   B. stiff hair   C. official order
    D. sweet fruit   E. broad stream

33. ABANDON
    A. look over   B. hold on   C. lift up
    D. fall down   E. give up

34. TARANTULA
    A. grape   B. highway   C. button   D. spider   E. verse

35. BARELY
    A. generally   B. scarcely   C. completely
    D. especially   E. gradually

36. MINUS
    A. about   B. through   C. across   D. less   E. into

37. MUTINY
    A. stranger   B. puzzle   C. rebellion   D. lemon   E. tenant

38. SNEER
    A. listen with interest   B. practice with care
    C. look with scorn   D. lift with ease
    E. dance with joy

39. ELIGIBLE
    A. lonesome   B. careless   C. qualified
    D. inferior   E. profound

40. A GUST is a sudden
    A. rush of wind   B. act of duty   C. increase of pain
    D. loss of friends   E. need of money

41. SASSAFRAS
    A. tree   B. wave   C. egg   D. board   E. yard
41.____

42. A GHETTO is a section of a
    A. story   B. wall   C. church   D. city   E. garden
42.____

43. MUFF
    A. water heater   B. hand warmer   C. glass cleaner
    D. paint dryer   E. wood burner
43.____

44. PENNANT
    A. route   B. flag   C. journal   D. speech   E. leader
44.____

45. EXCLUDE
    A. educate   B. excite   C. eliminate
    D. encourage   E. ensure
45.____

46. MANGO
    A. fruit   B. army   C. uncle   D. star   E. stone
46.____

47. JUVENILE
    A. haunted   B. youthful   C. intimate
    D. favorable   E. unable
47.____

48. STAGE
    A. step in a process   B. tear in a net
    C. condition in a treaty   D. light in a tower
    E. article in a newspaper
48.____

49. GORGE
    A. circle   B. chain   C. valley   D. hall   E. queen
49.____

50. JOLT
    A. justify   B. join   C. judge   D. jar   E. journey
50.____

KEY (CORRECT ANSWERS)

1. D	11. A	21. D	31. A	41. A
2. A	12. C	22. C	32. B	42. D
3. B	13. C	23. D	33. E	43. B
4. A	14. D	24. E	34. D	44. B
5. C	15. A	25. A	35. B	45. C
6. E	16. E	26. B	36. D	46. A
7. B	17. E	27. B	37. C	47. B
8. C	18. E	28. E	38. C	48. A
9. D	19. D	29. A	39. C	49. C
10. B	20. B	30. E	40. A	50. D

TEST 2

DIRECTIONS: Select the word or phrase which has the same meaning, or most nearly, the same meaning as the CAPITALIZED word. *PRINT THE LETTER OF THE CORRECT ANSWER IN THE SPACE AT THE RIGHT.*

1. GRATIFY
   A. heat   B. shout   C. hope   D. charge   E. please

   1.____

2. CARDIAC means of the
   A. arm   B. feet   C. heart   D. legs   E. head

   2.____

3. AGHAST
   A. similar   B. modern   C. lucky   D. limited   E. terrified

   3.____

4. DEMOTE
   A. invite   B. reduce   C. stroke   D. pause   E. excuse

   4.____

5. SITUATE
   A. wear   B. add   C. take   D. place   E. study

   5.____

6. THUS
   A. not   B. too   C. why   D. so   E. do

   6.____

7. SCAVENGE
   A. check certificates   B. change residence
   C. support legislation   D. divide inheritance
   E. remove rubbish

   7.____

8. RAFTER
   A. angel   B. canal   C. beam   D. lamb   E. trunk

   8.____

9. CURRICULUM
   A. school of fish   B. collection of pictures   C. type of window
   D. range of mountains   E. program of studies

   9.____

10. LANK
    A. slender   B. grateful   C. musical   D. lively   E. rare

    10.____

11. GRISTLE
    A. fortitude   B. cartilage   C. graphite
    D. arrogance   E. overture

    11.____

12. FACTION
    A. dinner   B. blood   C. group   D. passage   E. hill

    12.____

13. DECELERATE means
    A. velocity   B. disorder   C. enthusiasm
    D. hazards   E. expenditures

    13.____

14. CONSOLE
    A. compare   B. conclude   C. comfort
    D. command   E. collect

15. HORDE
    A. circle   B. shade   C. word   D. crowd   E. sand

16. MANIPULATE
    A. reserve   B. devote   C. handle   D. inquire   E. introduce

17. SUMAC
    A. prayer   B. reward   C. shrub   D. doctrine   E. porch

18. POTPOURRI
    A. tailor   B. embassy   C. schooner   D. medley   E. parson

19. CONCRETE
    A. clean   B. mean   C. low   D. nice   E. real

20. ALBACORE
    A. tire   B. soldier   C. box   D. fish   E. stick

21. MESQUITE
    A. office   B. tree   C. fire   D. store   E. gate

22. DESTITUTE
    A. respectful   B. divine   C. urgent
    D. slippery   E. needy

23. DISCREET
    A. fragrant   B. prudent   C. unpleasant
    D. radiant   E. gallant

24. ISOPOD
    A. advertisement   B. edifice   C. meteorite
    D. philanthropist   E. crustacean

25. JUJUBE
    A. candy   B. echo   C. poem   D. harvest   E. brick

26. SPUTUM
    A. saloon   B. sickle   C. shawl   D. saliva   E. sermon

27. MULLET
    A. bird   B. ball   C. dog   D. stone   E. fish

28. BASTION
    A. fortification   B. qualification   C. appropriation
    D. legislation   E. illustration

2 (#2)

183

29. FOREGO
    A. represent   B. sacrifice   C. justify
    D. determine   E. display

30. AFFLUX
    A. flow   B. fool   C. fall   D. fly   E. floor

31. MACKINTOSH
    A. raincoat   B. tractor   C. honeybee
    D. cartoon   E. saucepan

32. TRAJECTORY
    A. curved path   B. ill health   C. bold type
    D. glorious spirit   E. strong back

33. PICADOR
    A. statesman   B. horseman   C. conductor
    D. sultan   E. fisherman

34. GRACKLE
    A. chipmunk   B. pumpkin   C. strawberry
    D. blackbird   E. caterpillar

35. APROPOS
    A. instructive   B. respectful   C. forbidden
    D. pertinent   E. dominant

36. YEW
    A. evergreen tree   B. dismal day   C. shabby house
    D. twisty road   E. frightful dream

37. A POMANDER is
    A. magnetic   B. explosive   C. aromatic
    D. frail   E. rotten

38. NUBILOUS
    A. cloudy   B. incredible   C. liberal
    D. spiritual   E. ragged

39. A TRIPHTHONG is a combination of three
    A. fossils   B. cables   C. diagrams   D. vowels   E. atoms

40. BROB
    A. jail   B. pouch   C. tax   D. spike   E. cavern

41. WHIST
    A. captain   B. game   C. soul   D. finger   E. rock

4 (#2)

42. FETID
    A. exhausted B. stinking C. pathetic
    D. meager D. insane

42.____

43. ABSTRACTED
    A. unmoved B. insulated C. preoccupied
    D. dominated E. devastated

43.____

44. PINON
    A. piano B. pioneer C. pine D. pinch E. pint

44.____

45. TERRINE
    A. knife B. railway C. chicken D. wagon E. vessel

45.____

46. CONVENTICLE
    A. major enemy B. royal gentleman
    C. impossible question D. sharp object
    E. secret meeting

46.____

47. BEZANT
    A. hotel B. coin C. mill D. harbor E. desk

47.____

48. An EMIR is an Arabian
    A. drink B. farmer C. chief D. song E. horse

48.____

49. SCINTILLATE
    A. develop B. whistle C. ruin D. breathe E. flash

49.____

50. RUMMER
    A. union B. knight C. coal D. shoe E. glass

50.____

KEY (CORRECT ANSWERS)

1. E	11. B	21. B	31. A	41. B
2. C	12. C	22. E	32. A	42. B
3. E	13. A	23. B	33. B	43. C
4. B	14. C	24. E	34. D	44. C
5. D	15. D	25. A	35. D	45. E
6. D	16. C	26. D	36. A	46. E
7. E	17. C	27. E	37. C	47. B
8. C	18. D	28. A	38. A	48. C
9. E	19. E	29. B	39. D	49. E
10. A	20. D	30. A	40. D	50. E

TEST 3

DIRECTIONS: Select the word or phrase which has the same meaning, or most nearly, the same meaning as the CAPITALIZED word. *PRINT THE LETTER OF THE CORRECT ANSWER IN THE SPACE AT THE RIGHT.*

1. CINEREOUS
   A. ashen   B. precise   C. bashful   D. valiant   E. nimble
   1.____

2. SOREDIUM
   A. cell   B. building   C. convention
   D. powder   E. funeral
   2.____

3. GLIB
   A. unaware   B. fluent   C. reluctant
   D. philosophical   E. inquisitive
   3.____

4. DINT
   A. supply   B. wish   C. force   D. price   E. demand
   4.____

5. SARCOPHAGUS
   A. coffin   B. insect   C. interview
   D. wharf   D. mushroom
   5.____

6. ANTHEMION
   A. department   B. remedy   C. ornament
   D. punishment   E. election
   6.____

7. QUA
   A. during   B. as   C. while   D. if   E. when
   7.____

8. LARINE means like a
   A. sleigh   B. mirror   C. wreath   D. gull   E. matron
   8.____

9. FLABELLUM
   A. fort   B. frost   C. fan   D. file   E. flock
   9.____

10. TRINGLE
    A. wave   B. bench   C. light   D. rod   E. mirror
    10.____

11. FUSCOUS
    A. outrageous   B. austere   C. contagious
    D. swarthy   E. eloquent
    11.____

12. POCOCURANTE
    A. ignorant   B. frightened   C. distinguished
    D. indifferent   E. dainty
    12.____

2 (#3)

13. MAENAD MAENAD   13.____
    A. insidious laugh   B. picturesque scene
    C. unscrupulous master   D. caustic reply
    E. frenzied woman

14. DIABOLO   14.____
    A. bed   B. dance   C. game   D. mark   E. record

15. LEMPIRA   15.____
    A. chair   B. money   C. salt   D. earth   E. music

16. EDACIOUS   16.____
    A. auspicious   B. voracious   C. malicious
    D. atrocious   E. luscious

17. PYROPE   17.____
    A. reptile   B. heather   C. slogan   D. mantle   E. garnet

18. GARGANEY   18.____
    A. hero   B. frame   C. bush   D. skirt   E. duck

19. REDACT   19.____
    A. edit   B. invert   C. convict   D. inherit   E. afflict

20. JACONET   20.____
    A. tribe   B. gift   C. port   D. treaty   E. cloth

KEY (CORRECT ANSWERS)

1.	A	11.	D
2.	A	12.	D
3.	B	13.	E
4.	C	14.	C
5.	A	15.	B
6.	C	16.	B
7.	B	17.	E
8.	D	18.	E
9.	C	19.	A
10.	D	20.	E

EXAMINATION SECTION

TEST 1

DIRECTIONS: Select the word or phrase which has the same meaning, or most nearly the same meaning, as the word in capital letters. *PRINT THE LETTER OF THE CORRECT ANSWER IN THE SPACE AT THE RIGHT.*

1. The SHORE is by the
   A. sea   B. train   C. letter   D. table   E. paper

   1.____

2. INK is used to
   A. walk on   B. write with   C. cut with
   D. serve with   E. stand on

   2.____

3. EAGLE
   A. family   B. cup   C. lake   D. coat   E. bird

   3.____

4. A TRICYCLE is to
   A. hear with   B. ride on   C. lie on
   D. walk under   E. see through

   4.____

5. A MISTAKE is something done
   A. first   B. wrong   C. next   D. often   E. alone

   5.____

6. A WITNESS is a person who
   A. trains animals   B. bakes cakes
   C. observes actions   D. fixes machines
   E. grows wheat

   6.____

7. PUSS
   A. factory   B. devil   C. exercise   D. camp   E. cat

   7.____

8. ENCYCLOPEDIA
   A. woman   B. reason   C. nation   D. food   E. book

   8.____

9. ADVICE
   A. record   B. visit   C. bridge   D. opinion   E. minute

   9.____

10. TOMB
    A. baby   B. market   C. grave   D. roof   E. scale

    10.____

11. CORPS
    A. angry teacher   B. tired worker
    C. sick animal   D. military unit
    E. special vacation

    11.____

189

12. TREMENDOUS
    A. serious   B. enormous   C. religious
    D. famous   E. precious

13. APPROACH means to come
    A. through   B. with   C. into   D. between   E. near

14. ABANDON
    A. look over   B. hold on   C. lift up
    D. fall down   E. give up

15. TARANTULA
    A. grape   B. highway   C. button   D. spider   E. verse

16. MUTINY
    A. stranger   B. puzzle   C. rebellion   D. lemon   E. tenant

17. ELIGIBLE
    A. lonesome   B. careless   C. qualified
    D. inferior   E. profound

18. SASSAFRAS
    A. tree   B. wave   C. egg   D. board   E. yard

19. MUFF
    A. water heater   B. hand warmer   C. glass cleaner
    D. paint dryer   E. wood burner

20. STAGE
    A. step in a process   B. tear in a net
    C. condition in a treaty   D. light in a tower
    E. article in a newspaper

21. GRATIFY
    A. heat   B. shout   C. hope   D. charge   E. please

22. CARDIAC means of the
    A. arm   B. feet   C. heart   D. legs   E. head

23. THUS
    A. not   B. too   C. why   D. so   E. do

24. LANK
    A. slender   B. grateful   C. musical   D. lively   E. rare

25. FACTION
    A. dinner   B. blood   C. group   D. passage   E. hill

3 (#1)

26. CONSOLE
    A. compare   B. conclude   C. comfort
    D. command   E. collect

27. HORDE
    A. circle   B. shade   C. word   D. crowd   E. sand

28. POTPOURRI
    A. tailor   B. embassy   C. schooner
    D. medley   E. parson

29. ALBACORE
    A. tire   B. soldier   C. box   D. fish   E. stick

30. MESQUITE
    A. office   B. tree   C. fire   D. store   E. gate

31. DESTITUTE
    A. respectful   B. divine   C. urgent
    D. slippery   E. needy

32. JUJUBE
    A. candy   B. echo   C. poem   D. harvest   E. brick

33. A TRIPHTHONG is a combination of three
    A. fossils   B. cables   C. diagrams   D. vowels   E. atoms

34. PINON
    A. piano   B. pioneer   C. pine   D. pinch   E. pint

35. BEZANT
    A. hotel   B. coin   C. mill   D. harbor   E. desk

36. CINEREOUS
    A. ashen   B. precise   C. bashful   D. valiant   E. nimble

37. DINT
    A. supply   B. wish   C. force   D. price   E. demand

38. QUA
    A. during   B. as   C. while   D. if   E. when

39. REDACT
    A. edit   B. invert   C. convict   D. inherit   E. afflict

40. JACONET
    A. tribe   B. gift   C. port   D. treaty   E. cloth

KEY (CORRECT ANSWERS)

1.	A	11.	D	21.	E	31.	E
2.	B	12.	B	22.	C	32.	A
3.	E	13.	E	23.	D	33.	D
4.	B	14.	E	24.	A	34.	C
5.	B	15.	D	25.	C	35.	B
6.	C	16.	C	26.	C	36.	A
7.	E	17.	C	27.	D	37.	C
8.	E	18.	A	28.	D	38.	A
9.	D	19.	B	29.	D	39.	A
10.	C	20.	A	30.	B	40.	E

EXAMINATION SECTION
TEST 1

DIRECTIONS: Select the word or phrase which has the same meaning, or most nearly the same meaning, as the CAPITALIZED word. *PRINT THE LETTER OF THE CORRECT ANSWER IN THE SPACE AT THE RIGHT.*

1. A CAR is to

    A. start fires with   B. eat on   C. take pictures with
    D. ride in   E. draw with

    1.____

2. INK is used to

    A. walk on   B. write with   C. cut with
    D. serve with   E. stand on

    2.____

3. POOR means having very little

    A. money   B. hair   C. sun   D. time   E. snow

    3.____

4. COMBAT

    A. point   B. report   C. fight   D. start   E. admit

    4.____

5. A MISTAKE is something done

    A. first   B. wrong   C. next   D. often   E. alone

    5.____

6. HOWL

    A. roar   B. design   C. propose   D. depart   E. succeed

    6.____

7. PHONY

    A. tough   B. neutral   C. vivid   D. fake   E. hasty

    7.____

8. ADVICE

    A. record   B. visit   C. bridge   D. opinion   E. minute

    8.____

9. BURLAP

    A. tunnel   B. medicine   C. soil   D. engine   E. fabric

    9.____

10. A SEAMSTRESS is a woman who

    A. writes   B. sews   C. sings   D. paints   E. bakes

    10.____

11. APPROACH means to come

    A. through   B. with   C. into   D. between   E. near

    11.____

12. ABANDON

    A. look over   B. hold on   C. lift up   D. fall down   E. give up

    12.____

13. BARELY

    A. generally   B. scarcely   C. completely
    D. especially   E. gradually

    13.____

14. SNEER
    A. listen with interest   B. practice with care   C. look with scorn
    D. lift with ease   E. dance with joy

15. ELIGIBLE
    A. lonesome   B. careless   C. qualified   D. inferior   E. profound

16. EXCLUDE
    A. educate   B. excite   C. eliminate   D. encourage   E. ensure

17. JUVENILE
    A. haunted   B. youthful   C. intimate   D. favorable   E. unable

18. JOLT
    A. justify   B. join   C. judge   D. jar   E. journey

19. GRATIFY
    A. heat   B. shout   C. hope   D. charge   E. please

20. RAFTER
    A. angel   B. canal   C. beam   D. lamb   E. trunk

21. LANK
    A. slender   B. grateful   C. musical   D. lively   E. rare

22. CONSOLE
    A. compare   B. conclude   C. comfort   D. command   E. collect

23. MANIPULATE
    A. reserve   B. devote   C. handle   D. inquire   E. introduce

24. CONCRETE
    A. clean   B. mean   C. low   D. nice   E. real

25. DESTITUTE
    A. respectful   B. divine   C. urgent   D. slippery   E. needy

26. BASTION
    A. fortification   B. qualification   C. appropriation
    D. legislation   E. illustration

27. FOREGO
    A. represent   B. sacrifice   C. justify
    D. determine   E. display

28. MACKINTOSH 28.____
    A. raincoat   B. tractor   C. honeybee
    D. cartoon   E. saucepan

29. TRAJECTORY 29.____
    A. curved path   B. ill health   C. bold type
    D. glorious spirit   E. strong back

30. A TRIPHTHONG is a combination of three 30.____
    A. fossils   B. cables   C. diagrams
    D. vowels   E. atoms

31. WHIST 31.____
    A. captain   B. game   C. soul   D. finger   E. rock

32. FETID 32.____
    A. exhausted   B. stinking   C. pathetic
    D. meager   E. insane

33. BEZANT 33.____
    A. hotel   B. coin   C. mill   D. harbor   E. desk

34. SCINTILLATE 34.____
    A. develop   B. whistle   C. ruin   D. breathe   E. flash

35. GLIB 35.____
    A. unaware   B. fluent   C. reluctant
    D. philosophical E. inquisitive

36. DINT 36.____
    A. supply   B. wish   C. force   D. price   E. demand

37. SARCOPHAGUS 37.____
    A. coffin   B. insect   C. interview
    D. wharf   E. mushroom

38. DIABOLO 38.____
    A. bed   B. dance   C. game   D. mark   E. record

39. LEMPIRA 39.____
    A. chair   B. money   C. salt   D. earth   E. music

40. PYROPE 40.____
    A. reptile   B. heather   C. slogan   D. mantle   E. garnet

KEY (CORRECT ANSWERS)

1.	D	11.	E	21.	A	31.	B
2.	B	12.	E	22.	C	32.	B
3.	A	13.	B	23.	C	33.	B
4.	C	14.	C	24.	E	34.	E
5.	B	15.	C	25.	E	35.	B
6.	A	16.	C	26.	A	36.	C
7.	D	17.	B	27.	B	37.	A
8.	D	18.	D	28.	A	38.	C
9.	E	19.	E	29.	A	39.	B
10.	B	20.	C	30.	D	40.	E

VERBAL ANALOGIES
EXAMINATION SECTION
TEST 1

DIRECTIONS: Each question consists of two capitalized words which have a certain relationship to each other, followed by five lettered pairs of words in small letters. Choose the letter of the pair of words which are related to each other in the SAME way as the words of the capitalized pair are related to each other. *PRINT THE LETTER OF THE CORRECT ANSWER IN THE SPACE AT THE RIGHT.*

1. DISEASE : IMMUNITY :: _____ : _____ 1.____
   A. crime : pardon   B. custom : practice   C. debt : bankruptcy
   D. tax : exemption   E. travel : deduction

2. RESPONSIBILITY : RELEASE :: _____ : _____ 2.____
   A. duty : refrain   B. promise : renege   C. debt : honor
   D. blame : vindicate   E. position : retract

3. PENDULUM : SWING :: _____ : _____ 3.____
   A. pulley : ladder   B. hand : clock   C. lever : crowbar
   D. balance : seesaw   E. weight : fulcrum

4. NADIR : ZENITH :: _____ : _____ 4.____
   A. depression : recovery   B. perigee : apogamy
   C. earth : sky   D. appanage : station
   E. threshold : lintel

5. ROB : CONFISCATE :: _____ : _____ 5.____
   A. punish : revenge   B. walk : trespass   C. insult : offend
   D. murder : execute   E. take : accept

6. WORKER : UNEMPLOYED :: _____ : _____ 6.____
   A. crop : barren   B. property : useless
   C. purchase : unnecessary   D. visitor : unwelcome
   E. field : fallow

7. PROFUSION : AUSTERITY :: _____ : _____ 7.____
   A. capitalism : socialism   B. erudition : reprise
   C. logic : irrationality   D. affluence : frugality
   E. effluence : confluence

8. REPERTOIRE : OPERA :: _____ : _____ 8.____
   A. suits : closet   B. team : baseball   C. melody : harmony
   D. wardrobe : costume   E. chest : drawers

9. DISDAIN : AFFRONT :: _____ : _____
   A. perjury : boos
   B. pleasure : pain
   C. approval : applause
   D. age : wrinkle
   E. grimace : awry

10. SALES : ADVERTISING :: _____ : _____
    A. votes : campaigning
    B. savings : banking
    C. liquor : drinking
    D. troops : leading
    E. weakness : strength

11. ATTACK : MURDER :: _____ : _____
    A. filial : fraternal
    B. mind : body
    C. paroxysm : parricide
    D. sudden : poison
    E. diseased : dead

12. BALTIC : INDIAN :: _____ : _____
    A. Mediterranean : Pacific
    B. Atlantic : Caribbean
    C. Arctic : Gulf of Mexico
    D. Black Sea : Persian Gulf
    E. Antarctic : Andaman Sea

13. PROFESSION : STRUGGLE :: _____ : _____
    A. strong : weak
    B. métier : melee
    C. mixed : confusion
    D. vocation : trade
    E. expert : novice

14. ALLOYS : ATMOSPHERE :: _____ : _____
    A. weight : measure
    B. metallurgy : meteorology
    C. technology : science
    D. archaic : present

15. GRAM : KILOGRAM :: _____ : _____
    A. millimeter : centimeter
    B. dekameter : decimeter
    C. mile : kilometer
    D. micron : microbe
    E. Centigrade : Fahrenheit

16. PRESIDENT : FRANCE :: _____ : _____
    A. Queen Elizabeth : England
    B. king : Belgium
    C. president : United States
    D. governor : state
    E. king : Italy

17. HAND : DIAL :: _____ : _____
    A. time : number
    B. light : lamp
    C. ticking : talking
    D. clock : radio
    E. time : space

18. ANNEX : BUILDING :: _____ : _____
    A. pin : clasp
    B. stone : setting
    C. cell : prison
    D. branch : tree
    E. island : mainland

19. FLOOR : PARQUET :: _____ : _____
    A. elevator : escalator
    B. functional : ornamental
    C. filigree : scroll
    D. wreath : nosegay
    E. head : hair

20. DEVIL : DRUGGIST :: _____ : _____   20._____
    A. demon : farmer   B. demonology : pharmacology
    C. medieval : primitive   D. dispensed : compounded
    E. Faustian : Freudian

21. ELECTRICITY : GAS :: _____ : _____   21._____
    A. lighter : match   B. current : flow   C. fire : flame
    D. conductor : ignition   E. train : automobile

22. - : HYPHEN :: _____ : _____   22._____
    A. x : division   B. $: pound   C. symbol : word
    D. y : geometry   E. & : sum

23. WILD : DOMESTICATED :: _____ : _____   23._____
    A. jungle : forest   B. atavistic : masochistic
    C. cave : dwelling   D. animal : man
    E. primitive : civilized

24. INEPT : TACTLESS :: _____ : _____   24._____
    A. right : left   B. evil : sinful   C. clever : stupid
    D. depraved : foolish   E. maladroit : gauche

25. INTERVENE : INTERCEDE :: _____ : _____   25._____
    A. interfere : impute   B. interpose : intrude   C. arbitrate : argue
    D. meditate : mediate   E. space : species

KEY (CORRECT ANSWERS)

1. D
2. D
3. C
4. E
5. D

6. E
7. D
8. D
9. C
10. A

11. C
12. A
13. B
14. B
15. A

16. C
17. D
18. D
19. B
20. B

21. B
22. C
23. E
24. E
25. B

TEST 2

DIRECTIONS: Each question consists of two capitalized words which have a certain relationship to each other, followed by five lettered pairs of words in small letters. Choose the letter of the pair of words which are related to each other in the SAME way as the words of the capitalized pair are related to each other. *PRINT THE LETTER OF THE CORRECT ANSWER IN THE SPACE AT THE RIGHT.*

1. PITHY : BOMBASTIC :: _____ : _____ 1._____
   A. verbose : taciturn   B. garrulous : pompous
   C. meagre : replete   D. laconic : grandiloquent
   E. concise : precise

2. MANAGER : TEAM :: _____ : _____ 2._____
   A. President : Congress   B. Speaker : Senate
   C. captain : crew   D. minister : hierarchy
   E. principal : P.T.A.

3. STEEPLE : LEDGE :: _____ : _____ 3._____
   A. citadel : tower   B. spire : dungeon   C. warp : woof
   D. peak : summit   E. cone : roof

4. CREDULOUS : UNCTUOUS :: _____ : _____ 4._____
   A. ingenious : artful   B. ingenuous : urbane
   C. naïve : provincial   D. benign : benignant
   E. cantankerous : peevish

5. PHILIPPIC : ABUSE :: _____ : _____ 5._____
   A. eulogy : mirth   B. tirade : tears   C. sycophancy : music
   D. encomium : praise   E. intrepidity : fear

6. CUMULATIVE : ACCRETIVE :: _____ : _____ 6._____
   A. indigenous : spontaneous   B. reticence : verbosity
   C. philately : numismatics   D. indigence : poverty
   E. culvert : bridge

7. UNCONSTRAINED : IMPROVISED :: _____ : _____ 7._____
   A. unrehearsed : prepared   B. simultaneous : pithy
   C. premeditated : unpremeditated   D. extemporaneous : contemporaneous
   E. spontaneous : impromptu

8. INORDINACY : EXCESSIVE :: _____ : _____ 8._____
   A. applause : approval   B. anomaly : irregular
   C. remuneration : payable   D. provocation : irritate
   E. emulation : insidious

201

9. PLEBEIAN : PATRICIAN :: _____ : _____
    A. Democrat : Republican   B. Communist : Conservative
    C. serf : fief   D. vassal : lord
    E. common man : elite

10. FLEETING : EPHEMERAL :: _____ : _____
    A. permanent : temporary   B. casual : persistent
    C. transient : evanescent   D. temporary : permanent
    E. passing : perceptible

11. INSTRUMENTALIST : ORGANIST :: _____ : _____
    A. harmonist : contrapuntist   B. quartet : counterpoint
    C. lute : lutenist   D. singer : composition
    E. cello : violoncello

12. ADULTERATE : COMPOUND :: _____ : _____
    A. fusión : blend   B. commingle : miscellany
    C. interpretation : commingling D. interpolate : amalgamate
    E. mix : potpourri

13. QUIESCENCE : INDOLENCE :: _____ : _____
    A. lurk : abeyance   B. concealed : potential
    C. latency : dormancy   D. escape : observation
    E. suppress : inertia

14. BROGUE : JARGONIST :: _____ : _____
    A. patois : neologist   B. empathy : psychiatrist
    C. dialect : Anglicism   D. country : patriot
    E. gazette : journalist

15. DENIAL : DISCLAIMER :: _____ : _____
    A. veto : ignore   B. contradiction : convention
    C. cancel : canker   D. disavowal : negation
    E. gainsay : contradict

16. FATE : PREDESTINATION :: _____ : _____
    A. doom : destiny   B. appointed : office
    C. elect : fated   D. exigency : inevitability
    E. lot : choice

17. LETHARGY : EXHAUSTION :: _____ : _____
    A. laziness : weariness   B. continence : ennui
    C. enfeebled : haggard   D. exertion : tiredness
    E. lassitude : fatigue

18. QUALM : IRRESOLUTION :: _____ : _____
    A. fear : diffidence   B. fright : stampede
    C. awe : trust   D. sanguine : apprehensive
    E. nightmare : alarm

3 (#2)

19. WAR : SURRENDER :: _____ : _____ 19._____
    A. victor : accede   B. grant : scholarship   C. election : concede
    D. state : cede   E. prison : confess

20. BALD EAGLE : GROUSE :: _____ : _____ 20._____
    A. termite : cockroach   B. chanticleer : rooster   C. falcon : pheasant
    D. peacock : hen   E. vulture : hawk

21. ORANGUTAN : BRONCHO :: _____ : _____ 21._____
    A. antelope : trotter
    B. Wales : United States
    C. caribou : marmoset
    D. ewe : ram
    E. steeplechaser : pacer

22. UNITED STATES : FRANCE :: _____ : _____ 22._____
    A. official : citizen
    B. policeman : gendarme
    C. officer : attendant
    D. New York : Louisiana
    E. west : east

23. SEOUL : SOUTH KOREA :: _____ : _____ 23._____
    A. Estopil : Portugal   B. Pnom Penh : Laos   C. Barcelona : Spain
    C. London : England   E. Venezuela : Caracas

24. PERSECUTION : PARANOIA :: _____ : _____ 24._____
    A. altruism : megalomania
    B. neurosis : psychosis
    C. dichotomy : schizophrenia
    D. extraversion : claustrophobia
    E. disease : symptom

25. ONE : TWO :: _____ : _____ 25._____
    A. century : millennium
    B. planet : astronomy
    C. year : twenty
    D. month : year
    E. decade : score

KEY (CORRECT ANSWERS)

1. D
2. C
3. C
4. B
5. D

6. D
7. E
8. B
9. E
10. C

11. A
12. D
13. C
14. A
15. D

16. A
17. E
18. A
19. C
20. C

21. A
22. B
23. D
24. C
25. E

TEST 3

DIRECTIONS: Each question consists of two capitalized words which have a certain relationship to each other, followed by five lettered pairs of words in small letters. Choose the letter of the pair of words which are related to each other in the SAME way as the words of the capitalized pair are related to each other. *PRINT THE LETTER OF THE CORRECT ANSWER IN THE SPACE AT THE RIGHT.*

1. CHAFFER : BARGAIN :: _____ : _____   1.____
   A. scarify : cleanse   B. hector : befriend
   C. propitiate : placate   D. improvise : intercalate
   E. decollate : decode

2. SPANIEL : FAWNING PERSON :: _____ : _____   2.____
   A. cameo : miniature   B. nonage : minority   C. pediment : obstacle
   D. flacon : flag   E. marasca : wine

3. SEMINAL : ORIGINATIVE :: _____ : _____   3.____
   A. sullied : inflamed   B. beleaguered : besieged
   C. viable : moribund   D. amorphous : remanent
   E. quintan : fourth

4. SLAKE : ALLAY :: _____ : _____   4.____
   A. comport : frolic   B. beset : assail   C. parry : join
   D. revet : review   E. remonstrate : concur

5. SALAAM : OBEISANCE :: _____ : _____   5.____
   A. jape : hiatus   B. ethos : fundamental spirit of a culture
   C. gravamen : greeting   D. chanticleer : fox
   E. ablation : inhalation

6. SLATTERNLY : SLOVENLY :: _____ : _____   6.____
   A. complaisant : priggish   B. myopic : farsighted
   C. awry : convex   D. oblate : flattened at the poles
   E. slavish : sleazy

7. PREEN : SLEEK :: _____ : _____   7.____
   A. extrapolate : disengage   B. discountenance : disconcert
   C. bandy : banter   D. cense : ascribe
   E. cite : proscribe

8. SATRAP : EXECUTE :: _____ : _____   8.____
   A. rigmarole : prolix talk   B. apostasy : denunciation
   C. apogee : perigee   D. allotrophy : allusion
   E. chaldron : chalice

9. INCHOATE : NASCENT :: _____ : _____
   A. extirpative : invective
   B. contumacious : headstrong
   C. disinterested : prejudiced
   D. veracious : mendacious
   E. abandoned : manumitted

10. RAIL : REVILE :: _____ : _____
    A. abjure : appeal to
    B. vouchsafe : contemplate
    C. execrate : curse
    D. exorcise : criticize
    E. ablactate : abominate

11. ANTONYM : OPPOSITE :: _____ : _____
    A. antonym : unlike
    B. metaphor : poetry
    C. triangle : pyramid
    D. synonym : sme
    E. metonymy : versification

12. READER : PUNCTUATION :: _____ : _____
    A. telegraph operator : Morse
    B. vocabulary : alphabet
    C. English : pronunciation
    D. bicyclist : roadblock
    E. motorist : road sign

13. OCEAN : ROAD :: _____ : _____
    A. ship : hurricane
    B. canal : road
    C. storm : accident
    D. buoy : detour
    E. warning : signal

14. MATTER : ESSENCE :: _____ : _____
    A. play : outcome
    B. matter : particle
    C. molecule : atom
    D. paragraph : gist
    E. epitome : paraphrase

15. PENURIOUS : SLUM :: _____ : _____
    A. captive : jail
    B. parched : desert
    C. withered : plant
    D. inundated : flood
    E. glum : outlook

16. DEMEANOR : CHARACTER :: _____ : _____
    A. personality : qualities
    B. aspect : appearance
    C. vestibule : apartment
    D. facade : building
    E. front : affront

17. HAIR : TRIM :: _____ : _____
    A. beard : shave
    B. lawn : mow
    C. wool : shear
    D. shrub : prune
    E. scissors : cut

18. WORK : PUTTER :: _____ : _____
    A. bum : thief
    B. late : laggard
    C. regress : ingress
    D. diligent : tardy
    E. wait : loiter

19. EXILE : SANCTUARY :: _____ : _____
    A. child : bed
    B. refugee : haven
    C. berth : stowaway
    D. fish : bowl
    E. prisoner : dungeon

20. CAR : HORN :: _____ : _____   20.____
    A. air raid : siren   B. swimmer : bell buoy   C. singer : tune
    D. train : whistle   E. ship : anchor

21. SETTING : DIAMOND :: _____ : _____   21.____
    A. sash : window   B. frame : picture   C. shell : egg
    D. painting : canvas   E. border : exile

22. AFFECTION : PASSION :: _____ : _____ 22.____
    A. storm : sea   B. contraction : dilation
    C. atmospheric pressure : clear day   D. breeze : gale
    E. wind : gale

23. TEAR : CUT :: _____ : _____   23.____
    A. wrinkle : fold   B. paper : refuse   C. wrinkle : smooth
    D. steal : lose   E. sprinkle : rub

24. FIGHTER : BELL :: _____ : _____   24.____
    A. butterfly hunter : net   B. fencer : sword
    C. writer : pen   D. dog : whistle
    E. sprinter : gun

25. PLANT : FUNGUS :: _____ : _____   25.____
    A. transient : permanent   B. mate : captain
    C. sailor : pirate   D. police : thief
    E. wolf : prey

KEY (CORRECT ANSWERS)

1.	C	11.	D
2.	B	12.	E
3.	B	13.	D
4.	B	14.	D
5.	B	15.	B
6.	D	16.	D
7.	B	17.	D
8.	A	18.	E
9.	B	19.	B
10.	C	20.	D

21.	B
22.	E
23.	A
24.	E
25.	C

TEST 4

DIRECTIONS: Each question consists of two capitalized words which have a certain relationship to each other, followed by five lettered pairs of words in small letters. Choose the letter of the pair of words which are related to each other in the SAME way as the words of the capitalized pair are related to each other. *PRINT THE LETTER OF THE CORRECT ANSWER IN THE SPACE AT THE RIGHT.*

1. EVENING : MORNING :: _____ : _____ 1._____
   A. coming : going B. ten : five C. sunset : sunrise
   D. spring : autumn E. despair : hope

2. RUNG : RING :: _____ : _____ 2._____
   A. arisen : arise B. drunk : drink C. stroke : strike
   D. sang : sing E. clang : cling

3. ENTHUSIASTIC : APPROVING :: _____ : _____ 3._____
   A. disliking : liking B. pink : red
   C. frigid : cool D. bitter : sour
   E. apathetic : disapproving

4. MOLECULE : ATOM :: _____ : _____ 4._____
   A. kennel : dog B. shelf : book C. sea : fish
   D. regiment : soldier E. star : galaxy

5. ACT : PLAY :: _____ : _____ 5._____
   A. notes : staff B. harmony : counterpoint
   C. melody : harmony D. key : piano
   E. movement : symphony

6. APIARY : BEES :: _____ : _____ 6._____
   A. dog : kennel B. fish : aquarium C. mortuary : people
   D. corral : cattle E. breviary : priest

7. STRANDS : ROPE :: _____ : _____ 7._____
   A. sugar : cane B. warp : woof C. links : chain
   D. train : cars E. rivers : ocean

8. BODY : SKIN :: _____ : _____ 8._____
   A. window : door B. ink : crayon C. book : cover
   D. write : compose E. spelling : grammar

9. PENCIL : LEAD :: _____ : _____ 9._____
   A. lighter : fluid B. keys : typewriter C. cup : coffee
   D. book : page E. razor : blade

10. AIRPLANE : LOCOMOTION :: _____ : _____
    A. statement : contention   B. canoe : paddle
    C. hero : worship   D. spectacles : vision
    E. hay : horse

11. STREAM : RIVER :: _____ : _____
    A. land : water   B. village : suburb   C. cape : continent
    D. sea : ocean   E. city : country

12. RECTANGLE : SQUARE :: _____ : _____
    A. line : perimeter   B. triangle : square   C. square : diamond
    D. circle : square   E. oval : circle

13. EMOLUMENT : INCENTIVE :: _____ : _____
    A. deed : crime   B. play : plot   C. criminal : reward
    D. dance : movement   E. reward : capture

14. WOLF : PROWL :: _____ : _____
    A. rat : gnaw   B. monkey : mimic   C. reader : browse
    D. trooper : lurk   E. gang : highjack

15. FOND : INFATUATION :: _____ : _____
    A. affectionate : adumbration   B. calm : listless
    C. eager : sentimentality   D. glib : fluency
    E. enthusiastic : fervor

16. CONCORD : DISCORD :: _____ : _____
    A. alliance : organization   B. treaty : covenant
    C. conciliation : revolution   D. entreaty : parity
    E. pact : feud

17. EXTENUATE : CRIME :: _____ : _____
    A. condone : error   B. placate : pardon   C. expiate : sin
    D. moderate : tone   E. reprisal : retaliation

18. APPENDIX : PREFACE :: _____ : _____
    A. glossary : index   B. preface : table of contents
    C. progeny : proletariat   D. footnote : emendation
    E. epilogue : prologue

19. SUBSEQUENT : COINCIDENTAL :: _____ : _____
    A. posthumous : following   B. now : there
    C. consecutive : ensuing   D. posterior : simultaneous
    E. prolonged : before

20. MUNDANE : SPIRITUAL :: _____ : _____
    A. scientist : missionary   B. secular : altruistic
    C. municipal : ecclesiastical   D. pecuniary : musical
    E. student : teacher

3 (#4)

21. UNSCRUPULOUS : QUALMS :: _____ : _____ 21._____
    A. remorseless : compassion   B. intrepid : rashness
    C. opportunist : opportunity   D. querulous : lamentation
    E. impenitent : sin

22. SOPHISTRY : LOGIC :: _____ : _____ 22._____
    A. discretion : improvidence   B. spirit : spiritualism
    C. reason : rationalization   D. feeling : intuition
    E. wisdom : sophistication

23. TRESPASSER : BARK :: _____ : _____ 23._____
    A. snake : hiss   B. burglar : alarm   C. crossing : bell
    D. air raid : siren   E. ship : buoy

24. RESEARCH : FELLOWSHIP :: _____ : _____ 24._____
    A. honor : medal   B. merit : scholarship   C. student : bonus
    D. matrimony : dowry   E. study : grant

25. IMPEND : DEMISE :: _____ : _____ 25._____
    A. loom : disaster   B. question : puzzle   C. imminent : eminent
    D. howl : storm   E. hurt : penalty

KEY (CORRECT ANSWERS)

1.	C	11.	D
2.	B	12.	E
3.	D	13.	E
4.	E	14.	E
5.	E	15.	E
6.	D	16.	E
7.	C	17.	A
8.	C	18.	E
9.	E	19.	D
10.	D	20.	B

21. A
22. D
23. B
24. E
25. A

TEST 5

DIRECTIONS: Each question consists of two capitalized words which have a certain relationship to each other, followed by five lettered pairs of words in small letters. Choose the letter of the pair of words which are related to each other in the SAME way as the words of the capitalized pair are related to each other. *PRINT THE LETTER OF THE CORRECT ANSWER IN THE SPACE AT THE RIGHT.*

1. DEATH : DEMISE :: _____ : _____
   A. frightful : horrid   B. resistance : invasion
   C. asylum : insane   D. life : breath
   E. might : right
1._____

2. DRAGON : DINOSAUR :: _____ : _____
   A. descendant : ancestor   B. medieval : prehistoric
   C. fabulous : real   D. creditable : veritable
   E. amphibian : reptile
2._____

3. SHIP : NAVIGATION :: _____ : _____
   A. promoter : event   B. victory : leader
   C. conduct : conscience   D. state : army
   E. nation : patriotism
3._____

4. GUFFAW : LAUGH :: _____ : _____
   A. lament : cry   B. wail : whimper   C. face : mouth
   D. chuckle : snicker   E. smirk : simper
4._____

5. ANARCHY : CHAOS :: _____ : _____
   A. government : order   B. beast : beauty   C. government : law
   D. rule : order   E. totalitarian : mob
5._____

6. INFINITE : FINITE :: _____ : _____
   A. second : minute   B. hour : minute   C. era : decade
   D. month : day   E. immortality : mortality
6._____

7. WATER : BOAT :: _____ : _____
   A. locomotive : steam   B. wagon : horse   C. air : dirigible
   D. lion : tiger   E. gasoline : taxi
7._____

8. INAUGURATION : PRESIDENT :: _____ : _____
   A. promulgation : list   B. matriculation : student
   C. election : candidate   D. promotion : officer
   E. ordination : priest
8._____

9. OMNIPOTENT : VASSAL :: _____ : _____
   A. soldier : civilian   B. policeman : prisoner
   C. master : slave   D. captain : tar
   E. native : alien
9._____

10. SAME : SYNONYM :: _____ : _____ 10.____
   A. bell : bellows   B. false : pseudonym   C. same : homonym
   D. botanist : biologist   E. opposite : antonym

KEY (CORRECT ANSWERS)

1.	A	6.	E
2.	C	7.	C
3.	C	8.	E
4.	B	9.	C
5.	A	10.	E

READING COMPREHENSION
UNDERSTANDING AND INTERPRETING WRITTEN MATERIAL
EXAMINATION SECTION
TEST 1

DIRECTIONS: Each question has five suggested answers, lettered A to E. Decide which one is the BEST answer. *PRINT THE LETTER OF THE CORRECT ANSWER IN THE SPACE AT THE RIGHT.*

1. Some specialists are willing to give their services to the Government entirely free of charge; some feel that a nominal salary, such as will cover traveling expenses, is sufficient for a position that is recognized as being somewhat honorary in nature; many other specialists value their time so highly that they will not devote any of it to public service that does not repay them at a rate commensurate with the fees that they can obtain from a good private clientele.
   The paragraph BEST supports the statement that the use of specialists by the Government
   A. is rare because of the high cost of securing such persons
   B. may be influenced by the willingness of specialists to serve
   C. enables them to secure higher salaries in private fields
   D. has become increasingly common during the past few years
   E. always conflicts with private demands for their services

   1.____

2. The fact must not be overlooked that only about one-half of the international trade of the world crosses the oceans. The other half is merely exchanges of merchandise between countries lying alongside each other or at least within the same continent.
   The paragraph BEST supports the statement that
   A. the most important part of any country's trade is transoceanic
   B. domestic trade is insignificant when compared with foreign trade
   C. the exchange of goods between neighboring countries is not considered international trade
   D. foreign commerce is not necessarily carried on by water
   E. about one-half of the trade of the world is international

   2.____

3. Individual differences in mental traits assume importance in fitting workers to jobs because such personal characteristics are persistent and are relatively little influenced by training and experience.
   The paragraph BEST supports the statement that training and experience
   A. are limited in their effectiveness in fitting workers to jobs
   B. do not increase a worker's fitness for a job
   C. have no effect upon a person's mental traits
   D. have relatively little effect upon the individual's chances for success
   E. should be based on the mental traits of an individual

   3.____

4. The competition of buyers tends to keep prices up, the competition of sellers to send them down. Normally, the pressure of competition among sellers is stronger than that among buyers since the seller has his article to sell and must get rid of it, whereas the buyer is not committed to anything.
The paragraph BEST supports the statement that low prices are caused by
   A. buyer competition
   B. competition of buyers with sellers
   C. fluctuations in demand
   D. greater competition among sellers than among buyers
   E. more sellers than buyers

5. In seventeen states, every lawyer is automatically a member of the American Bar Association. In some other states and localities, truly representative organizations of the Bar have not yet come into being, but are greatly needed.
The paragraph IMPLIES that
   A. representative Bar Associations are necessary in states where they do not now exist
   B. every lawyer is required by law to become a member of the Bar
   C. the Bar Association is a democratic organization
   D. some states have more lawyers than others
   E. every member of the American Bar Association is automatically a lawyer in seventeen states

KEY (CORRECT ANSWERS)

1. B
2. D
3. A
4. D
5. A

TEST 2

DIRECTIONS: Each question has five suggested answers, lettered A to E. Decide which one is the BEST answer. *PRINT THE LETTER OF THE CORRECT ANSWER IN THE SPACE AT THE RIGHT.*

1. We hear a great deal about the new education, and see a great deal of it in action. But the school house, though prodigiously magnified in scale, is still very much the same old school house.
   The paragraph IMPLIES
   A. the old education was, after all, better than the new
   B. although the modern school buildings are larger than the old ones, they have not changed very much in other respects
   C. the old school houses do not fit in with modern educational theories
   D. a fine school building does not make up for poor teachers
   E. schools will be schools

   1.____

2. No two human beings are of the same pattern—not even twins and the method of bringing out the best in each one necessarily according to the nature of the child.
   The paragraph IMPLIES that
   A. individual differences should be considered in dealing with children
   B. twins should be treated impartially
   C. it is an easy matter to determine the special abilities of children
   D. a child's nature varies from year to year
   E. we must discover the general technique of dealing with children

   2.____

3. Man inhabits today a world very different from that which encompassed even his parents and grandparents. It is a world geared to modern machinery—automobiles, airplanes, power plants; it is linked together and served by electricity.
   The paragraph IMPLIES that
   A. the world has no changed much during the last few generations
   B. modern inventions and discoveries have brought about many changes in man's way of living
   C. the world is run more efficiently today than it was in our grandparents' time
   D. man is much happier today than he was a hundred years ago
   E. we must learn to see man as he truly is, underneath the veneers of man's contrivances

   3.____

4. Success in any study depends largely upon the interest taken in that particular subject by the student. This being the case, each teacher earnestly hopes that her students will realize at the vey onset that shorthand can be made an intensely fascinating study.
   The paragraph IMPLIES that
   A. Everyone is interested in shorthand
   B. success in a study is entirely impossible unless the student finds the study very interesting

   4.____

C. if a student is eager to study shorthand, he is likely to succeed in it
D. shorthand is necessary for success
E. anyone who is not interested in shorthand will not succeed in business

5. The primary purpose of all business English is to move the reader to agreeable and mutually profitable action. This action may be indirect or direct, but in either case a highly competitive appeal for business should be clothed with incisive diction tending to replace vagueness and doubt with clarity, confidence, and appropriate action.
   The paragraph IMPLIES that the
   A. ideal business letter uses words to conform to the reader's language level
   B. business correspondent should strive for conciseness in letter writing
   C. keen competition of today has lessened the value of the letter as an appeal for business
   D. writer of a business letter should employ incisive diction to move the reader to compliant and gainful action
   E. the writer of a business letter should be himself clear, confident, and forceful

KEY (CORRECT ANSWERS)

1. B
2. A
3. B
4. C
5. D

TEST 3

DIRECTIONS: Each question has five suggested answers, lettered A to E. Decide which one is the BEST answer. *PRINT THE LETTER OF THE CORRECT ANSWER IN THE SPACE AT THE RIGHT.*

1. To serve the community best, a comprehensive city plan must coordinate all physical improvements, even at the possible expense of subordinating individual desires, to the end that a city may grow in a more orderly way and provide adequate facilities for its people
   The paragraph IMPLIES that
   A. city planning provides adequate facilities for recreation
   B. a comprehensive city plan provides the means for a city to grow in a more orderly fashion
   C. individual desires must always be subordinated to civic changes
   D. the only way to serve a community is to adopt a comprehensive city plan
   E. city planning is the most important function of city government

1.____

2. Facility in writing letters, the knack of putting into these quickly written letters the same personal impression that would mark an interview, and the ability to boil down to a one-page letter the gist of what might be called a five- or ten-minute conversation —all these are essential to effective work under conditions of modern business organization.
   The paragraph IMPLIES that
   A. letters are of more importance in modern business activities than ever before
   B. letters should be used in place of interviews
   C. the ability to write good letters is essential to effective work in modern business organization
   D. business letters should never be more than one page in length
   E. the person who can write a letter with great skill will get ahead more readily than others

2.____

3. The general rule is that it is the city council which determines the amount to be raised by taxation and which therefore determines, within the law, the tax rates. As has been pointed out, however, no city council or city authority has the power to determine what kind of taxes should be levied.
   The paragraph IMPLIES that
   A. the city council has more authority than any other municipal body
   B. while the city council has a great deal of authority in the levying of taxes, its power is not absolute
   C. the kinds of taxes levied in different cities vary greatly
   D. the city council appoints the tax collectors
   E. the mayor determines the kinds of taxes to be levied

3.____

4. The growth of modern business has made necessary mass production, mass distribution, and mass selling. As a result, the problems of personnel and industrial relations have increased so rapidly that grave injustice in the handling of personal relationships have frequently occurred. Personnel administration is complex because, as in all human problems, many intangible elements are involved. Therefore a thorough, systematic, and continuous study of the psychology of human behavior is essential to the intelligent handling of personnel.
The paragraph IMPLIES that
   A. complex modern industry makes impossible the personal relationships which formerly existed between employer and employee
   B. mass decisions are successfully applied to personnel problems
   C. the human element in personnel administration makes continuous study necessary to is intelligent application
   D. personnel problems are less important than the problems of mass production and mass distribution
   E. since personnel administration is so complex and costly, it should be subordinated to the needs of good industrial relations

5. The Social Security Act is striving toward the attainment of economic security for the individual and for his family. It was stated, in outlining this program, that security for the individual and for the family concerns itself with three factors: (1) decent homes to live in; (2) development of the natural resources of the country so as to afford the fullest opportunity to engage in productive work; and (3) safeguards against the major misfortunes of life. The Social Security Act is concerned with the third of these factors —"safeguards against misfortunes which cannot be wholly eliminated in this man-made world of ours."
The paragraph IMPLIES that the
   A. Social Security Act is concerned primarily with supplying to families decent homes in which to live
   B. development of natural resources is the only means of offering employment to the masses of the unemployed
   C. Social Security Act has attained absolute economic security for the individual and his family
   D. Social Security Act deals with the first (1) factor as stated in the paragraph above
   E. Social Security Act deals with the third (3) factor as stated in the paragraph above

KEY (CORRECT ANSWERS)

1. B
2. C
3. B
4. C
5. E

TEST 4

DIRECTIONS: Each question has five suggested answers, lettered A to E. Decide which one is the BEST answer. *PRINT THE LETTER OF THE CORRECT ANSWER IN THE SPACE AT THE RIGHT.*

PASSAGE 1

Free unrhymed verse has been practiced for some thousands of years and reaches back to the incantation which linked verse with the ritual dance. It provided a communal emotion; the aim of the cadenced phrases was to create a state of mind. The general coloring of free rhythms in the poetry of today is that of speech rhythm, composed in the sequence of the musical phrase, not in the sequence of the metronome, the regular beat. In the twenties, conventional rhyme fell into almost complete disuse. This liberation from rhyme became as well a liberation of rhyme. Freed of its exacting task of supporting lame verse, it would be applied with greater effect where wanted for some special effect. Such break in the tradition of rhymed verse had the healthy effect of giving it a fresh start, released from the hampering convention of too familiar cadences. This refreshing and subtilizing of the use of rhythm can be seen everywhere in the poetry today.

1. The title below that BEST expresses the ideas of this paragraph is: 1.____
    A. Primitive Poetry
    B. The Origin of Poetry
    C. Rhyme and Rhythm in Modern Verse
    D. Classification of Poetry
    E. Purposes in All Poetry

2. Free verse had its origin in primitive   2.____
    A. fairytales   B. literature   C. warfare
    D. chants   E. courtship

3. The object of early free verse was to   3.____
    A. influence the mood of the people   B. convey ideas
    C. produce mental pictures   D. create pleasing sounds
    E. provide enjoyment

PASSAGE 2

Control of the Mississippi had always been goals of nations having ambitions in the New World. LaSalle claimed it for France in 1682. Iberville appropriated it to France when he colonized Louisiana in 1700. Bienville founded New Orleans, its principal port, as a French city in 1718. The fleur-de-lis were the blazon of the delta country until 1762. Then Spain claimed all of Louisiana. The Spanish were easy neighbors. American products from western Pennsylvania and the Northwest Territory were barged down the Ohio and Mississippi to New Orleans; here they were reloaded on ocean-going vessels that cleared for the great seaports of the world.

4. The title below that BEST expresses the ideas of this paragraph is: 4.____
   A. Importance of Seaports
   B. France and Spain in the New World
   C. Early Control of the Mississippi
   D. Claims of European Nations
   E. American Trade on the Mississippi

5. Until 1762, the lower Mississippi area was held by 5.____
   A. England   B. Spain   C. the United States
   D. France   E. Indians

6. In doing business with Americans, the Spaniards were 6.____
   A. easy to outsmart
   B. friendly to trade
   C. inclined to charge high prices for use of their ports
   D. shrewd
   E. suspicious

PASSAGE 3

Our humanity is by no means so materialistic as foolish talk is continually asserting it to be. Judging by what I have learned about men and women, I am convinced that there is far more in them of idealistic willpower than ever comes to the surface of the world. Just as the water of streams is small in amount compared to that which flows underground, so the idealism which becomes visible is small in amount compared with that which men and women bear locked in their hearts, unreleased or scarcely released. To unbind what is bound, to bring the underground waters to the surface—mankind is waiting and longing for men who can do that.

7. The title below that BEST expresses the ideas of the paragraph is: 7.____
   A. Releasing Underground Riches
   B. The Good and Bad in Man
   C. Materialism in Humanity
   D. The Surface and the Depths of Idealism
   E. Unreleased Energy

8. Human beings are more idealistic than 8.____
   A. the water in underground streams
   B. their waiting and longing proves
   C. outward evidence shows
   D. the world
   E. other living creatures

PASSAGE 4

The total impression made by any work of fiction cannot be rightly understood without a sympathetic perception of the artistic aims of the writer. Consciously or unconsciously, he has accepted certain facts, and rejected or suppressed other facts, in order to give unity to the particular aspect of human life which he is depicting. No novelist possesses the impartiality, the indifference, the infinite tolerance of nature. Nature displays to use, with complete unconcern, the beautiful and the ugly, the precious and the trivial, the pure and the impure. But a writer must select the aspects of nature and human nature which are demanded by the work in hand. He is forced to select, to combine, to create.

9. The title below that BEST expresses the ideas of this paragraph is:
   A. Impressionists in Literature
   B. Nature as an Artist
   C. The Novelist as an Imitator
   D. Creative Technic of the Novelist
   E. Aspects of Nature

10. A novelist rejects some facts because they
    A. are impure and ugly
    B. would show he is not impartial
    C. are unrelated to human nature
    D. would make a bad impression
    E. mar the unity of his story

11. It is important for a reader to know
    A. the purpose of the author
    B. what facts the author omits
    C. both the ugly and the beautiful
    D. something about nature
    E. what the author thinks of human nature

PASSAGE 5

If you watch a lamp which is turned very rapidly on and off, and you keep your eyes open, "persistence of vision" will bridge the gaps of darkness between the flashes of light, and the lamp will seem to be continuously lit. This "topical afterglow" explains the magic produced by the stroboscope, a new instrument which seems to freeze the swiftest motions while they are still going on, and to stop time itself dead in its tracks. The "magic" is all in the eye of the beholder.

12. The "magic" of the stroboscope is due to
    A. continuous lighting
    B. intense cold
    C. slow motion
    D. behavior of the human eye
    E. a lapse of time

13. "Persistence of vision" is explained by
    A. darkness
    B. winking
    C. rapid flashes
    D. gaps
    E. after impression

KEY (CORRECT ANSWERS)

1.	C	6.	B	11.	A
2.	D	7.	D	12.	D
3.	A	8.	C	13.	E
4.	C	9.	D		
5.	D	10.	E		

TEST 5

DIRECTIONS: Each question has five suggested answers, lettered A to E. Decide which one is the BEST answer. *PRINT THE LETTER OF THE CORRECT ANSWER IN THE SPACE AT THE RIGHT.*

PASSAGE 1

During the past fourteen years, thousands of top-lofty United States elms have been marked for death by the activities of the tiny European elm bark beetle. The beetles, however, do not do fatal damage. Death is caused by another importation, Dutch elm disease, a fungus infection which the beetles carry from tree to tree. Up to 1941, quarantine and tree-sanitation measures kept the beetles and the disease pretty well confined within 510 miles around metropolitan New York. War curtailed these measures and made Dutch elm disease a wider menace. Every household and village that prizes an elm-shaded lawn or commons must now watch for it. Since there is as yet no cure for it, the infected trees must be pruned or felled, and the wood must be burned in order to protect other healthy trees.

1. The title below that BEST expresses the ideas of this paragraph is: 1.____
   A. A Menace to Our Elms
   B. Pests and Diseases of the Elm
   C. Our Vanishing Elms
   D. The Need to Protect Dutch Elms
   E. How Elms are Protected

2. The danger of spreading the Dutch elm disease was increased by 2.____
   A. destroying infected trees   B. the war
   C. the lack of a cure   D. a fungus infection
   E. quarantine measures

3. The European elm bark beetle is a serious threat to our elms because it 3.____
   A. chews the bark
   B. kills the trees
   C. is particularly active on the eastern seaboard
   D. carries infection
   E. cannot be controlled

PASSAGE 2

It is elemental that the greater the development of man, the greater the problems he has to concern him. When he lived in a cave with stone implements, his mind no less than his actions was grooved into simple channels. Every new invention, every new way of doing things posed fresh problems for him. And, as he moved along the road, he questioned each step, as indeed he should, for he trod upon the beliefs of his ancestors. It is equally elemental to say that each step upon this later road posed more questions than the earlier ones. It is only the educated man who realizes the results of his actions; it is only the thoughtful one who questions his own decisions.

4. The title below that BEST expresses the ideas of this paragraph is: 4._____
   A. Channels of Civilization
   B. The Mark of a Thoughtful Man
   C. The Cave Man in Contrast with Man Today
   D. The Price of Early Progress
   E. Man's Never-Ending Challenge

PASSAGE 3

Spring is one of those things that man has no hand in, any more than he has a part in sunrise or the phases of the moon. Spring came before man was here to enjoy it, and it will go right on coming even if man isn't here some time in the future. It is a matter of solar mechanics and celestial order. And for all our knowledge of astronomy and terrestrial mechanics, we haven't yet been able to do more than bounce a radar beam off the moon. We couldn't alter the arrival of the spring equinox by as much as one second, if we tried.

Spring is a matter of growth, of chlorophyll, of bud and blossom. We can alter growth and change the time of blossoming in individual plants; but the forests still grow in nature's way, and the grass of the plains hasn't altered its nature in a thousand years. Spring is a magnificent phase of the cycle of nature; but man really hasn't any guiding or controlling hand in it. He is here to enjoy it and benefit by it. And April is a good time to realize it; by May perhaps we will want to take full credit.

5. The title below that BEST expresses the ideas of this passage is: 5._____
   A. The Marvels of the Spring Equinox
   B. Nature's Dependence on Mankind
   C. The Weakness of Man Opposed to Nature
   D. The Glories of the World
   E. Eternal Growth

6. The author of the passage states that   6._____
   A. man has a part in the phases of the moon
   B. April is a time for taking full-credit
   C. April is a good time to enjoy nature
   D. man has a guiding hand in spring
   E. spring will cease to be if civilization ends

PASSAGE 4

The walled medieval town was as characteristic of its period as the cut of a robber baron's beard. It sprang out of the exigencies of war, and it was not without its architectural charm, whatever is hygienic deficiencies may have been. Behind its high, thick walls not only the normal inhabitants but the whole countryside fought and cowered in an hour of need. The capitals of Europe now forsake the city when the sirens scream and death from the sky seems imminent. Will the fear of bombs accelerate the slow decentralization which began with the automobile and the wide distribution of electrical energy and thus reverse the medieval flow to the city?

3 (#5)

7. The title below that BEST expresses the ideas in this paragraph is: 7.____
   A. A Changing Function of the Town
   B. The Walled Medieval Town
   C. The Automobile's Influence on City Life
   D. Forsaking the City
   E. Bombs Today and Yesterday

8. Conditions in the Middle Ages made the walled town 8.____
   A. a natural development
   B. the most dangerous of all places
   C. a victim of fires
   D. lacking in architectural charm
   E. healthful

9. Modern conditions may 9.____
   A. make cities larger
   B. make cities more hygienic
   C. protect against floods
   D. cause people to move from population centers
   E. encourage good architecture

PASSAGE 5

The literary history of this nation began when the first settler from abroad of sensitive mind paused in his adventure long enough to feel that he was under a different sky, breathing new air and that a New World was all before him with only his strength and Providence for guides. With him began a new emphasis upon an old theme in literature, the theme of cutting loose and faring forth, renewed, under the powerful influence of a fresh continent for civilized literature, whose other flow has come from a nostalgia for the rich culture of Europe, so much of which was perforce left behind.

10. The title below that BEST expresses the ideas of this paragraph is: 10.____
    A. America's Distinctive Literature   B. Pioneer Authors
    C. The Dead Hand of the Past   D. Europe's Literary Grandchild
    E. America Comes of Age

11. American writers, according to the author, because of their colonial experiences 11.____
    A. were antagonistic to European writers
    B. cut loose from Old World influences
    C. wrote only on New World events and characters
    D. created new literary themes
    E. gave fresh interpretation to an old literary idea

KEY (CORRECT ANSWERS)

1. A
2. B
3. D
4. E
5. C
6. C
7. A
8. A
9. D
10. A
11. E

TEST 6

DIRECTIONS: Each question has five suggested answers, lettered A to E. Decide which one is the BEST answer. *PRINT THE LETTER OF THE CORRECT ANSWER IN THE SPACE AT THE RIGHT.*

1. Any business not provided with capable substitutes to fill all important positions is a weak business. Therefore, a foreman should train each man not on to perform his own particular duties but also to do those of two or three positions.
   The paragraph BEST supports the statement that
   A. dependence on substitutes is a sign of weak organization
   B. training will improve the strongest organization
   C. the foreman should be the most expert at any particular job under him
   D. every employee can be trained to perform efficiency work other than his own
   E. vacancies in vital positions should be provided for in advance

   1.____

2. The coloration of textile fabrics composed of cotton and wool generally requires two processes, as the process used in dyeing wool is seldom capable of fixing the color upon cotton. The usual method is to immerse the fabric in the requisite baths to dye the wool and then to treat the partially dyed material in the manner found suitable for cotton.
   The paragraph BEST supports the statement that the dyeing of textile fabrics composed of cotton and wool is
   A. less complicated than the dyeing of wool alone
   B. more successful when the material contains more cotton than wool
   C. not satisfactory when solid colors are desired
   D. restricted to two colors for any one fabric
   E. usually based upon the methods required for dyeing the different materials

   2.____

3. The serious investigator must direct his whole effort toward success in his work. If he wishes to succeed in each investigation, his work will be by no means easy, smooth, or peaceful; on the contrary, he will have to devote himself completely and continuously to a task that requires all his ability.
   The paragraph BEST supports the statement that an investigator's success depends most upon
   A. ambition to advance rapidly in the service
   B. persistence in the face of difficulty
   C. training and experience
   D. willingness to obey orders without delay
   E. the number of investigations which he conducts

   3.____

4. Honest people in one nation find it difficult to understand the viewpoint of honest people in another. State departments and their ministers exist for the purpose of explaining the viewpoints of one nation in terms understood by another. Some of their most important work lies in this direction.

   4.____

The paragraph BEST supports the statement that
- A. people of different nations may not consider matters in the same light
- B. it is unusual for many people to share similar ideas
- C. suspicion prevents understanding between nations
- D. the chief work of state departments is to guide relations between nations united by a common cause
- E. the people of one nation must sympathize with the viewpoints of others

5. Economy once in a while is just not enough. I expect to find it at every level of responsibility, from cabinet member to the newest and youngest recruit. Controlling waste is something like bailing a boat; you have to keep at it. I have no intention of easing up on my insistence on getting a dollar of value for each dollar we spend.
The paragraph BEST supports the statement that
- A. we need not be concerned about items which cost less than a dollar
- B. it is advisable to buy the cheaper of two items
- C. the responsibility of economy is greater at high levels than at low levels
- D. economy becomes easy with practice
- E. economy is a continuing responsibility

KEY (CORRECT ANSWERS)

1. E
2. E
3. B
4. A
5. E

TEST 7

DIRECTIONS: Each question has five suggested answers, lettered A to E. Decide which one is the BEST answer. *PRINT THE LETTER OF THE CORRECT ANSWER IN THE SPACE AT THE RIGHT.*

1. On all permit imprint mail the charge for postage has been printed by the mailer before he presents it for mailing and pays the postage. Such mail of any class is mailable only at the post office that issued a permit covering it. Since the postage receipts for such mail represent only the amount of permit imprint mail detected and verified, employees in receiving, handling, and outgoing sections must be alert constantly to route such mail to the weighing section before it is handled or dispatched.
The paragraph BEST supports the statement that, at post offices where permit mail is received for dispatch,
    A. dispatching units make a final check on the amount of postage payable on permit imprint mail
    B. employees are to check the postage chargeable on mail received under permit
    C. neither more nor less postage is to be collected than the amount printed on permit imprint mail
    D. the weighing section is primarily responsible for failure to collect postage on such mail
    E. unusual measures are taken to prevent unstamped mail from being accepted

1.____

2. Education should not stop when the individual has been prepared to make a livelihood and to live in modern society. Living would be mere existence were there were no appreciation and enjoyment of the riches of art, literature, and science.
The paragraph BEST supports the statement that true education
    A. is focused on the routine problems of life
    B. prepares one for full enjoyment of life
    C. deals chiefly with art, literature, and science
    D. is not possible for one who does not enjoy scientific literature
    E. disregards practical ends

2.____

3. Insured and c.o.d. air and surface mail is accepted with the understanding that the sender guarantees any necessary forwarding or return postage. When such mail is forwarded or returned, it shall be rated up for collection of postage; except that insured or c.o.d. air mail weighing 8 ounces or less and subject to the 40 cents an ounce rate shall be forwarded by air if delivery will be advanced, and returned by surface means without additional postage.
The paragraph BEST supports the statement that the return postage for undeliverable insured mail is
    A. included in the original prepayment on air mail parcels
    B. computed but not collected before dispatching surface patrol post mail to sender

3.____

C. not computed or charged for any air mail that is returned by surface transportation
D. included in the amount collected when the sender mails parcel post
E. collected before dispatching for return if any amount due has been guaranteed

4. All undeliverable first-class mail, except first-class parcels and parcel post paid with first-class postage, which cannot be returned to the sender, is sent to a dead-letter branch. Undeliverable matter of the third- and fourth-classes of obvious value for which the sender does not furnish return postage and undeliverable first-class parcels and parcel-post matter bearing postage of the first-class, which cannot be returned, is sent to a dead parcel-post branch.
The paragraph BEST supports the statement that matter that is sent to a dead parcel-post branch includes all undeliverable
   A. mail, except for first-class letter mail, that appears to be valuable
   B. mail, except that of the first-class, on which the sender failed to prepay the original mailing costs
   C. parcels on which the mailer prepaid the first-class rate of postage
   D. third- and fourth-class matter on which the required return postage has not been paid
   E. parcels on which first-class postage has been prepaid, when the sender's address is not known

5. Civilization started to move rapidly when man freed himself of the shackles that restricted his search for truth.
The passage BEST supports the statement that the progress of civilization
   A. came as a result of man's dislike for obstacles
   B. did not begin until restrictions on learning were removed
   C. has been aided by man's efforts to find the truth
   D. is based on continually increasing efforts
   E. continues at a constantly increasing rate

KEY (CORRECT ANSWERS)

1. B
2. B
3. B
4. E

TEST 8

DIRECTIONS: Each question has five suggested answers, lettered A to E. Decide which one is the BEST answer. *PRINT THE LETTER OF THE CORRECT ANSWER IN THE SPACE AT THE RIGHT.*

1. E-mails should be clear, concise, and brief. Omit all unnecessary words. The parts of speech most often used in e-mails are nouns, verbs, adjectives, and adverbs. If possible, do without pronouns, prepositions, articles, and copulative verbs. Use simple sentences, rather than complex and compound.
   The paragraph BEST supports the statement that in writing e-mails one should always use
   A. common and simple words
   B. only nouns, verbs, adjectives, and adverbs
   C. incomplete sentences
   D. only words essential to the meaning
   E. the present tense of verbs

   1._____

2. The function of business is to increase the wealth of the country and the value and happiness of life. It does this by supplying the material needs of men and women. When the nation's business is successfully carried on, it renders public service of the highest value.
   The paragraph BEST supports the statement that
   A. all businesses which render public service are successful
   B. human happiness is enhanced only by the increase of material wants
   C. the value of life is increased only by the increase of wealth
   D. the material needs of men and women are supplied by well-conducted business
   E. business is the only field of activity which increases happiness

   2._____

3. In almost every community, fortunately, there are certain men and women known to be public-spirited. Others, however, may be selfish and act only as their private interests seem to require.
   The paragraph BEST supports the statement that those citizens who disregard others are
   A. fortunate   B. needed
   C. found only in small communities   D. not known
   E. not public spirited

   3._____

KEY (CORRECT ANSWERS)

1. D
2. D
3. E

NONVERBAL REASONING

DIRECTIONS: In each question, there are five drawings (A-E presented from left to right). One drawing does NOT belong with the other four. You are to decide which drawing does NOT belong and PRINT THE LETTER of that drawing on your answer sheet.

EXAMPLES

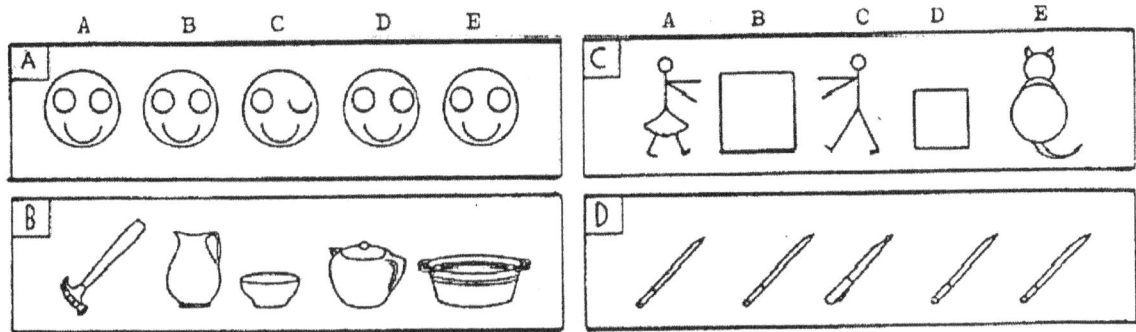

EXAMPLE A:
C does NOT belong because the eye is incomplete.

EXAMPLE B:
A does not belong because it is a hammer and the rest are objects relating to food.

EXAMPLE C:
E does not belong because while there are 2 each of the straight stick figures and squares, there is only one cat made of circular strokes.

EXAMPLE D:
C does not belong because it is thicker than the other pens, has a clip on its cap and it is a fountain pen while the rest are ballpoint pens.

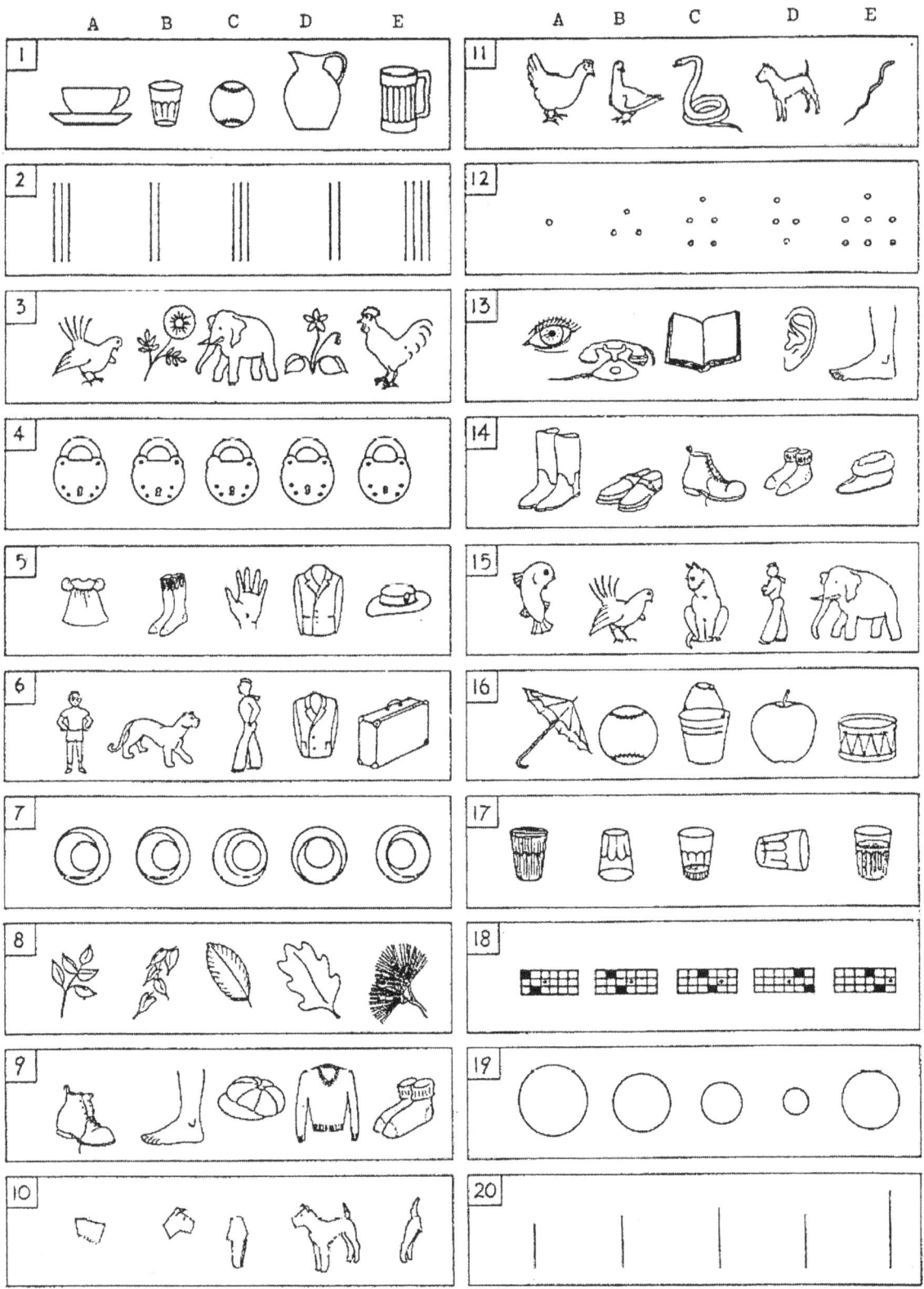

3 (#1)

4 (#1)

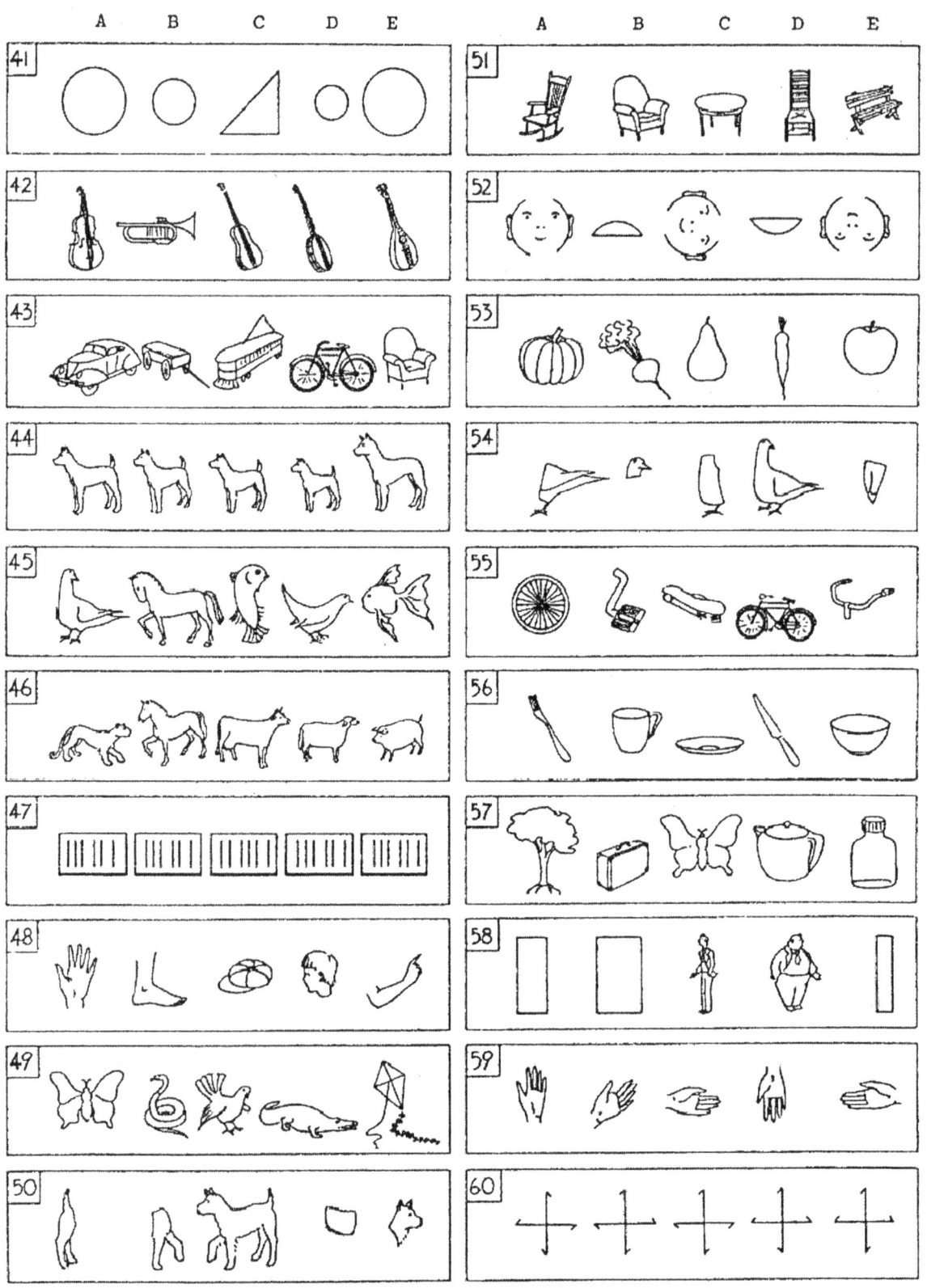

KEY (CORRECT ANSWERS)

1. C	16. D	31. E	46. A
2. E	17. D	32. B	47. C
3. C	18. D	33. A	48. C
4. C	19. E	34. D	49. E
5. C	20. D	35. C	50. C
6. B	21. C	36. C	51. C
7. C	22. E	37. D	52. C
8. E	23. C	38. A	53. A
9. B	24. C	39. D	54. D
10. D	25. C	40. B	55. D
11. D	26. B	41. C	56. C
12. D	27. D	42. B	57. A
13. E	28. A	43. E	58. A
14. D	29. A	44. E	59. B
15. D	30. D	45. B	60. D